Home Education

Home Education

by

Charlotte Mason

First Edition

Bottom of the Hill Publishing
www.BottomoftheHillPublishing.com

ISBN: 978-1-935785-66-8

Table of Contents

Preface to the Home Education Series

The educational outlook is rather misty and depressing both at home and abroad. That science should be a staple of education, that the teaching of Latin, of modern languages, of mathematics, must be reformed, that nature and handicrafts should be pressed into service for the training of the eye and hand, that boys and girls must learn to write English and therefore must know something of history and literature; and, on the other hand, that education must be made more technical and utilitarian—these, and such as these, are the cries of expedience with which we take the field. But we have no unifying principle, no definite aim; in fact, no philosophy of education. As a stream can rise no higher than its source, so it is probable that no educational effort can rise above the whole scheme of thought which gives it birth; and perhaps this is the reason of all the fallings from us, vanishings, failures, and disappointments which mark our educational records.

Those of us, who have spent many years in pursuing the benign and elusive vision of Education, perceive her approaches are regulated by a law, and that this law has yet to be evoked. We can discern its outlines, but no more. We know that it is pervasive; there is no part of a child's home life or school work which the law does not penetrate. It is illuminating, too, showing the value, or lack of value, of a thousand systems and expedients. It is not only a light, but a measure, providing a standard whereby all things, small and great, belonging to educational work must be tested. The law is liberal, taking in whatsoever things are true, honest, and of good report, and offering no limitation or hindrance save where excess should injure. And the path indicated by the law is continuous and progressive, with no transition stage from the cradle to the grave, except that maturity takes up the regular self direction to which immaturity has been trained. We shall doubtless find, when we apprehend the law, that certain German thinkers—Kant, Herbart, Lotze, Froebel—are justified; that, as they say, it is necessary to believe in God; that, therefore, the knowledge of God is the principal knowledge, and the chief end of education. By one more character shall we be able to recognise this perfect law of educational liberty when it shall be made evident. It has been said that The best idea which we can form of absolute truth is that it is viable to meet every condition by which it can be tested. This we shall expect of our law—that it shall meet every test of experiment and every test of rational investigation.

Not having received the tables of our law, we fall back upon Froebel or upon Herbart; or, if we belong to another School, upon Locke or Spencer; but we are not satisfied. A discontent, is it a divine discontent? Is upon us; and assuredly we should hail a workable, effectual philosophy of education as a deliverance from much perplexity. Before this great deliverance comes to us it is probable that many tentative efforts will be put forth, having more or less of the characters of a philosophy; notably, having a central idea, a body of thought with various members working in vital harmony.

Such a theory of education, which need not be careful to call itself a system of psychology, must be in harmony with the thought movements of the age; must regard education, not as a shut off compartment, but as being as much a part of life as birth or growth, marriage or work; and it must leave the pupil attached to the world at many points of contact. It is true that educationalists are already eager to establish such contact in several directions, but their efforts rest upon an axiom here and an idea there, and there is no broad unifying basis of thought to support the whole.

Fools rush in where angels fear to tread; and the hope that there may be tentative efforts towards a philosophy of education, and that all of them will bring us nearer to the magnum opus, encourages me to launch one such attempt. The central thought, or rather body of thought, upon which I found, is the somewhat obvious fact that the child is a person with all the possibilities and powers included in personality. Some of members which develop from this nucleus have been exploited from time to time by educational thinkers, and exist vaguely in the general common sense, a notion here, another there. One thesis, which is, perhaps, new, that Education is the Science of Relations, appears to me to solve the question of curricula, as showing that the object of education is to put a child in living touch as much as may be of the life of Nature and of thought. Add to this one or two keys to self knowledge, and the educated youth goes forth with some idea of self management, with some pursuits, and many vital interests. My excuse for venturing to offer a solution, however tentative and passing, to the problem of education is twofold. For between thirty and forty years I have laboured without pause to establish a working and philosophic theory of education; and in the next place, each article of the educational faith I offer has been arrived at by inductive processes; and has, I think, been verified by a long and wide series of experiments. It is, however, with sincere diffidence that I venture to offer the results of this long labour; because I know that in this field there are many labourers far more able and expert than I—the angels who fear to tread, so precarious is the footing!

But, if only pour encourager les autres, I append a short synopsis of education theory advanced in the volumes of the Home Education Series.

The treatment is not methodic, but incidental; here a little, there a little, as seemed to me most likely to meet the occasions of parents and teachers. I should add that in the course of a number of years the various essays have been prepared for the use of the Parents National Education Union in the hope that that Society might witness for a more or less coherent body of educational thought.

"The consequence of truth is great; therefore the judgment of it must not be negligent."—Whichcote

1. Children are born persons.

2. They are not born either good or bad, but with possibilities for either good or evil.

3. The principles of authority on the one hand and obedience on the other, are natural, necessary and fundamental; but

4. These principles are limited by the respect due to the personality of children, which must not be encroached upon, whether by fear or love, suggestion or influence, or undue play upon any one natural desire.

5. Therefore we are limited to three educational instruments—the atmosphere of environment, the discipline of habit, and the presentation of living ideas.

6. By the saying, Education is an atmosphere, it is not meant that a child should be isolated in what may be called a 'child environment,' especially adapted and prepared; but that we should take into account the educational value of his natural home atmosphere, both as regards persons and things, and should let him live freely among his proper conditions. It stultifies a child to bring down his world to a 'child's' level.

7. By Education is a discipline, is meant the discipline of habits formed definitely and thoughtfully, whether habits of mind or body. Physiologists tell us of the adaptation of brain structure to habitual lines of thought—i.e. to our habits.

8. In the saying that Education is a life, the need of intellectual and moral as well as of physical sustenance is implied. The mind feeds on ideas, and therefore children should have a generous curriculum.

9. But the mind is not a receptacle into which ideas must be dropped, each idea adding to an 'apperception mass' of its like, the theory upon which the Herbartian doctrine of interest rests.

10. On the contrary, a child's mind is no mere sac to hold ideas; but is rather, if the figure may be allowed, a spiritual organism, with an appetite for all knowledge. This is its proper diet, with which it is prepared to deal, and which it can digest and assimilate as the body does foodstuffs.

11. This difference is not a verbal quibble. The Herbartian doctrine lays the stress of education—the preparation of knowledge in enticing morsels, presented in due order—upon the teacher. Children taught upon this principle are in danger of receiving much teaching with little knowledge; and the teacher's axiom is, 'What a child learns matters less than how he learns it.'

12. But, believing that the normal child has powers of mind that fit him to deal with all knowledge proper to him, we must give him a full and generous curriculum; taking care, only, that the knowledge offered to him is vital—that is, the facts are not presented without their informing ideas. Out of this conception comes the principle that,

13. Education is the Science of Relations; that is, that a child has natural relations with a vast number of things and thoughts: so we must train him upon physical exercises, nature, handicrafts, science and art, and upon many living books; for we know

that our business is, not to teach him all about anything, but to help him make valid, as many as may be of 'Those first born affinities, 'That fit our new existence to existing things.'

14. There are also two secrets of moral and intellectual self management which should be offered to children; these we may call the Way of the Will and the Way of the Reason.

15. The Way of the Will.—Children should be taught (a) To distinguish between 'I want' and 'I will.' (b) That the way to will effectively is to turn our thoughts from that which we desire but do not will. (c) That the best way to turn our thoughts is to think of or do some quite different thing, entertaining or interesting. (d) That, after a little rest in this way, the will returns to its work with new vigour. (This adjunct of the will is familiar to us as diversion, whose office is to ease us for a time from will effort, that we may 'will' again with added power. The use of suggestion—even self suggestion—as an aid to the will, is to be deprecated, as tending to stultify and stereotype character. It would seem that spontaneity is a condition of development, and that human nature needs the discipline of failure as well as of success.)

16. The Way of the Reason.—We should teach children, too, not to 'lean' (too confidently) 'unto their own understanding,' because of the function of reason is, to give logical demonstration (a) of mathematical truth; and (b) of an initial idea, accepted by the will. In the former case reason is, perhaps, an infallible guide, but in the second it is not always a safe one, for whether that initial idea be right or wrong, reason will confirm it by irrefragable proofs.

17. Therefore children should be taught, as they become mature enough to understand such teaching that the chief responsibility which rests on them as persons is the acceptance or rejection of initial ideas. To help them in this choice we should give them principles of conduct and a wide range of the knowledge fitted for them. These three principles (15, 16 and 17) should save children from some of the loose thinking and heedless action which cause most of us to live at a lower level than we need.

18. We should allow no separation to grow up between the intellectual and 'spiritual' life of children; but should teach them that the divine Spirit has constant access to their spirits, and is their continual helper in all the interests, duties and joys of life.

The 'Home Education' Series is so called from the title of the first volume, and not as dealing, wholly or principally with 'Home' as opposed to 'School" education.

Preface to the Fourth Edition

My attempt in the following volume is to the suggest to parents and teachers a method of education resting upon a basis of natural law; and to touch, in this connection, upon a mother's duties to her children. In venturing to speak on this latter subject, I do so with the sincerest deference to mothers, believing that, in the words of a wise teacher of men, "the woman receives from the Spirit of God Himself the intuitions into the child's character, the capacity of appreciating its strength and its weakness, the faculty of calling forth the one and sustaining the other, in which lies the mystery of education, apart from which all its rules and measures are utterly vain and ineffectual." But just in proportion as a mother has this peculiar insight as regards her own children she will, I think, feel her need of a knowledge of the general principles of education, founded upon the nature and the needs of all children. And this knowledge of the science of education, not the best of mothers will get from above, seeing that we do not often receive as a gift that which we have the means of getting by our own efforts.

I venture to hope that teachers of young children, also, may find this volume of use. This period of a child's life between his sixth and his ninth year should be used to lay the basis of a liberal education, and of the habit of reading for instruction. During these years the child should enter upon the domain of knowledge, in a good many directions, in a reposeful, consecutive way, which is not to be attained through the somewhat exciting medium of oral lessons. I hope that teachers may find the approach (from a new standpoint), to the hackneyed "subjects of instruction" proper for little children at any rate interesting and stimulating; and possibly the methods which this fresh standpoint indicates may prove suggestive and helpful.

The particular object of this volume, as a member of the 'Home Education' Series, is to show the bearing of the physiology of habit upon education; why certain physical, intellectual, and moral habits are a valuable asset to a child, and what may be done towards the formation of such habits. I beg to acknowledge my indebtedness to Dr Carpenter's Mental Physiology for valuable teaching on the subject of habits contained in some two or three chapters of that work. Also, I would renew my grateful thanks to those medical friends who have given careful and able revision to such parts of the work as rest upon a physiological basis.

I should add that some twenty years ago (1885) the greater part of this volume was delivered as 'Lectures to Ladies,' in which form the papers were originally published (1886) under the title which is still retained.

Lectures VII. and VIII. and the Appendix of the original volume have been transferred from this to other volumes of the Series. The whole has been very carefully revised, and much new matter introduced, especially in Part V., 'Lessons as Instruments of Education,' which now offers a fairly complete introduction to methods of teaching subjects fit for children between the ages of six and nine.

The rest of the volume attempts to deal with the whole of education from infancy until the ninth year of life.

C. M. Mason

Scale How, Ambleside.

1905

Part I
Some Preliminary Considerations

Not the least sign of the higher status they have gained, is the growing desire for work that obtains amongst educated women. The world wants the work of such women; and presently, as education becomes more general, we shall see all women with the capacity to work falling into the ranks of working women, with definite tasks, fixed hours, and for wages, the pleasure and honour of doing useful work if they are under no necessity to earn money.

Children are a Public Trust.—Now, that work which is of most importance to society is the bringing up and instruction of the children—in the school, certainly, but far more in the home, because it is more than anything else the home influences brought to bear upon the child that determine the character and career of the future man or woman. It is a great thing to be a parent: there is no promotion, no dignity, to compare with it. The parents of but one child may be cherishing what shall prove a blessing to the world. But then, entrusted with such a charge, they are not free to say, "I may do as I will with mine own." The children are, in truth, to be regarded less as personal property than as public trusts, put into the hands of parents that they may make the very most of them for the good of society. And this responsibility is not equally divided between the parents: it is upon the mothers of the present that the future of the world depends, in even a greater degree than upon the fathers, because it is the mothers who have the sole direction of the children's early, most impressible years. This is why we hear so frequently of great men who have had good mothers—that is, mothers who brought up their children themselves, and did not make over their gravest duty to indifferent persons.

Mothers owe a 'thinking love' to their Children.—"The mother is qualified," says Pestalozzi, "and qualified by the Creator Himself, to become the principal agent in the development of her child; … and what is demanded of her is—a thinking love … God has given to the child all the faculties of our nature, but the grand point remains undecided—how shall this heart, this head, these hands be employed? to whose service shall they be dedicated? A question the answer to which involves a futurity of happiness or misery to a life so dear to thee. Maternal love is the first agent in education."

We are waking up to our duties and in proportion as mothers become more highly educated and efficient, they will doubtless feel the more strongly that the education of their children during the first six years of life is an undertaking hardly to be entrusted to any hands but their own. And they will take it up as their profession—that is, with the diligence, regularity, and punctuality which men bestow on their professional labours.

That the mother may know what she is about, may come thoroughly furnished to her work, she should have something more than a hearsay acquaintance with the theory of education, and with those conditions of the child's nature upon which such theory rests.

The training of Children 'dreadfully defective.'—"The training of children, says Mr. Herbert Spencer—"physical, moral and intellectual—is dreadfully defective. And in great measure it is so, because parents are devoid of that knowledge by which this training alone can be rightly guided. What is to be expected when one of the most intricate of problems is undertaken by those who have given scarcely a thought to the principle on which its solution depends? For shoemaking or housebuilding, for the management of a ship or of a locomotive engine, a long apprenticeship is needful. Is it, then, that the unfolding of a human being in body and mind is so comparatively simple a process that any one may superintend and regulate it with no preparation whatever? If not—if the process is, with one exception, more complex than any in Nature, and the task of ministering to it one of the surpassing difficulty—is it not madness to make no provision for such a task!? Better sacrifice accomplishments than omit this all essential instruction ... Some acquaintance with the first principles of physiology and the elementary truths of psychology is indispensable for the right bringing up of children. ... Here are the indisputable facts: that the development of children in mind and body follows certain laws; that unless these laws are in some degree conformed to by parents, death is inevitable; that unless they are in a great degree conformed to, and that only when they are completely conformed to, can a perfect maturity be reached. Judge, then, whether all who may one day be parents should not strive with some anxiety to learn what these laws are." (Herbert Spencer, Education)

How Parents Usually Proceed.—The parent begins instinctively by regarding his child as an unwritten tablet, and is filled with great resolves as to what he shall write thereon. By-and-by, traits of disposition appear, the child has little ways of his own; and, at first, every new display of personality is a delightful surprise. That the infant should show pleasure at the sight of his father, that his face should cloud in sympathy with his mother, must always be wonderful to us. But the wonder stales; his parents are used to the fact by the time the child shows himself as a complete human being like themselves, with affections, desires, powers; taking to his book, perhaps, as a duck to the water; or to the games which shall make a man of him. The notion of doing all for the child with which the parents began gradually recedes. So soon as he shows that he has a way of his own he is encouraged to take it. Father and mother have no greater delight than to watch the individuality of their child unfold as a flower unfolds. But Othello loses his occupation. The more the child shapes his own course, the less do the parents find to do, beyond feeding him with food convenient, whether of love, or thought, or of bodily meat and drink. And here, we may notice, the parents need only supply; the child knows well enough how to appropriate. The parents' chief care is, that that which they supply shall be wholesome and nourishing, whether in the way of picture books, lessons, playmates, bread and milk, or mother's love. This is education as most parents understand it, with more of meat, more of love, more of culture, according to their kind and degree. They let their children alone, allowing human nature to develop on its own lines, modified by facts of environment and descent.

Nothing could be better for the child than this 'masterly inactivity,' so far as it goes. It is well he should be let grow and helped to grow according to his nature; and so long as the parents do not step in to spoil him, much good and no very evident harm comes of letting him alone. But this philosophy of 'let him be,' while it covers a part, does not cover the serious part of the parents' calling; does not touch the strenuous incessant efforts upon lines of law which go to the producing of a human being at his best.

Nothing is trivial that concerns a child; his foolish-seeming words and ways are pregnant with meaning for the wise. It is in the infinitely little we must study in the infinitely great; and the vast possibilities, and the right direction of education, are indicated in the open book of the little child's thoughts.

A generation ago, a great teacher amongst us never wearied of reiterating that in the Divine plan "the family is the unit of the nation": not the individual, but the family. There is a great deal of teaching in the phrase, but this lies on the surface; the whole is greater than the part, the whole contains the part, owns the part, orders the part; and this being so, the children are the property of the nation, to be brought up for the nation as is best for the nation, and not according to the whim of individual parents. The law is for the punishment of evil doers, for the praise of them that do well; so, practically, parents have very free play; but it is as well we should remember that the children are a national trust whose bringing up is the concern of all—even of those unmarried and childless persons whose part in the game is the rather dreary one of 'looking on.'

I.—A Method of Education

Traditional Methods of Education.—Never was it more necessary for parents to face for themselves this question of education in all its bearings. Hitherto, children have been brought up upon traditional methods mainly. The experience of our ancestors, floating in a vast number of educational maxims, is handed on from lip to lip; and few or many of these maxims form the educational code of every household.

But we hardly take in how complete a revolution advancing science is effecting in the theory of education. The traditions of the elders have been tried and found wanting; it will be long before the axioms of the new school pass into the common currency; and, in the meantime, parents are thrown upon their own resources, and absolutely must weigh principles, and adopt a method, of education for themselves.

For instance, according to the former code, a mother might use her slipper now and then, to good effect and without blame; but now, the person of the child is, whether rightly or wrongly, held sacred and the infliction of pain for moral purposes is pretty generally disallowed.

Again, the old rule of the children's table was, 'the plainer the better, and let hunger bring sauce'; now the children's diet must be at least as nourishing and as varied as that of their elders; and appetite, the cravings for certain kinds of food, hitherto a vicious tendency to be repressed, is now within certain limitations the parents' most trustworthy guide in arranging a dietary for their children.

That children should be trained to endure hardness, was a principle of the old regime. "I shall never make a sailor if I can't face the wind and rain," said a little fellow of five who was taken out on a bitter night to see a torchlight procession; and, though, shaking with cold, he declined the shelter of a shed. Nowadays, the shed is everything; the children must not be permitted to suffer from fatigue or exposure.

That children should do as they are bid, mind their books, and take pleasure as it offers when nothing stands in the way, sums up the old theory; now, the pleasures of children are apt to be made more account than their duties.

Formerly, they were brought up in subjection; now, the elders give place, and the world is made for the children.

English people rarely go so far as the parents of that story in French Home Life, who arrived an hour late at a dinner party, because they had been desired by their girl of three to undress and go to bed when she did, and were able to steal away only when the child was asleep. We do not go so far, but that is the direction in which we are now moving; and how far the new theories of education are wise and humane, the outcome of more widely spread physiological and psychological knowledge, and how far they just pander to child worship to which we are all succumbing, is not a question to be decided off hand.

At any rate, it is not too much to say that a parent who does not follow reasonably a method of education, fully thought out, fails—now, more than ever before—to fulfil the claims his children have upon him.

Method a Way to an End.—Method implies two things—a way to an end, and a step by step progress in that way. Further, the following of a method implies an idea, a mental image, of the end of object to be arrived at. What do you propose that education shall effect in and for your child? Again, method is natural; easy, yielding, unobtrusive, simple as the ways of Nature herself; yet, watchful, careful, all pervading, all compelling. Method, with the end of education in view, presses the most unlikely matters into service to bring about that end; but with no more tiresome mechanism than the sun employs when it makes the winds to blow and the waters to flow only by shining. The parent who sees his way—that is, the exact force of method—to educate his child, will make use of every circumstance of the child's life almost without intention on his own part, so easy and spontaneous is a method of education based upon Natural Law. Does the child eat or drink, does he come, or go, or play—all the time he is being educated, though he is as little aware of it as he is of the act of breathing. There is always the danger that a method, a bona fide method, should degenerate into a mere system. The Kindergarten Method, for instance, deserves the name, as having been conceived and perfected by large hearted educators to aid the many sided evolution of the living, growing, most complex human being; but what a miserable wooden system does it become in the hands of ignorant practitioners!

A System easier than a Method.—A 'system of education' is an alluring fancy; more so, on some counts, than a method, because it is pledged to more definite calculable results. By means of a system certain developments may be brought about through the observance of given rules. Shorthand, dancing, how to pass examinations, how to become a good accountant, or a woman of society, may all be learned upon systems.

System—the observing of rules until the habit of doing certain things, of behaving in certain ways, is confirmed, and, therefore, the art is acquired—is so successful in achieving precise results, that it is no wonder there should be endless attempts to straiten the whole field of education to the limits of a system.

If a human being were a machine, education could do more for him than to set him in action in prescribed ways, and the work of the educator would be simply to adopt a good working system or set of systems.

But the educator has to deal with a self-acting, self-developing being, and his business is to guide, and assist in, the production of the latent good in that being, the dissipation of the latent evil, the preparation of the child to take his place in the world at his best, with every capacity for good that is in him developed into a power.

Though system is a highly useful as an instrument of education, a 'system of education' is mischievous, as producing only mechanical action instead of the vital growth and movement of a living being.

It is worth while to point out the differing characters of a system and a method, because parents let themselves be run away with often enough by some plausible 'system,' the object of which is to produce development in one direction—of the muscles, of the memory, of the reasoning faculty—were a complete all-round education. This easy satisfaction arises from the sluggishness of human nature, to which any definite scheme is more agreeable than the constant watchfulness, the unforeseen action, called for when the whole of a child's existence is to be used as the means of his education. But who is sufficient for an education so comprehensive, so incessant? A parent may be willing to undergo any definite labours for his child's sake; but to be always catering to his behoof, always contriving that circumstances shall play upon him for his good, is the part of a god and not of a man! A reasonable objection enough, if one looks upon education as an endless series of independent efforts, each to be thought out and acted out on the spur of the moment; but the fact is, that a few broad essential principles cover the whole field, and these once fully laid hold of, it is as easy and natural to act upon them as it is to act upon our knowledge of such facts as that fire burns and water flows. My endeavour in this and the following chapters will be to put these few fundamental principles before you in their practical bearing. Meantime, let us consider one or two preliminary questions.

II.—The Child's Estate

The Child in the Midst.—And first, let us consider where and what the little being is who is entrusted to the care of human parents. A tablet to be written upon? A twig to be bent? Wax to be moulded? Very likely; but he is much more—a being belonging to an altogether higher estate than ours; as it were, a prince committed to the fostering care of peasants. Hear Wordsworth's estimate of the child's estate:—

> "Our birth is but a sleep and a forgetting:
>
> The soul that rises with us, our life's star,
>
> Hath had elsewhere in its setting,
>
> And cometh from afar;
>
> Not in entire forgetfulness,
>
> And not in utter nakedness,
>
> But in trailing clouds of glory do we come
>
> From God, who is our home:
>
> Heaven lies about us in our infancy!
>
>
> Thou, whose exterior semblance doth belie
>
> Thy soul's immensity;
>
> Thou best philosopher, who yet dost keep
>
> Thy heritage; thou eye among the blind,
>
> That, deaf and silent, read'st the eternal deep,
>
> Haunted for ever by the eternal mind
>
> Mighty Prophet! Seer blest!
>
> On whom those truths do rest,
>
> Which we are toiling all our lives to find
>
> Thou, over whom they immortality
>
> Broods like a day, a master o'er a slave,
>
> A presence which is not be put by;
>
> Thou little child, yet glorious in the might
>
> Of heaven born freedom, on they being's height"—

and so on, through the whole of that great ode [Intimiations of Immortality from Reflections of Early Childhood], which next after the Bible, shows the deepest insight into what is peculiar to the children in their nature and estate. "Of such is the kingdom of heaven." "Except ye become as little children ye shall in no case enter the kingdom of heaven." "Who is the greatest in the kingdom of heaven?" "And He called a little child, and set him in the midst." Here is the Divine estimate of the child's estate. It is worth while for parents to ponder every utterance in the Gospels about these children, divesting themselves of the notion that these sayings belong, in the first place, to the grown up people who have become as little children. What these profound sayings are, and how much they may mean, it is beyond us to discuss here; only they appear to cover far more than Wordsworth claims for the children in his sublimest reach

"Trailing clouds of glory do we come

From God, who is our home."

Code of Education in the Gospels.—It may surprise parents who have not given much attention to the subject to discover also a code of education in the Gospels, expressly laid down by Christ. It is summed up in three commandments, and all three have a negative character, as if the chief thing required of grown-up people is that they should do no sort of injury to the children: Take heed that ye offend not—despise not—hinder not—one of these little ones.

So run the three educational laws of the New Testament, which, when separately examined, appear to me to cover all the help we can give the children and all the harm we can save them from—that is, whatever is included in training up a child in the way he should go. Let us look upon these three great laws as prohibitive, in order to clear the ground for the consideration of a method of education; for if we once settle with ourselves what we may not do, we are greatly helped to see what we may do, and must do. But, as a matter of fact, the positive is included in the negative, what we are bound to do for the child in what we are forbidden to do to his hurt.

III.—Offending the Children

Offences.—The first and second of the Divine edicts appear to include our sins of commission and of omission against the children: we offend them, when we do by them that which we ought not to have done; we despise them, when we leave undone those things which, for their sakes, we ought to have done. An offence, we know, is literally a stumbling-block, that which trips up the walker and causes him to fall. Mothers know what it is to clear the floor of every obstacle when a baby takes his unsteady little runs from chair to chair, from one pair of loving arms to another. The table-leg, the child's toy on the floor, which has caused a fall and a pitiful cry, is a thing to be deplored; why did not somebody put it out of the way, so that the baby should not stumble? But the little child is going out into the world with uncertain tottering steps in many directions.

There are causes of stumbling not so easy to remove as an offending footstool; and woe to him who causes the child to fall!

Children are born Law-abiding.—'Naughty baby!' says the mother; and the child's eyes droop, and a flush rises over neck and brow. It is very wonderful; very 'funny,' some people think, and say, 'Naughty baby!' when the baby is sweetly good, to amuse themselves with the sight of the infant soul rising visibly before their eyes. But what does it mean, this display of feeling, conscience, in the child, before any human teaching can have reached him? No less than this, that he is born a law abiding being, with a sense of may, and must not, of right and wrong. That is how children are sent into the world with the warning, "Take heed that ye offend not one of these little ones." And—this being so—who has not met big girls and boys, the children of right-minded parents, who yet do not know what must means, who are not moved by ought, whose hearts feel no stir at the solemn name of Duty, who know no higher rule of life than 'I want,' and 'I don't want,' 'I like,' and 'I don't like'? Heaven help parents and children when it has come to that!

But how has it been brought about that the babe, with an acute sense of right and wrong even when it can understand little of human speech, should grow into the boy or girl already proving 'the curse of lawless heart'? By slow degrees, here a little and there a little, as all that is good or bad in character comes to pass. 'Naughty!' says the mother, again, when a little hand is thrust into the sugar bowl; and when a pair of roguish eyes seek hers furtively, to measure, as they do unerringly, how far the little pilferer may go. It is very amusing; the mother 'cannot help laughing'; and the little trespass is allowed to pass: and, what the poor mother has not thought of, an offence, a cause of stumbling, has been cast into the path of her two-year-old child. He has learned already that which is 'naughty' may yet be done with some impunity, and he goes on improving his knowledge. It is needless to continue; everybody knows the steps by which the mother's 'no' comes to be disregarded, her refusal teased into consent. The child has learned to believe that he has nothing to overcome but his mother's disinclination; if she choose to let him do this and that, there is no reason why she should not; he can make her choose to let him do the next thing forbidden, and then he may do it. The next step in the argument is not too great for childish wits: if his mother does what she chooses, of course he will do what he chooses, if he can; and henceforward the child's life becomes an endless struggle to get his own way; a struggle in which a parent is pretty sure to be worsted, having many things to think of, while the child sticks persistently to the thing which has his fancy for the moment.

They must perceive that their Governors are Law-compelled.—Where is the beginning of this tangle, spoiling the lives of parent and child alike? In this: that the mother began with no sufficient sense of duty; she thought herself free to allow and disallow, to say and unsay, at pleasure, as if the child were hers to do what she liked with. The child has never discovered a background of must behind is mother's decisions; he does not know that she must not let him break his sister's playthings, gorge himself with cake, spoil the pleasure of other people, because these things are not right. Let the child perceive that his parents are law-compelled as well as he, that they simply cannot allow him to do the things which have been forbidden, and he submits with the sweet meekness which belongs to his age. To give reasons to a child is usually out of place, and is a sacrifice of parental dignity; but he is quick enough to read the 'must' and 'ought' which rule her, in his mother's face and manner, and in the fact that she is not to be moved from a resolution on any question of right and wrong.

Parents may Offend their Children by Disregarding the Laws of Health.—This, of allowing him in what is wrong, is only one of the many ways in which the loving mother may offend her child. Through ignorance, or wilfulness, which is worse, she may not only allow wrong in him, but do wrong by him. She may cast a stumbling-block in the way of physical life by giving him unwholesome food, letting him sleep and live in ill-ventilated rooms, by disregarding any or every of the simple laws of health, ignorance of which is hardly to be excused in the face of the pains taken by scientific men to bring this necessary knowledge within the reach of every one.

And the Intellectual Life.—Almost as bad is the way the child's intellectual life may be wrecked at its outset by a round of dreary, dawdling lessons in which definite progress is the last thing made or expected, and which, so far from educating in any true sense, stultify his wits in a way he never gets over. Many a little girl, especially, leaves the home schoolroom with a distaste for all manner of learning, an aversion to mental effort, which lasts her lifetime, and that is why she grows up to read little but trashy novels, and to talk all day about her clothes.

And of the Moral Life.—And her affections—the movements of the outgoing tender child-heart—how are they treated? There are few mothers who do not take pains to cherish the family affections; but when the child comes to have dealings with outsiders, do not worldly maxims and motives ever nip the buds of childish love? Far worse than this happens when the child's love finds no natural outlets within her home: when she is the plain or the dull child of the family, and is left out in the cold, while the parents' affection is lavished on the rest. Of course she does not love her brothers and sisters, who monopolise what should have been hers too. And how is she to love her parents? Nobody knows the real anguish which many a child in the nursery suffers from this cause, nor how many lives are embittered and spoiled through the suppression of these childish affections. "My childhood was made miserable," a lady said to me a while ago, "by my mother's doting fondness for my little brother; there was not a day when she did not make me wretched by coming into the nursery to fondle and play with him, and all the time she had not a word nor a look nor a smile for me, any more than if I had not been in the room. I have never got over it; she is very kind to me now, but I never feel quite natural with her. And how can we two, brother and sister, feel for each other as we should if we had grown up together in love in the nursery?"

IV.—Despising the Children

Children should have the best of their Mothers.—Suppose that a mother may offend her child, how is it possible that she should not despise him? "Despise: to have a low opinion of, to undervalue"—thus the dictionary; and, as a matter of fact, however much we may delight in them, we grown-up people have far too low an opinion of children. If the mother did not undervalue her child, would she leave him to the society of an ignorant nursemaid during the early years when his whole nature is, like the photographer's sensitive plate, receiving momently indelible impressions? Not but that his nurse is good for the child. Very likely it would not answer for educated people to have their children always about them. The constant society of his parents might be too stimulating for the child; and frequent change of thought, and the society of other people, make the mother all the fresher for her children. But they should have the best of their mother, her freshest, brightest hours; while, at the same time, she is careful to choose her nurses wisely, train them carefully, and keep a vigilant eye upon all that goes on in the nursery.

'Nurse.'—Mere coarseness and rudeness in his nurse does the tender child lasting harm. Many a child leaves the nursery with his moral sense blunted, and with an alienation from his heavenly Father set up which many last his lifetime. For the child's moral sense is exceedingly quick; he is all eyes and ears for the slightest act or word of unfairness, deception, shiftiness. His nurse says, "If you'll be a good boy, I won't tell"; and the child learns that things may be concealed from his mother, who should be to him as God, knowing all his good and evil. And it is not as if the child noted the slips of his elders with aversion. He knows better, it is true, but then he does not trust his own intuitions; he shapes his life on any pattern set before him, and with the fatal tint of human nature upon him he is more ready to imitate a bad pattern than a good. Give him a nurse who is coarse, violent, and tricky, and before the child is able to speak plainly he will have caught these dispositions.

Children's Faults are Serious.—One of many ways in which parents are apt to have too low an opinion of their children is in the matter of their faults. A little child shows some ugly trait—he is greedy, and gobbles up his sister's share of the goodies as well as his own; he is vindictive, ready to bite or fight the hand that offends him; he tells a lie;—no, he did not touch the sugar-bowl or the jam-pot. The mother puts off the evil day: she knows she must sometime reckon with the child for those offences, but in the meantime she says, "Oh, it does not matter this time; he is very little, and will know better by-and-by." To put the thing on no higher grounds, what happy days for herself and her children would the mother secure if she would keep watch at the place of the letting out of waters! If the mother settle it in her own mind that the child never does wrong without being aware of his wrong-doing, she will see that is not too young to have his fault corrected or prevented. Deal with a child on his first offence, and a grieved look is enough to convict the little transgressor; but let him go on until a habit of wrong-doing is formed, and the cure is a slow one; then the mother has no chance until she has formed in him a contrary habit of well-doing. To laugh a ugly tempers and let them pass because the child is small, is to sow the wind.

V.—Hindering the Children

A Child's Relationship with Almighty God.—The most fatal way of despising the child falls under the third educational law of the Gospels; it is to overlook and make light of his natural relationship with Almighty God. "Suffer the little children to come unto Me," says the Saviour, as if that were the natural thing for the children to do, the thing they do when they are not hindered by their elders. And perhaps it is not too beautiful a thing to believe in this redeemed world, that, as the babe turns to his mother though he has no power to say her name, as the flowers turn to the sun, so the hearts of the children turn to their Saviour and God with unconscious delight and trust.

Nursery Theology.—Now listen to what goes on in many a nursery:—'God does not love you, you naughty, wicked boy!' 'He will send you to the bad, wicked place!,' and so on; and this is all the practical teaching about the ways of his 'almighty Lover' that the child gets!—never a word of how God does love and cherish the little children all day long, and fill their hours with delight. Add to this, listless perfunctory prayers, idle discussions of Divine things in their presence, light use of holy words, few signs whereby the child can read that the things of God are more to his parents than any things of the world, and the child is hindered, tacitly forbidden to "come unto Me,"—and this, often, by parents who in the depths of their hearts desire nothing in comparison with God. This mischief lies in that same foolish undervaluing of the children, in the notion that the child can have no spiritual life until it please his elders to kindle the flame.

VI.—Conditions of Healthy Brain-Activity

Having just glanced at the wide region of forbidden ground, we are prepared to consider what it is, definitely and positively, that the mother owes to her child under the name of Education.

All Mind Labour means Wear of Brain.—And first of all, the more educable powers of the child—his intelligence, his will, his moral feelings—have their seat in his brain; that is to say, as the eye is the organ of sight, so is the brain, or some part of it, the organ of thought and will, of love and worship. Authorities differ as to how far it is possible to localise the functions of the brain; but this at least seems pretty clear—that none of the functions of mind are performed without real activity in the mass of grey and white nervous matter named 'the brain.' Now, this is not a matter for the physiologist alone, but for every mother and father of a family; because that wonderful brain, by means of which we do our thinking, if it is to act healthily and in harmony with the healthful action of the members, should act only under such conditions of exercise, rest, and nutrition as secure health in every other part of the body.

Exercise.—Most of us have met with a few eccentric and a good many silly persons, concerning whom the question forces itself, Were these people born with less brain power than others? Probably not; but if they were allowed to grow up without the daily habit of appropriate moral and mental work, if they were allowed to dawdle through youth without regular and sustained efforts of thought or will, the result would be the same, and the brain which should have been invigorated by daily exercise has become flabby and feeble as a healthy arm would be after carried for years in a sling. The large active brain is not content with entire idleness; it strikes out lines for itself and works fitfully, and the man or woman becomes eccentric, because wholesome mental effort, like moral, must be carried on under the discipline of rules. A shrewd writer suggests that mental indolence may have been in some measure the cause of those pitiable attacks of derangement and depression from which poor Cowper suffered; the making of graceful verses when the 'maggot bit' did not afford him the amount of mental labour necessary for his well being.

The outcome of which is—Do not let the children pass a day without distinct efforts, intellectual, moral, volitional; let them brace themselves to understand; let them compel themselves to do and to bear; and let them do right at the sacrifice of ease and pleasure: and this for many higher reasons, but, in the first and lowest place, that the mere physical organ of mind and will may grow vigorous with work.

Rest.—Just as important is it that the brain should have due rest; that is, should rest and work alternately. And here two considerations come into play. In the first place, when the brain is actively at work it is treated as is every other organ of the body in the same circumstances; that is to say, a large additional supply of blood is attracted to the head for the nourishment of the organ which is spending its substance in hard work. Now, there is not an indefinite quantity of what we will for the moment call surplus blood in the vessels. The supply is regulated on the principle that only one set of organs shall be excessively active at one time—now the limbs, now the digestive organs, now the brain; and all the blood in the body that can be spared goes to the support of those organs which, for the time being, are in a state of labour.

Rest after Meals.—The child has just had his dinner, the meal of the day which most severely taxes his digestive organs; for as much as two or three hours after, much labour is going on in these organs, and the blood that can be spared from elsewhere is present to assist. Now, send the child out for a long walk immediately after dinner—the blood goes to the labouring extremities, and the food is left half digested; give the child a regular course of such dinners and walks, and he will grow up a dyspeptic. Set him to his books after a heavy meal, and the case is as bad; the blood which should have been assisting in the digestion of the meal goes to the labouring brain.

It follows that the hours for lessons should be carefully chosen, after periods of mental rest—sleep or play, for instance—and when there is no excessive activity in any other part of the system. Thus, the morning, after breakfast (the digestion of which lighter meal is not a severe task), is much the best time for lessons and every sort of mental work; if the whole afternoon cannot be spared for out-of-door recreation, that is the time for mechanical tasks such as needlework, drawing, practising; the children's wits are bright enough in the evening, but the drawback to evening work is, that the brain, once excited, is inclined to carry on its labours beyond bed-time, and dreams, wakefulness, and uneasy sleep attend the poor child who has been at work until the last minute. If the elder children must work in the evening, they should have at least one or two pleasant social hours before they go to bed; but, indeed, we owe it to the children to abolish evening 'preparation.'

Change of Occupation.—"There is," says Huxley, "no satisfactory proof at present, that the manifestation of any particular kind of mental faculty is especially allotted to, or connected with, the activity of any particular region or the cerebral hemispheres," a dictum against the phrenologists, but coming to us on too high authority to be disputed. It is not possible to localise the 'faculties'—to say you are cautious with this fraction of your brain, and music-loving with another; but this much is certain, and is very important to the educator: the brain, or some portion of the brain, becomes exhausted when any given function has been exercised too long. The child has been doing sums for some time, and is getting unaccountably stupid: take away his slate and let him read history, and you find his wits fresh again. Imagination, which has had no part in the sums, is called into play by the history lesson, and the child brings a lively unexhausted power to his new work. School time-tables are usually drawn up with a view to give the brain of the child variety of work; but the secret of weariness children often show in the home school room is, that no such judicious change of lessons is contrived.

Nourishment.—Again, the brain cannot do its work well unless it be abundantly and suitably nourished; somebody has made a calculation of how many ounces of brain went to the production of such a work—say Paradise Lost—how many to such another, and so on. Without going into mental arithmetic of this nature, we may say with safety that every sort of intellectual activity wastes the tissues of the brain; a network of vessels supplies an enormous quantity of blood to the organ, to make up for this waste of material; and the vigour and health of the brain depend upon the quality and quantity of this blood-supply.

Certain Causes affect the Quality of the Blood.—Now, the quality of the blood is affected by three or four causes. In the first place, the blood is elaborated from the food; the more nutritious and easy of digestion the food, the more vital will be the properties of the blood. The food must be varied, too, a mixed diet, because various ingredients are required to make up for the various waste in the tissues. The children are shocking spendthrifts; their endless goings and comings, their restlessness, their energy, the very wagging of their tongues, all mean expenditure of substance: the loss is not appreciable, but they lose something by every sudden sally, out of doors or within. No doubt the gain of power which results from exercise is more than compensation for the loss of substance; but, all the same, this loss must be promptly made good. And not only is the body of the child more active, proportionately, than that of the man: the child's brain as compared with a man's is in a perpetual flutter of endeavour. It is calculated that though the brain of a man weighs no more than a fortieth part of his body, yet a fifth or sixth of his whole complement of blood goes to nourish this delicate and intensely active organ; but, in the child's case, a considerably larger proportion of the blood that is in him is spent on the sustenance of his brain. And all the time, with these excessive demands upon him, the child has to grow! not merely to make up for waste, but to produce new substance in brain and body.

Concerning Meals.—What is the obvious conclusion? That the child must be well fed. Half the people of low vitality we come across are the victims of low-feeding during their childhood; and that more often because their parents were not alive to their duty in this respect, then because they were not in a position to afford their children the diet necessary to their full physical and mental development. Regular meals at, usually, unbroken intervals—dinner, never more than five hours after breakfast; luncheon, unnecessary; animal food, once certainly, in some lighter form, twice a day—are the suggestions of common sense followed out in most well-regulated households. But it is not the food which is eaten, but the food which is digested, that nourishes body and brain. And here so many considerations press, that we can only glance at two or three of the most obvious. Everybody knows that children should not eat pastry, or pork, or fried meats, or cheese, or rich, highly-flavoured food of any description; that pepper, mustard, and vinegar, sauces and spices, should be forbidden, with new bread, rich cakes and jams, like plum or gooseberry, in which the leathery coat of the fruit is preserved; that milk, or milk and water, and that not too warm, or cocoa, is the best drink for children, and that they should be trained not to drink until they have finished eating; that fresh fruit at breakfast is invaluable; that, as serving the same end, oatmeal porridge and treacle, and the fat of toasted bacon, are valuable breakfast foods; and that a glass of water, also, taken the last thing at night, and the first thing in the morning, is useful in promoting those regular habits on which much of the comfort of life depends.

Talk at Meals.—All this and much of the same kind it is needless to urge; but again let me say, it is digested food that nourishes the system, and people are apt to forget how far mental and moral conditions affect the processes of digestion. The fact is, that the gastric juices which act as solvents to the viands are only secreted freely when the mind is in a cheerful and contented frame. If the child dislike his dinner, he swallows it, but the digestion of that distasteful meal is a laborious, much-impeded process: if the meal be eaten in silence, unrelieved by pleasant chat, the child loses much of the 'good' of his dinner. Hence it is not a matter of pampering them at all, but a matter of health, of due nutrition, that the children should enjoy their food, and that their meals should be eaten in gladness; though, by the way, joyful excitement is as mischievous as its opposite in destroying that even, cheerful tenor of mind favourable to the processes of digestion. No pains should be spared to make the hours of meeting round the family table the brightest hours of the day. This is supposing that the children are allowed to sit at the same table with their parents; and, if it is possible! to let them do so at every meal excepting a late dinner, the advantage to the little people is incalculable. Here is the parents' opportunity to train them in manners and morals, to cement family love, and to accustom the children to habits, such as that of thorough mastication, for instance, as important on the score of health as on that of propriety.

Variety in Meals.—But, given pleasant surroundings and excellent food, and even then the requirements of these exacting little people are not fully met: plain as their food should be, they must have variety. A leg of mutton every Tuesday, the same cold on Wednesday, and hashed on Thursday, may be very good food; but the child who has this diet week after week is inadequately nourished, simply because he is tired of it. The mother should contrive a rotation for her children that will last at least a fortnight, without the same dinner recurring twice. Fish, especially if the children dine off it without meat to follow, is excellent as a change, the more so as it is rich in phosphorus—a valuable brain food. The children's puddings deserve a good deal of consideration, because they do not commonly care for fatty foods, but prefer to derive the warmth of their bodies from the starch and sugar of their puddings. But give them a variety; do not let it be 'everlasting tapioca.' Even for tea and breakfast the wise mother does not say, 'I always give my children' so and so. They should not have anything 'always'; every meal should have some little surprise. But is this the way, to make them think overmuch of what they shall eat and drink? On the contrary, it is the underfed children who are greedy, and unfit to be trusted with any unusual delicacy.

Air as important as Food.—The quality of the blood depends almost as much on the air we breathe as on the food we eat; in the course of every two or three minutes, all the blood in the body passes through the endless ramifications of the lungs, for no other purpose than that, during the instant of its passage, it should be acted upon by the oxygen contained in the air which is drawn into the lungs in the act of breathing. But what can happen to the blood in the course of an exposure of so short duration? Just this- the whole character, the very colour, of the blood is changed: it enters the lungs spoiled, no longer capable of sustaining life; it leaves them, a pure vital fluid. Now, observe, the blood is only fully oxygenated when the air contains its full proportion of oxygen, and every breathing and burning object withdraws some oxygen from the atmosphere. Hence the importance of giving the children daily airings, and abundant exercise of limb and lung in unvitiated, unimpoverished air.

The Children Walk every Day.—'The children walk every day; they are never out less than an hour when the weather is suitable.' That is better than nothing; so is this: An East London school mistress notices the pale looks of one of her best girls. "Have you had any dinner, Nellie?" "Ye-es" (with hesitation). "What have you had?" "Mother gave Jessie and me a halfpenny to buy our dinners, and we bought a haporth of aniseed drops—they go further than bread"—with an appeal in her eyes against possible censure for extravagance. Children do not develop at their best upon aniseed drops for dinner, nor upon an hour's 'constitutional' daily. Possibly science will bring home to us more and more the fact that animal life, pent under cover, is supported under artificial conditions, just as is plant life in a glass house. Here is where most Continental nations have the advantage over us; they keep up the habit of out-of-door life; and as a consequence, the average Frenchman, German, Italian, Bulgarian, is more joyous, more simple, and more hardy than the average Englishman Climate? Did not Charles II—and he knew—declare for the climate of England because you could be abroad "more hours in the day and more days in the year" in England than "in any other country"? We lose sight of the fact that we are not like the historical personage who live upon "nothing but victuals and drink." "You can't live upon air!" we say to the invalid who can't eat. No; we cannot live upon air; but, if we must choose among the three sustainers of life, air will support us the longest. We know all about it; we are deadly weary of the subject; let but the tail of your eye catch 'oxygenation' on a page, and the well trained organ skips that paragraph of its own accord. No need to tell Macaulay's schoolboy, or anybody else, how the blood of the body is brought to the lungs and there spread about in a huge extent of innumerable 'pipes' that it may be exposed momentarily to the oxygen of the air; how the air is made to blow upon the blood, so spread out in readiness, by the bellows-like action of breathing; how the air penetrates the very thin walls of the pipes; and then, behold, a magical (or chemical) transmutation; the worthless sewage of the system becomes on the instant the rich vivifying fluid whose function it is to build up the tissues of muscle and nerve. And the Prospero that wears the cloak? Oxygen, his name!; and the marvel that he effects within us some fifteen times in the course of a minute is possibly without parallel in the whole array of marvels which we 'tot up' with easy familiarity, setting down 'life,' and carrying—a cypher!

Oxygenation has its Limitations.—We know all about it; what we forget, perhaps, is, that even oxygen has its limitation: nothing can act but where it is, and, waste attends work, hold true for this vital gas as for other matters. Fire and lamp and breathing beings are all consumers of the oxygen which sustains them. What follows? Why, that this element, which is present in the ration of twenty-three parts to the hundred in pure air, is subject to an enormous drain within the four walls of a house, where the air is more or less stationary. I am not speaking just now of the vitiation of air—only of the drain upon its life-sustaining element. Think, again, of the heavy drain upon the oxygen which must support the multitudinous fires and many breathing beings congregated in a large town! 'What follows?' is a strictly vital question. Man can enjoy the full measure of vigorous joyous existence possible to him only when his blood is fully aerated; and this takes place when the air he inhales contains its full complement of oxygen. Is it too much to say that vitality is reduced, other things being equal in proportion as persons are house dwellers rather than open-air dwellers? The impoverished air sustains life at a low and feeble level; wherefore in the great towns, stature dwindles, the chest contracts, men hardly live to see their children's children. True, we must needs have houses for shelter from the weather by day and for rest at night; but in proportion as we cease to make our houses 'comfortable,' as we regard them merely as necessary shelters when we cannot be out of doors, shall we enjoy to the full the vigorous vitality possible to us.

Unchanged Air.—Parents of pale faced town children, think of these things! The gutter children who feed on the pickings of the streets are better off (and healthier looking) in this one respect than your cherished darlings, because they have more of the first essential of life—air. There is some circulation of air even in the slums of the city, and the child who spends its days in the streets is better supplied with oxygen than he who spends most of his hours in the unchanged air of a spacious apartment. But it is not the air of the streets the children want. It is the delicious life-giving air of the country. The outlay of the children in living is enormously in excess of the outlay of the adult. The endless activity of the child, while it develops muscle, is kept up at the expense of very great waste of tissue. It is the blood which carries material for the reparation of this loss. The child must grow, every part of him, and it is the blood which brings material for the building up new tissues. Again, we know the brain is, out of all proportion to its size, the great consumer of the blood supply, but the brain of the child, what with its eager activity, what with its twofold growth, is insatiable in its demands!

'I feed Alice on beef tea.'—'I feed Alice on beef tea, cod-liver oil, and all sorts of nourishing things; but it's very disheartening, the child doesn't gain flesh!' It is probable that Alice breathes for twenty-two of the twenty-four hours the impoverished and more or less vitiated air pent within the four walls of a house. The child is practically starving; for the food she eats is very imperfectly and inadequately converted into the aerated blood that feeds the tissues of the body.

And if she is suffering from bodily inanition, what about the eager, active, curious, hungering mind of the little girl? 'Oh, she has her lessons regularly every day.' Probably: but lessons which deal with words, only the signs of things, are not what the child wants. There is no knowledge so appropriate to the early years of a child as that of the name and look and behaviour in situ of every natural object he can get at. "He hath so done His marvellous works that they ought to be had in remembrance."

> "Three years she grew in sun and shower,
> Then Nature said, 'A lovelier flower
> On earth was never sown:
> This child I to myself will take:
> She shall be mine, and I will make
> A lady of my own.
>
> " 'She shall be sportive as the fawn,
> That wild with glee across the lawn
> Or up the mountain springs;
> And hers shall be the breathing balm,
> And hers the silence and the calm
> Of mute, insensate things.
>
> " 'The stars of midnight shall be dear
> To her; and she shall lean her ear
> In many a secret place
> Where rivulets dance their wayward round,

And beauty born of murmuring sound

Shall pass into her face.' "

Indoor Airings.—About out-of-door airings we shall have occasion to speak more fully; but indoor airings are truly as important, because, if the tissues be nourished upon impure blood for all the hours the child spends in the house, the mischief will not be mended in the shorter intervals spent out of doors. Put two or three breathing bodies, as well as fire and gas, into a room, and it is incredible how soon the air becomes vitiated unless it be constantly renewed; that is, unless the room be well ventilated. We know what is to come in out of the fresh air and complain that a room feels stuffy; but sit in the room a few minutes, and you get accustomed to its stuffiness; the senses are no longer a safe guide.

Ventilation.—Therefore, regular provision must be made for the ventilation of rooms regardless of the feelings of their inmates; at least an inch of window open at the top, day and night, renders a room tolerably safe, because it allows the escape of the vitiated air, which, being light, ascends, leaving room for the influx of colder, fresher air by cracks and crannies in doors and floors. An open chimney is a useful, though not a sufficient, ventilator; it is needless to say that the stopping-up of chimneys in sleeping-rooms is suicidal. It is particularly important to accustom children to sleep with an inch or two, or more, of open window all through the year—as much more as you like in the summer.

Night Air Wholesome.—There is a popular notion that night air is unwholesome; but if you reflect that wholesome air is that which contains its full complement of oxygen, and no more than its very small complement of carbonic acid gas, and that all burning objects—fire, furnace, gas-lamp—give forth carbonic acid gas and consume oxygen, you will see that night air is, in ordinary circumstances, more wholesome than day air, simply because there is a less exhaustive drain upon its vital gas. When the children are out of a room which they commonly occupy, day nursery or breakfast room, then is the opportunity to air it thoroughly by throwing windows and doors wide open and producing a thorough draught.

Sunshine.—But it is not only air, and pure air, the children must have if their blood is to be of the 'finest quality,' as the advertisements have it. Quite healthy blood is exceedingly rich in minute, red disc-like bodies, known as red corpuscles, which in favourable circumstances are produced freely in the blood itself. Now, it is observed that people who live much in the sunshine are of a ruddy countenance—that is,   a great many of these red corpuscles are present in their blood; while the poor souls who live in cellars and sunless alleys have skins the colour of whity-brown paper. Therefore, it is concluded that light and sunshine are favourable to the production of red corpuscles in the blood; and, therefore—to this next 'therefore' is but a step for the mother—the children's rooms should be on the sunny side of the house, with a south aspect if possible. Indeed, the whole house should be kept light and bright for their sakes; trees and outbuildings that obstruct the sunshine and make the children's rooms dull should be removed without hesitation.

Free Perspiration.—Another point must be attended to, in order to secure that the brain be nourished by healthy blood. The blood receives and gets ride of the waste of the tissues, and one of the most important agents by means of which it does this necessary scavenger's work is the skin. Millions of invisible pores perforate the skin, each the mouth of a minute many-folded tube, and each such pore is employed without a moment's cessation, while the body is in health, in discharging perspiration—that is, the waste of the tissues—upon the skin.

Insensible Perspiration.—When the discharge is excessive, we are aware of moisture upon the skin; but, aware of it or not, the discharge is always going on; and, what is more, if it be checked, or if a considerable portion of the skin be glazed, so that it becomes impervious, death will result. This is why people die in consequence of scalds or burns which injure a large surface of the skin, although they do not touch any vital organ; multitudes of minute tubes which should carry off injurious matters from the blood are closed, and, though the remaining surface of the skin and the other excretory organs take extra work upon them, it is impossible to make good the loss of what may be called efficient drainage over a considerable area. Therefore, if the brain is to be duly nourished, it is important to keep the whole surface of the skin in a condition to throw off freely the excretion of blood.

Daily Bath and Porous Garments.—Two considerations follow: of the first, the necessity for the daily bath, followed by vigorous rubbing of the skin, it is needless to say a word here. But possibly it is not so well understood that children should be clothed in porous garments which admit of the instant passing off of the exhalations of the skin. Why did delicate women faint, or, at any rate, 'feel faint,' when it was the custom to go to church in sealskin coats? Why do people who sleep under down, or even under silk or cotton quilts, frequently rise unrefreshed? From the one cause: their coverings have impeded the passage of the insensible perspiration, and so have hindered the skin in its function of relieving the blood of impurities. It is surprising what a constant loss of vitality many people experience from no other cause than the unsuitable character of their clothing. The children cannot be better dressed throughout than in loosely woven woollen garments, flannels and serges, of varying thicknesses for summer and winter wear. Woollens have other advantages over cotton and linen materials besides that of being porous. Wool is a bad conductor, and therefore does not allow of the too free escape of the animal heat; and it is absorbent, and therefore relieves the skin of the clammy sensations which follow sensible perspiration. We should be the better for it if we could make up our minds to sleep in wool, discarding linen or cotton in favour of sheets made of some lightly woven woolen material.

We might say much on this one question, the due nutrition of brain, upon which the very possibility of healthy education depends. But something will have been effected if the reason why of only two or three practical rules of health is made so plain that they cannot be evaded without a sense of law-breaking.

I fear the reader may be inclined to think that I am inviting his attention for the most part to a few physiological matters—the lowest round of the educational ladder. The lowest round it may be, but yet it is the lowest round, the necessary step to all the rest. For it is not too much to say that, in our present state of being, intellectual, moral, even spiritual life and progress depend greatly upon physical conditions. That is to say, not that he who has a fine physique is necessarily a good and clever man; but that the good and clever man requires much animal substance to make up for the expenditure of tissue brought about in the exercise of his virtue and his intellect. For example, is it easier to be amiable, kindly, candid, with or without a headache or an attack of neuralgia?

VII—'The Reign of Law' in Education

Common Sense and Good Intentions.—Besides, though this physical culture of the brain may be only the groundwork of education, the method of it indicates what should be the method of all education; that is, orderly, regulated progress under the guidance of Law. The reason why education effects so much less than it should effect is just this— that in nine cases out of ten, sensible good parents trust too much to their common sense and their good intentions, forgetting that common sense must be at the pains to instruct itself in the nature of the case, and that well-intended efforts come to little if they are not carried on in obedience to divine laws, to be read in many cases, not in the Bible, but in the facts of life.

Law-abiding Lives often more blameless than Pious Lives.—It is a shame to believing people that many whose highest profession is that they do not know, and therefore do not believe, should produce more blameless lives, freer from flaws of temper, from the vice of selfishness, than do many sincerely religious people. It is a fact that will confront the children by-and-by, and one of which they require an explanation; and what is more, it is a fact that will have more weight, should it confront them in the person of a character which they cannot but esteem and love, than all the doctrinal teaching they have had in their lives. This appears to me the threatening danger to that confessed dependence upon and allegiance to Almighty God which we recognise as religion—not the wickedness, but the goodness of a school which refuses to admit any such dependence and allegiance.

My sense of this danger is my reason for offering the little I have to say upon the subject of education,—my sense of the danger, and the assurance I feel that it is no such great danger after all, but one that parents of the cultivated class are competent to deal with, and are precisely the only persons who can deal with it.

Mind and Matter equally governed by Law.—As for this superior morality of some non-believers, supposing we grant it, what does it amount to? Just to this, that the universe of mind, as the universe of matter, is governed by unwritten laws of God; that the child cannot blow soap bubbles or think his flitting thoughts otherwise than in obedience to divine laws; that all safety, progress, and success in life come out of obedience to law, to the laws of mental, moral or physical science, or of that spiritual science which the

Bible unfolds; that it is possible to ascertain laws and keep laws without recognizing the Lawgiver, and that those who do ascertain and keep any divine law inherit the blessing due to obedience, whatever be their attitude towards the Lawgiver; just as the man who goes out into blazing sunshine is warmed, though he may shut his eyes and decline to see the sun. Conversely, that they who take no pains to study the principles which govern human action and human thought miss the blessings of obedience to certain laws, though they may inherit the better blessings which come of acknowledged relationship with the Lawgiver.

Antagonism to Law shown by some Religious Persons.—These last blessings are so unspeakably satisfying, that often enough the believer who enjoys them wants no more. He opens his mouth and draws in his breath for the delight he has in the law, it is true; but it is the law of the spiritual life only. Towards the other laws of God which govern the universe he sometimes takes up an attitude of antagonism, almost of resistance, worthy of an infidel.

It is nothing to him that he is fearfully and wonderfully made; he does not care to know how the brain works, nor how the more subtle essence we call mind evolves and develops in obedience to laws. There are pious minds to which a desire to look into these things savours of unbelief, as if it were to dishonour the Almighty to perceive that He carries on His glorious works by means of glorious Laws. They will have to do with no laws excepting the laws of the kingdom of grace. In the meantime, the non-believer, who looks for no supernatural aids, lays himself out to discover and conform to all the laws which regulate natural life—physical, mental, moral; all the laws of God, in fact, excepting those of the spiritual life which the believer appropriates as his peculiar inheritance. But these laws which are left to Esau are laws of God also, and the observance of them is attended with such blessings, that the children of the believers say, Look, how is it that these who do not acknowledge the Law as of God are better than we who do?

Parents must acquaint themselves with the Principles of Physiology and Moral Science.—Now, believing parents have no right to lay up this crucial difficulty for their children. They have no right, for instance, to pray that their children may be made truthful, diligent, upright, and at the same time neglect to acquaint themselves with those principles of moral science the observance of which will guide into truthfulness, diligence, and uprightness of character. For this, also, is the law of God. Observe, not into the knowledge of God, the thing best worth living for: no mental science, and no moral science, is pledged to reveal that. What I contend for is, that these sciences have their part to play in the education of the human race, and that the parent may not disregard them with impunity. My endeavour in this and the following volumes of the series will be to sketch out roughly a method of education which, as resting upon a basis of natural law, may look, without presumption, to inherit the Divine blessing. Any sketch I can offer in this short compass must be very imperfect and very incomplete; but a hint here and there may be enough to put intelligent parents on profitable lines of thinking with regard to the education of their children.

Part II
Out-of-Door Life for the Children

I.—A Growing Time

Meals out of Doors.—People who live in the country know the value of fresh air very well, and their children live out of doors, with intervals within for sleeping and eating. As to the latter, even country people do not make full use of their opportunities. On fine days when it is warm enough to sit out with wraps, why should not tea and breakfast, everything but a hot dinner, be served out of doors? For we are an overwrought generation, running to nerves as a cabbage runs to seed; and every hour spent in the open is a clear gain, tending to the increase of brain power and bodily vigour, and to the lengthening of life itself. They who know what it is to have fevered skin and throbbing brain deliciously soothed by the cool touch of the air are inclined to make a new rule of life, Never be within doors when you can rightly be without.

Besides, the gain of an hour or two in the open air, there is this to be considered: meals taken al fresco are usually joyous, and there is nothing like gladness for converting meat and drink into healthy blood and tissue. All the time, too, the children are storing up memories of a happy childhood. Fifty years hence they will see the shadows of the boughs making patterns on the white tablecloth; and sunshine, children's laughter, hum of bees, and scent of flowers are being bottled up for after refreshment.

For Dwellers in Towns and Suburbs.—But it is only the people who live, so to speak, in their own gardens who can make a practice of giving their children tea out of doors. For the rest of us, and the most of us, who live in towns or the suburbs of towns, that is included in the larger question—How much time daily in the open air should the children have? And how is it possible to secure this for them? In this time of extraordinary pressure, educational and social, perhaps a mothers first duty to her children is to secure for them a quiet growing time, a full six years of passive receptive life, the waking part of it spent for the most part out in the fresh air. And this, not for the gain in bodily health alone—body and soul, heart and mind, are nourished with food convenient for them when the children are let alone, let to live without friction and without stimulus amongst happy influences which incline them to be good.

Possibilities of a Day in the Open.—I make a point, says a judicious mother, of sending my children out, weather permitting, for an hour in the winter, and two hours a day in the summer months. That is well; but it is not enough. In the first place, do not send them; if it is anyway possible, take them; for, although the children should be left much to themselves, there is a great deal to be done and a great deal to be prevented during these long hours in the open air. And long hours they should be; not two, but four, five, or six hours they should have on every tolerably fine day, from April till October. Impossible! Says an overwrought mother who sees her way to no more for her children than a daily hour or so on the pavements of the neighbouring London squares. Let me repeat, that I venture to suggest, not what is practicable in any household, but what seems to me absolutely best for the children; and that, in the faith that mothers work wonders once they are convinced that wonders are demanded of them. A journey of twenty minutes by rail or omnibus, and a luncheon basket, will make a day in the country possible to most town dwellers; and if one day, why not many, even every suitable day?

Supposing we have got them, what is to be done with these golden hours, so that every one shall be delightful? They must be spent with some method, or the mother will be taxed and the children bored. There is a great deal to be accomplished in this large fraction of the children's day. They must be kept in a joyous temper all the time, or they will miss some of the strengthening and refreshing held in charge for them by the blessed air. They must be let alone, left to themselves a great deal, to take in what they can of the beauty of earth and heavens; for of the evils of modern education few are worse than this—that the perpetual cackle of his elders leaves the poor child not a moment of time, nor an inch of space, wherein to wonder—and grow. At the same time, here is the mother's opportunity to train the seeing eye, the hearing ear, and to drop seeds of truth into the open soul of the child, which shall germinate, blossom, and bear fruit, without further help or knowledge of hers. Then, there is much to be got by perching in a tree or nestling in heather, but muscular development comes of more active ways, and an hour or two should be spent in vigorous play; and last, and truly least, a lesson or two must be got in.

No Story-Books.—Let us suppose mother and children arrived at some breezy open wherein it seemeth always afternoon. In the first place, it is not her business to entertain the little people: there should be no story-books, no telling of tales, as little talk as possible, and that to some purpose. Who thinks to amuse children with tale or talk at a circus or pantomime? And here, is there not infinitely more displayed for their delectation? Our wise mother, arrived, first sends the children to let off their spirits in a wild scamper, with cry, hallo, and hullaballo, and any extravagance that comes into their young heads. There is no distinction between big and little; the latter love to follow in the wake of their elders, and, in lessons or play, to pick up and do according to their little might. As for the baby, he is in bliss: divested of his garments, he kicks and crawls, and clutches the grass, laughs soft baby laughter, and takes in his little knowledge of shapes and properties in his own wonderful fashion—clothed in a woollen gown, long and loose, which is none the worse for the worst usage it may get.

II.—Sight-Seeing

By-and-by the others come back to their mother, and, while wits are fresh and eyes are keen, she sends them off on an exploring expedition—Who can see the most, and tell the most, about yonder hillock or brook, hedge, or copse. This is an exercise that delights children, and may be endlessly varied, carried on in the spirit of a game, and yet with the exactness and carefulness of a lesson.

How to See.—Find out all you can about that cottage at the foot of the hill; but do not pry about too much. Soon they are back, and there is a crowd of excited faces, and a hubbub of tongues, and random observations are shot breathlessly into the mother's ear. 'There are bee-hives.' 'We saw a lot of bees going into one.' 'There is a long garden.' 'Yes, and there are sunflowers in it.' 'And hen-and-chicken daisies and pansies.' 'And there's a great deal of pretty blue flowers with rough leaves, mother; what do you suppose it is?' 'Borage for the bees, most likely; they are very fond of it.' 'Oh, and there are apple and pear and plum trees on one side; there's a little path up the middle, you know.' 'On which hand side are the fruit trees?' 'The right—no, the left; let me see, which is my thimble-hand? Yes, it is the right-hand side.' 'And there are potatoes and cabbages, and mint and things on the other side.' 'Where are the flowers, then?' 'Oh, they are just the borders, running down each side of the path.' 'But we have not told mother about the wonderful apple tree; I should think there are a million apples on it, all ripe and rosy!' 'A million, Fanny?' 'Well, a great many, mother; I don't know how many.' And so on, indefinitely; the mother getting by degrees a complete description of the cottage and its garden.

Educational Uses of Sight-Seeing.—This is all play to the children, but the mother is doing invaluable work; she is training their powers of observation and expression, increasing their vocabulary and their range of ideas by giving them the name and the uses of an object at the right moment,—when they ask, 'What is it?' and 'What is it for?' And she is training her children in truthful habits, by making them careful to see the fact and to state it exactly, without omission or exaggeration. The child who describes, 'A tall tree, going up into a point, with rather roundish leaves; not a pleasant tree for shade, because the branches all go up,' deserves to learn the name of the tree, and anything her mother has to tell her about it. But the little bungler, who fails to make it clear whether he is describing an elm or a beech, should get no encouragement; not a foot should his mother move to see his tree, no coaxing should draw her into talk about it, until, in despair, he goes off, and comes back with some more certain note—rough or smooth bark, rough or smooth leaves,—then the mother considers, pronounces, and, full of glee, he carries her off to see for himself.

Discriminating Observation.—By degrees the children will learn discriminatingly every feature of the landscapes with which they are familiar; and think what a delightful possession for old age and middle life is a series of pictures imaged, feature by feature, in the sunny glow of the child's mind! The miserable thing about the childish recollections of most persons is that they are blurred, distorted, incomplete, no more pleasant to look upon than a fractured cup or a torn garment; and the reason is, not that the old scenes are forgotten, but that they were never fully seen. At the time, there was no more than a hazy impression that such and such objects were present, and naturally, after a lapse of years those features can rarely be recalled of which the child was not cognisant when he saw them before him.

III.—'Picture-Painting'

Method of.—So exceedingly delightful is this faculty of taking mental photographs, exact images, of the beauties of Nature we go about the world for the refreshment of seeing, that it is worth while to exercise children in another way towards this end, bearing in mind, however, that they see the near and the minute, but can only be made with an effort to look at the wide and the distant. Get the children to look well at some patch of landscape, and then to shut their eyes and call up the picture before them, if any bit of it is blurred, they had better look again. When they have a perfect image before their eyes, let them say what they see. Thus: 'I see a pond; it is shallow on this side, but deep on the other; trees come to the waters edge on that side, and you can see their green leaves and branches so plainly in the water that you would think there was a wood underneath. Almost touching the trees in the water is a bit of blue sky with a soft white cloud; and when you look up you see that same little cloud, but with a great deal of sky instead of a patch, because there are no trees up there. There are lovely little water-lilies round the far edge of the pond, and two or three of the big round leaves are turned up like sails. Near where I am standing three cows have come to drink, and one has got far into the water, nearly up to her neck,' etc.

Strain on the Attention.—This, too, is an exercise children delight in, but, as it involves some strain on the attention, it is fatiguing, and should only be employed now and then. It is, however, well worth while to give children the habit of getting a bit of landscape by heart in this way, because it is the effort of recalling and reproducing that is fatiguing; while the altogether pleasurable act of seeing, fully and in detail, is likely to be repeated unconsciously until it becomes a habit by the child who is required now and then to reproduce what he sees.

Seeing Fully and in Detail.—At first the children will want a little help in the art of seeing. The mother will say, 'Look at the reflection of the trees! There might be a wood under the water. What do those standing up leaves remind you of?' And so on, until the children have noticed the salient points of the scene. She will even herself learn off two or three scenes, and describe them with closed eyes for the children's amusement; and such little mimics are they, and at the same time so sympathetic, that any graceful fanciful touch which she throws into her descriptions will be reproduced with variations in theirs.

The children will delight in this game of picture-painting all the more if the mother introduce it by describing some great picture gallery she has seen—pictures of mountains, of moors, of stormy seas, of ploughed fields, of little children at play, of an old woman knitting,—and goes on to say, that though she does not paint her pictures on canvas and have them put in frames, she carries about with her just such a picture gallery; for whenever she sees anything lovely or interesting, she looks at it until she has the picture in her mind's eye; and then she carries it away with her, her own for ever, a picture on view just when she wants it.

A Means of After-Solace and Refreshment.—It would be difficult to overrate this habit of seeing and storing as a means of after-solace and refreshment. The busiest of us have holidays when we slip our necks out of the yoke and come face to face with Nature, to be healed and blessed by

"The breathing balm,

The silence and the calm

Of mute, insensate things."

This immediate refreshment is open to everybody according to his measure; but it is a mistake to suppose that everybody is able to carry away a refreshing image of that which gives him delight. Only a few can say with Wordsworth, of scenes they have visited

"Though absent long,

These forms of beauty have not been to me

As is a landscape to a blind mans eye;

But oft, in lonely rooms, and mid the din

Of towns and cities, I have owed to them,

In hours of weariness, sensations sweet,

Felt in the blood, and felt along the heart;

And passing even into my purer mind,

With tranquil restoration.

And yet this is no high poetic gift which the rest of us must be content to admire, but a common reward for taking pains in the act of seeing which parents may do a great deal to confer upon their children.

The mother must beware how she spoils the simplicity, the objective character of the child's enjoyment, by treating his little descriptions as feats of cleverness to be repeated to his father or to visitors; she had better make a vow to suppress herself, 'to say nothing to nobody,' in his presence at any rate, though the child should show himself a born poet.

IV. Flowers and Trees

Children should know Field-crops.—In the course of this 'sight-seeing' and 'picture-painting,' opportunities will occur to make the children familiar with rural objects and employments. If there are farm-lands within reach, they should know meadow and pasture, clover, turnip, and corn field, under every aspect, from the ploughing of the land to the getting in of the crops.

Field Flowers and the Life-History of Plants.—Milkwort, eyebright, rest-harrow, lady's-bedstraw, willow-herb, every wild flower that grows in their neighbourhood, they should know quite well; should be able to describe the leaf—its shape, size, growing from the root or from the stem; the manner of flowering—a head of flowers, a single flower, a spike, etc. And, having made the acquaintance of a wild flower, so that they can never forget it or mistake it, they should examine the spot where they find it, so that they will know for the future in what sort of ground to look for such and such a flower. 'We should find wild thyme here!' 'Oh, this is the very spot for marsh marigolds; we must come here in the spring.' If the mother is no great botanist, she will find Miss Ann Pratt's Wild Flowers [see Appendix] very useful, with its coloured plates, like enough to identify the flowers, by common English names, and pleasant facts and fancies that the children delight in. To make collections of wild flowers for the several months, press them, and mount them neatly on squares of cartridge paper, with the English name, habitat, and date of finding each, affords much happy occupation and, at the same time, much useful training: better still is it to accustom children to make careful brush drawings for the flowers that interest them, of the whole plant where possible.

The Study of Trees.—Children should be made early intimate with the trees, too; should pick out half a dozen trees, oak, elm, ash, beech, in their winter nakedness, and take these to be their year-long friends. In the winter, they will observe the light tresses of the birch, the knotted arms of the oak, the sturdy growth of the sycamore. They may wait to learn the names of the trees until the leaves come. By-and-by, as the spring advances, behold a general stiffening and look of life in the still bare branches; life stirs in the beautiful mystery of the leaf-buds, a nest of delicate baby leaves lying in downy warmth within many waterproof wrappings; oak and elm, beech and birch, each has its own way of folding and packing its leaflets; observe the 'ruby budded lime' and the ash, with its pretty stag's foot of a bud, not green but black—

"More black than ash-buds in the front of March."

The Seasons should be followed.—But it is hard to keep pace with the wonders that unfold themselves in the 'bountiful season bland.' There are the dangling catkins and the little ruby eyed pistil-late flowers of the hazel—clusters of flowers, both of them, two sorts on a single tree; and the downy staminate catkins of the willow; and the festive breaking out of all the trees into lovely leafage; the learning the patterns of the leaves as they come out, and the naming of the trees from this and other signs. Then the flowers come, each shut up tight in the dainty casket we call a bud, as cunningly wrapped as the leaves in their buds, but less carefully guarded, for these 'sweet nurslings' delay their coming for the most part until earth has a warm bed to offer, and the sun a kindly welcome.

Leigh Hunt on Flowers.—"Suppose," says Leigh Hunt, "suppose flowers themselves were new! Suppose they had just come into the world, a sweet reward for some new goodness... Imagine what we should feel when we saw the first lateral stem bearing off from the main one, and putting forth a leaf. How we should watch the leaf gradually unfolding its little graceful hand; then another, then another; then the main stalk rising and producing more; then one of them giving indications of the astonishing novelty—a bud! then this mysterious bud gradually unfolding like the leaf, amazing us, enchanting us, almost alarming us with delight, as if we knew not what enchantment were to ensue, till at length, in all its fairy beauty, and odorous voluptuousness, and the mysterious elaboration of tender and living sculpture, shines forth the blushing flower." The flowers, it is true, are not new; but the children are; and it is the fault of their elders if every new flower they come upon is not to them a Picciola, a mystery of beauty to be watched from day to day with unspeakable awe and delight.

Meanwhile, we have lost sight of those half-dozen forest-trees which the children have taken into a sort of comradeship for the year. Presently they have the delight of discovering that the great trees have flowers, too, flowers very often of the same hue as their leaves, and that some trees have put off having their leaves until their flowers have come and gone. By-and-by there is the fruit, and the discovery that every tree—with exceptions which they need not learn yet—and every plant bears fruit, 'fruit and seed after his kind.' All this is stale knowledge to older people, but one of the secrets of the educator is to present nothing as stale knowledge, but to put himself in the position of the child, and wonder and admire with him; for every common miracle which the child sees with his own eyes makes of him for the moment another Newton.

Calendars.—It is a capital plan for the children to keep a calendar—the first oak-leaf, the first tadpole, the first cowslip, the first catkin, the first ripe blackberries, where seen, and when. The next year they will know when and where to look out for their favourites, and will, every year, be in a condition to add new observations. Think of the zest and interest, the object, which such a practice will give to daily walks and little excursions. There is hardly a day when some friend may not be expected to hold a first 'At Home.'

Nature Diaries.—As soon as he is able to keep it himself, a nature-diary is a source of delight to a child. Every day's walk gives him something to enter: three squirrels in a larch tree, a jay flying across such a field, a caterpillar climbing up a nettle, a snail eating a cabbage leaf, a spider dropping suddenly to the ground, where he found ground ivy, how it was growing and what plants were growing with it, how bindweed or ivy manages to climb. Innumerable matters to record occur to the intelligent child. While he is quite young (five or six), he should begin to illustrate his notes freely with brush drawings; he should have a little help at first in mixing colours, in the way of principles, not directions. He should not be told to use now this and now that, but, 'we get purple by mixing so and so,' and then he should be left to himself to get the right tint. As for drawing, instruction has no doubt its time and place; but his nature diary should be left to his own initiative. A child of six will produce a dandelion, poppy, daisy, iris, with its leaves, impelled by the desire to represent what he sees, with surprising vigour and correctness.

An exercise book [Nature note-books may be had at the P.N.E.U Office. See Appendix] with stiff covers serves for a nature diary, but care is necessary in choosing paper that answers both for writing and brush drawing.

'I can't stop thinking.'—'But I can't stop thinking; I can't make my mind to sit down!' Poor little girl! All children owe you thanks for giving voice to their dumb woes. And we grown up people have so little imagination, that we send a little boy with an over-active brain to play by himself in the garden in order to escape the fag of lessons. Little we know how the brain-people swarm in and out and rush about!

> "The human (brain) is like a millstone, turning ever round and round;
>
> If it have nothing else to grind, it must itself be ground."

Set the child to definite work by all means, and give him something to grind. But, pray, let him work with things and not with signs—the things of Nature in their own places, meadow and hedgerow, woods and shore.

V. 'Living Creatures'

A Field of Interest and Delight.—Then, as for the 'living creatures,' here is a field of unbounded interest and delight. The domesticated animals are soon taken into kindly fellowship by the little people. Perhaps they live too far from the 'real country' for squirrels and wild rabbits to be more to them than a dream of possible delights. But surely there is a pond within reach—by road or rail—where tadpoles may be caught, and carried home in a bottle, fed, and watched through all their changes—fins disappearing, tails getting shorter and shorter, until at last there is no tail at all, and a pretty pert little frog looks you in the face. Turn up any chance stone, and you may come upon a colony of ants. We have always known that it becomes us to consider their ways and be wise; but now, think of all Lord Avebury has told us to make that twelve-year-old ant of his acquaintance quite a personage. Then, there are the bees. Some of us may have heard the late Dean Farrar describe that lesson he was present at, on 'How doth the little busy bee'— the teacher bright, but the children not responsive; they took no interest at all in little busy bees. He suspected the reason, and questioning the class, found that not one of them had ever seen a bee. 'Had never seen a bee! Think for a moment,' said he, 'of how much that implies'; and then we were moved by an eloquent picture of the sad child-life from which bees and birds and flowers are all shut out. But how many children are there who do not live in the slums of London, and yet are unable to distinguish a bee from a wasp, or even a 'humble' from a honey-bee!

Children should be encouraged to Watch.—Children should be encouraged to watch, patiently and quietly, until they learn something of the habits and history of bee, ant, wasp, spider, hairy caterpillar, dragon-fly, and whatever of larger growth comes in their way. 'The creatures never have any habits while I am looking!' a little girl in some story-book is made to complain; but that was her fault; the bright keen eyes with which children are blest were made to see, and see into, the doings of creatures too small for the unaided observation of older people. Ants may be brought under home observation in the following way: Get two pieces of glass 1 foot square, three strips of glass 11 1/2 inches long, and one strip 11 inches long, these all 1/4 inch wide. The glass must be carefully cut so as to fit exactly. Place the four strips of glass upon one of the sheets of glass and fix in an exact square, leaving a 1/2 inch opening, with seccotine or any good fixer. Get from an ant-hill about twelve ants (the yellow ants are best, as the red are inclined to be quarrelsome), a few eggs, and one queen. The queen will be quite as large as an ordinary ant, and so can be easily seen. Take some of the earth of the ant-hill. Put the earth with your ants and eggs upon the sheet of glass and fix the other sheet above, leaving only the small hole in one corner, made by the shorter strip, which should be stopped with a bit of cotton-wool. The ants will be restless for perhaps forty-eight hours, but will then begin to settle and arrange the earth. Remove the wool plug once a week, and replace it after putting two or three drops of honey on it. Once in three weeks remove the plug to drop in with a syringe about ten drops of water. This will not be necessary in the winter while the ants are asleep. This 'nest' will last for years.

With regard to the horror which some children show of beetle, spider, worm, that is usually a trick picked up from grown-up people. Kingsley's children would run after their 'daddy' with a 'delicious worm,' a 'lovely toad,' a 'sweet beetle' carried tenderly in both hands. There are real antipathies not to be overcome, such as Kingsley's own horror of a spider; but children who are accustomed to hold and admire caterpillars and beetles from their babyhood will not give way to affected horrors. The child who spends an hour in watching the ways of some new 'grub' he has come upon will be a man of mark yet. Let all he finds out about it be entered in his diary—by his mother, if writing be a labour to him,—where he finds it, what it is doing, or seems to him to be doing; its colour, shape, legs: some day he will come across the name of the creature, and will recognise the description of an old friend.

The Force of Public Opinion in the Home.—Some children are born naturalists, with a bent inherited, perhaps, from an unknown ancestor; but every child has a natural interest in the living things about him which it is the business of his parents to encourage; for, but few children are equal to holding their own in the face of public opinion; and if they see that the things which interest them are indifferent or disgusting to you, their pleasure in them vanishes, and that chapter in the book of Nature is closed to them. It is likely that the Natural History of Selborne would never have been written had it not been that the naturalist's father used to take his boys on daily foraging expeditions, when not a moving or growing thing, not a pebble nor a boulder within miles of Selborne, escaped their eager examination. Audubon, the American ornithologist, is another instance of the effect of this kind of early training. "When I had hardly learned to walk," he says, "and to articulate those first words always so endearing to parents, the productions of Nature that lay spread all around were constantly pointed out to me . . . My father generally accompanied my steps, procured birds and flowers for me, and pointed out the elegant movements of the former, the beauty and softness of their plumage, the manifestations of their pleasure, or their sense of danger, and the always perfect forms and splendid attire of the latter. He would speak of the departure and return of the birds with the season, describe their haunts, and, more wonderful than all, their change of livery, thus exciting me to study them, and to raise my mind towards their great Creator."

What Town Children can Do.—Town children may get a great deal of pleasure in watching the ways of sparrows—knowing little birds, and easily tamed by a dole of crumbs,— and their days out will bring them in the way of new acquaintances. But much may be done with sparrows. A friend writes:—"Have you seen the man in the gardens of Tuileries feeding and talking to dozens of them? They sit on his hat, his hands, and feed from his fingers. When he raises his arms they all flutter up and then settle again on him and round him. I have watched him call a sparrow from a distance by name and refuse food to all others till 'petit chou,' a pretty pied sparrow, came for his destined bit. Others had their names and came at call, but I could not see any distinguishing feature; and the crowd of sparrows on the walk, benches and railing, formed a most attentive audience to the bright French talk which kept them in constant motion as they were, here one and there another, invited to come for a tempting morsel. Truly a St. Francis and the birds!"

The child who does not know the portly form and spotted breast of the thrush, the graceful flight of the swallow, the yellow bill of the blackbird, the gush of song which the skylark pours from above, is nearly as much to be pitied as those London children who 'had never seen a bee.' A pleasant acquaintance, easy to pick up, is the hairy caterpillar. The moment to seize him is when he is seen shuffling along the ground in a great hurry; he is on the look-out for quiet quarters in which to lie up: put him in a box, then, and cover the box with net, through which you may watch his operations. Food does not matter—he has other things to attend to. By-and-by he spins a sort of white tent or hammock, into which he retires; you may see through it and watch him, perhaps at the very moment when his skin splits asunder, leaving him, for months to come, an egg-shaped mass without any sign of life. At last the living thing within breaks out of this bundle, and there it is, the handsome tiger-moth, fluttering feeble wings against the net. Most children of six have had this taste of a naturalist's experience, and it is worth speaking of only because, instead of being merely a harmless amusement, it is a valuable piece of education, of more use to the child than the reading of a whole book of natural history, or much geography and Latin. For the evil is, that children get their knowledge of natural history, like all their knowledge, at second hand. They are so sated with wonders, that nothing surprises them; and they are so little used to see for themselves, that nothing interests them. The cure for this blasé condition is, to let them alone for a bit, and then begin on new lines. Poor children, it is no fault of theirs if they are not as they were meant to be—curious eager little souls, all agog to explore so much of this wonderful world as they can get at, as quite their first business in life.

"He prayeth best who loveth best

All things both great and small;

For the dear God who loveth us,

He made and loveth all."

Nature Knowledge the most important for Young Children.—It would be well if we all persons in authority, parents and all who act for parents, could make up our minds that there is no sort of knowledge to be got in these early years so valuable to children as that which they get for themselves of the world they live in. Let them once get touch with Nature, and a habit is formed which will be a source of delight through life. We were all meant to be naturalists, each in his degree, and it is inexcusable to live in a world so full of the marvels of plant and animal life and to care for none of these things.

Mental Training of a Child Naturalist.—Consider, too, what an unequalled mental training the child-naturalist is getting for any study or calling under the sun—the powers of attention, of discrimination, of patient pursuit, growing with his growth, what will they not fit him for? Besides, life is so interesting to him, that he has no time for the faults of temper which generally have their source in ennui; there is no reason why he should be peevish or sulky or obstinate when he is always kept well amused.

Nature Work especially valuable for Girls.—I say 'he' from force of habit, as speaking of the representative sex, but truly that she should be thus conversant with Nature is a matter of infinitely more importance to the little girl: she it is who is most tempted to indulge in ugly tempers (as child and woman) because time hangs heavy on her hands; she, whose idler, more desultory habits of mind want the spur and bridle of an earnest absorbing pursuit; whose feebler health demands to be braced by an out-of-door life full of healthy excitement. Moreover, is it to the girls, little and big, a most true kindness to lift them out of themselves and out of the round of petty personal interests and emulations which too often hem in their lives; and then, with whom but the girls must it rest to mould the generations yet to be born?

VI.—Field-Lore and Naturalists' Books

Reverence for Life.—Is it advisable, then, to teach the children the elements of natural science, of biology, botany, zoology? on the whole, no: the dissection even of a flower is painful to a sensitive child, and, during the first six or eight years of life, I would not teach them any botany which should necessitate the pulling of flowers to bits; much less should they be permitted to injure or destroy any (not noxious) form of animal life. Reverence for life, as a wonderful and awful gift, which a ruthless child may destroy but never can restore, is a lesson of first importance to the child:—

"Let knowledge grow from more to more;

But more of reverence in us dwell."

The child who sees his mother with reverent touch lift an early snowdrop to her lips, learns a higher lesson than the 'print-books' can teach. Years hence, when the children are old enough to understand that science itself is in a sense sacred and demands some sacrifices, all the 'common information' they have been gathering until then, and the habits of observation they have acquired, will form a capital groundwork for a scientific education. In the meantime, let them consider the lilies of the field and the fowls of the air.

Rough Classification at First Hand.—For convenience in describing they should be able to name and distinguish petals, sepals, and so on; and they should be encouraged to make such rough classifications as they can with their slight knowledge of both animal and vegetable forms. Plants with heart-shaped or spoon-shaped leaves, with whole or divided leaves; leaves with criss-cross veins and leaves with straight veins; bell-shaped flowers and cross-shaped flowers; flowers with three petals, with four, with five; trees which keep their leaves all the year, and trees which lose them in autumn; creatures with a backbone and creatures without; creatures that eat grass and creatures that eat flesh, and so on. To make collections of leaves and flowers, pressed and mounted, and arranged according to their form, affords much pleasure, and, what is better, valuable training in the noticing of differences and resemblances. Patterns for this sort of classification of leaves and flowers will be found in every little book for elementary botany.

The power to classify, discriminate, distinguish between things that differ, is amongst the highest faculties of the human intellect, and no opportunity to cultivate it should be let slip; but a classification got out of books, that the child does not make for himself, cultivates no power but that of verbal memory, and a phrase or two of 'Tamil' or other unknown tongue, learnt off, would serve that purpose just as well.

Uses of 'Naturalists' ' Books.—The real use of naturalists' books at this stage is to give the child delightful glimpses into the world of wonders he lives in, to reveal the sorts of things to be seen by curious eyes, and fill him with desire to make discoveries for himself. There are many [Kingsley's Water Babies and Madam How and Lady Why. All Mrs. Brightwen's books. Miss Buckley's (Mrs. Fisher) 'Eyes and no Eyes' Series. Life and her Children, etc. All Seton-Thompson's books. Long's The School of the Woods, The Little Brother of the Bear. Kearton's Wild Nature's Ways. Living Animals of the World.] to be had, all pleasant reading, many of them written by scientific men, and yet requiring little or no scientific knowledge for the enjoyment.

Mothers and Teachers should know about Nature.—The mother cannot devote herself too much to this kind of reading, not only that she may read tit-bits to her children about matters they have come across, but that she may be able to answer their queries and direct their observations. And not only the mother, but any woman, who is likely ever to spend an hour or two in the society of children, should make herself mistress of this sort of information; the children will adore her for knowing what they want to know, and who knows but she may give its bent for life to some young mind designed to do great things for the world.

VII.—The Child Gets Knowledge By Means Of His Senses

Nature's Teaching.—Watch a child standing at gaze at some sight new to him—a plough at work, for instance—and you will see he is as naturally occupied as is a babe at the breast; he is, in fact, taking in the intellectual food which the working faculty of his brain at this period requires. In his early years the child is all eyes; he observes, or, more truly, he perceives, calling sight, touch, taste, smell, and hearing to his aid, that he may learn all that is discoverable by him about every new thing that comes under his notice. Everybody knows how a baby fumbles over with soft little fingers, and carries to his mouth, and bangs that it may produce what sound there is in it, the spoon or doll which supercilious grown-up people give him to 'keep him quiet.' The child is at his lessons, and is learning all about it at a rate utterly surprising to the physiologist, who considers how much is implied in the act of 'seeing,' for instance: that to the infant, as to the blind adult restored to sight, there is at first no difference between a flat picture and a solid body,—that the ideas of form and solidity are not obtained by sight at all, but are the judgments of experience.

Then, think of the vague passes in the air the little fist makes before it lays hold of the object of desire, and you see how he learns the whereabouts of things, having as yet no idea of direction. And why does he cry for the moon? Why does he crave equally, a horse or a house-fly as an appropriate plaything? Because far and near, large and small, are ideas he has yet to grasp. The child has truly a great deal to do before he is in a condition to 'believe his own eyes'; but Nature teaches so gently, so gradually, so persistently, that he is never overdone, but goes on gathering little stores of knowledge about whatever comes before him.

And this is the process the child should continue for the first few years of his life. Now is the storing time which should be spent in laying up images of things familiar. By-and-by he will have to conceive of things he has never seen: how can he do it except by comparison with things he has seen and knows? By-and-by he will be called upon to reflect, understand, reason; what material will he have, unless he has a magazine of facts to go upon? The child who has been made to observe how high in the heavens the sun is at noon on a summer's day, how low at noon on a day in mid-winter, is able to conceive of the great heat of the tropics under a vertical sun, and to understand the climate of a place depends greatly upon the mean height the sun reaches above the horizon.

Overpressure.—A great deal has been said lately about the danger of overpressure, of requiring too much mental work from a child of tender years. The danger exists; but lies, not in giving the child too much, but in giving him the wrong thing to do, the sort of work for which the present state of his mental development does not fit him. Who expects a boy in petticoats to lift half a hundredweight? But give the child work that Nature intended for him, and the quantity he can get through with ease is practically unlimited. Whoever saw a child tired of seeing, of examining in his own way, unfamiliar things? This is the sort of mental nourishment for which he has an unbounded appetite, because it is that food of the mind on which, for the present, he is meant to grow.

Object Lessons.—Now, how far is this craving for natural sustenance met? In infant and kindergarten schools, by the object lesson, which is good so far as it goes, but is sometimes like that bean a day on which the Frenchman fed his horse. The child at home has more new things brought under his noticed, if with less method. Neither at home nor at school is much effort made to set before the child the abundant 'feast of eyes' which his needs demand.

A Child learns from 'Things.'—We older people, partly because of our maturer intellect, partly because of our defective education, get most of our knowledge through the medium of words. We set the child to learn in the same way, and find him dull and slow. Why? Because it is only with a few words in common use that he associates a definite meaning; all the rest are no more to him than the vocables of a foreign tongue. But set him face to face with a thing, and he is twenty times as quick as you are in knowledge about it; knowledge of things flies to the mind of a child as steel filings to magnet. And, pari passu with his knowledge of things, his vocabulary grows; for it is a law of the mind that what we know, we struggle to express. This fact accounts for many of the apparently aimless questions of children; they are in quest, not of knowledge, but of words to express the knowledge they have. Now, consider what a culpable waste of intellectual energy it is to shut up a child, blessed with this inordinate capacity for seeing and knowing, within the four walls of a house, or the dreary streets of a town. Or suppose that he is let run loose in the country where there is plenty to see, it is nearly as bad to let this great faculty of the child's dissipate itself in random observations for want of method and direction.

The Sense of Beauty comes from Early Contact with Nature.—There is no end to the store of common information, got in such a way that it will never be forgotten, with which an intelligent child may furnish himself before he begins his school career. The boy who can tell you off-hand where to find each of the half-dozen most graceful birches, the three or four finest ash trees in the neighbourhood of his home, has chances in a life a dozen to one compared with the lower, slower intelligence that does not know an elm from an oak—not merely chances of success, but chances of a larger, happier life, for it is curious how certain feelings are linked with the mere observation of Nature and natural objects. "The aesthetic sense of the beautiful," says Dr. Carpenter, "of the sublime, of the harmonious, seems in its most elementary form to connect itself immediately with the Perceptions which arise of out of the contact of our minds with external Nature"; while he quotes Dr. Morrell, who says still more forcibly that "All those who have shown a remarkable appreciation of form and beauty date their first impressions from a period lying far behind the existence of definite ideas or verbal instruction."

Most Grown Men lose the Habit of Observation.—Thus, we owe something to Mr. Evans for taking his little daughter Mary Anne with him on his long business drives among the pleasant Warwickshire lanes; the little girl stood up between her father's knees, seeing much and saying little; and the outcome was the scenes of rural life in Adam Bede and The Mill on the Floss. Wordsworth, reared amongst the mountains, becomes a very prophet of Nature; while Tennyson draws endless imagery from the levels of the eastern counties where he was brought up. Little David Copperfield was "a very observant child, though," says he, "I think the memory of most of us can go farther back into such times than many of us suppose; just as I believe the power of observation in numbers of very young children to be quite wonderful for its closeness and accuracy. Indeed, I think that most grown men who are remarkable in this respect may with greater propriety be said not to have lost the faculty, than to have acquired it; the rather, as I generally observe such men to retain a certain freshness, and gentleness, and capacity of being pleased, which are also an inheritance they have preserved from their childhood";—in which remark Dickens makes his hero talk sound philosophy as well as kindly sense.

VIII.—The Child Should Be Made Familiar With Natural Objects

An Observant Child should be put in the way of Things worth Observing.—But what is the use of being a 'very observant child,' if you are not put in the way of things worth observing? And here is the difference between the streets of a town and the sights and sounds of the country. There is plenty to be seen in a town and children accustomed to the ways of the streets become nimble-witted enough. But the scraps of information to be picked up in a town are isolated fragments; they do not hang on to anything else, nor come to anything more; the information may be convenient, but no one is the wiser for knowing which side of the street is Smith's, and which turning leads to Thompson's shop.

Every Natural Object a Member of a Series.—Now take up a natural object, it does not matter what, and you are studying one of a group, a member of a series; whatever knowledge you get about it is so much towards the science which includes all of its kind. Break off an elder twig in the spring; you notice a ring of wood round a centre of pith, and there you have at a glance a distinguishing character of a great division of the vegetable world. You pick up a pebble. Its edges are perfectly smooth and rounded: why? you ask. It is water-worn, weatherworn. And that little pebble brings you face to face with disintegration, the force to which, more than to any other, we owe the aspects of the world which we call picturesque—glen, ravine, valley, hill. It is not necessary that the child should be told anything about disintegration or dicotyledon, only that he should observe the wood and pith in the hazel twig, the pleasant roundness of the pebble; by-and-by he will learn the bearing of the facts with which he is already familiar—a very different thing from learning the reason why of facts which have never come under his notice.

Power will pass, more and more, into the hands of Scientific Men.—It is infinitely well worth of the mother's while to take some pains every day to secure, in the first place, that her children spend hours daily amongst rural and natural objects; and, in the second place, to infuse into them, or rather to cherish in them, the love of investigation. "I say it deliberately," says Kingsley, "as a student of society and of history: power will pass more and more into the hands of scientific men. They will rule, and they will act—cautiously, we may hope, and modestly, and charitably—because in learning true knowledge they will have learnt also their own ignorance, and the vastness, the complexity, the mystery of Nature. But they will also be able to rule, they will be able to act, because they have taken the trouble to learn the facts and the laws of Nature."

Intimacy with Nature makes for Personal Well-being.—But to enable them to swim with the stream is the least of the benefits this early training should confer on the children; a love of Nature, implanted so early that it will seem to them hereafter to have been born in them, will enrich their lives with pure interests, absorbing pursuits, health, and good humour. "I have seen," says the same writer, "the young man of fierce passions and uncontrollable daring expend healthily that energy which threatened daily to plunge him into recklessness, if not into sin, upon hunting out and collecting, through rock and bog, snow and tempest, every bird and egg of the neighbouring forest . . . I have seen the young London beauty, amid all the excitement and temptation of luxury and flattery, with her heart pure, and her mind occupied in a boudoir full of shells and fossils, flowers and seaweeds, keeping herself unspotted from the world, by considering the lilies of the fields of the field, how they grow."

IX.—Out-Of-Door Geography

Small Things may teach Great.—After this long digression, intended to impress upon mothers the supreme importance of stirring up in their children a love of Nature and of natural objects—a deep-seated spring to send up pure waters into the driest places of after-life—we must return to the mother whom we have left out of doors all this time, waiting to know what she is to do next. This pleasant earth of ours is not to be overlooked in the out-of-door education of the children. 'How do you get time for so much?' 'Oh, I leave out subjects of no educational value; I do not teach geography, for instance,' said an advanced young theorist with all sorts of certificates.

Pictorial Geography.—But the mother, who knows better, will find a hundred opportunities to teach geography by the way: a duck-pond is a lake or an inland sea; any brooklet will serve to illustrate the great rivers of the world; a hillock grows into a mountain—an Alpine system; a hazel-copse suggests the mighty forests of the Amazon; a reedy swamp, the rice-fields of China; a meadow, the boundless prairies of the West; the pretty purple flowers of the common mallow is a text whereon to hang the cotton fields of the Southern States: indeed, the whole field of pictorial geography—maps may wait until by-and-by—may be covered in this way.

The Position of the Sun.—And not only this: the children should be taught to observe the position of the sun in the heavens from hour to hour, and by his position, to tell the time of day. Of course they will want to known why the sun is such an indefatigable traveller, and thereby hangs a wonderful tale, which they may as well learn in the 'age of faith,' of the relative sizes of sun and earth, and of the nature and movements of the latter.

Clouds, Rain, Snow, and Hail.—"Clouds and rain, snow and hail, winds and vapours, fulfilling His Word"—are all everyday mysteries that the mother will be called upon to explain faithfully, however simply. There are certain ideas which children must get from within a walking radius of their own home if ever they are to have a real understanding of maps and of geographical terms.

Distance is one of these, and the first idea of distance is to be attained by what children find a delightful operation. A child walks at his usual pace; somebody measures and tells him the length of his pace, and then he measures the paces of his brothers and sisters. Then such a walk, such a distance, here and there, is solemnly paced, and a little sum follows—so many inches or feet covered by each pace equals so many yards in the whole distance. Various short distances about the child's home should be measured in this way; and when the idea of covering distance is fully established, the idea of times as a means of measurement should be introduced. The time taken to pace a hundred yards should be noted down. Having found out that it takes two minutes to pace a hundred yards, children will be able for the next step—that if they have walked for thirty minutes, the walk should measure fifteen hundred yards; in thirty-five minutes they would have walked a mile, or rather seventeen hundred and fifty yards, and then they could add the ten yards more which would make a mile. The longer the legs the longer the pace, and most grown people can walk a mile in twenty minutes.

Direction.—By the time they have got somewhat familiar with the idea of distance, that of direction should be introduced. The first step is to make children observant of the progress of the sun. The child who observes the sun for a year and notes down for himself, or dictates, the times of his rising and setting for the greater part of the year, and the points of his rising and setting, will have secured a basis for a good deal of definite knowledge. Such observation should take in the reflection of the sun's light, the evening light reflected by east windows, the morning light by west windows, the varying length and intensity of shadows, the cause of shadows, to be learned by the shadow cast by a figure between the blind and a candle. He should associate, too, the hot hours of the day with the sun high overhead, and the cool hours of the morning and evening with a low sun; and should be reminded, that if he stands straight before the fire, he feels the heat more than if he were in a corner of the room. When he is prepared by a little observation in the course of the sun, he is ready to take in the idea of direction, which depends entirely upon the sun.

East and West.—Of course the first two ideas are that the sun rises in the east and sets in the west; from this fact he will be able to tell the direction in which the places near his own home, or the streets of his own town, lie. Bid him stand so that his right is towards the east where the sun rises, and his left towards the west where the sun sets. Then he is looking towards the north and his back is towards the south. All the houses, streets and towns on his right hand are to the east of him, those on the left are to the west. The places he must walk straight forward to reach are north of him, and the places behind him are to the south. If he is in a place new to him where he has never seen the sun rise or set and wants to know in what direction a certain road runs, he must notice in what direction his own shadow falls at twelve o'clock, because at noon the shadows of all objects fall towards the north. Then if he face the north, he has, as before, the south behind him, the east on his right hand, the west on his left; or if he face the sun at noon, he faces south.

Practice in finding Direction.—This will throw an interesting light for him on the names of our great railways. A child may become ready in noticing the directions of places by a little practice. Let him notice how each of the windows of his schoolroom faces, or the windows of each of the rooms in his home; the rows of houses he passes in his walks, and which are north, south, east and west sides of the churches he knows. He will soon be prepared to notice the direction of the wind by noticing the smoke from the chimneys, the movement of branches, corn, grass, etc. If the wind blow from the north—'The north wind doth blow and we shall have snow.' If it blow from the west, a west wind, we expect rain. Care must be taken at this point to make it clear to the child that the wind is named after the quarter it comes from, and not from the point it blows towards—just as he is English because he was born in England, and not French because he goes to France. The ideas of distance and direction may now be combined. Such a building is two hundred yards to the east of a gate, such a village two miles to the west. He will soon come across the difficulty, that a place is not exactly east or west, north or south. It is well to let him give, in a round-about way, the direction of places as—'more to the east than the west, 'very near the east but not quite,' 'half-way between east and west.' He will value the exact means of expression all the more for having felt the need of them.

Later, he should be introduced to the wonders of the mariner's compass, should have a little pocket compass of his own, and should observe the four cardinal and all other points. These will afford him the names for directions that he has found it difficult to describe.

Compass Drill.—Then he should do certain compass drills in this way: Bid him hold the N of the compass towards the north. "Then, with the compass in your hand, turn towards the east, and you will see a remarkable thing. The little needle moves, too, but moves quite by itself in just the other direction. Turn to the west, and again the needle moves in the opposite direction to that in which you move. However little you turn, a little quiver of the needle follows your movement. And you look at it, wondering how the little thing could perceive you had moved, when you hardly knew it yourself. Walk straight on in any direction, and the needle is fairly steady; only fairly steady, because you are sure, without intending it, to move a little to the right or left. Turn round very slowly, a little bit at a time, beginning at the north and turning towards the east, and you may make the needle also move round in a circle. It moves in the opposite direction to yourself, for it is trying to get back to the north from which you are turning."

Boundaries.—The children having got the idea of direction, it will be quite easy to introduce that of boundaries—such and such a turnip field, for instance, is bounded by the highroad on the south, by a wheat crop on the south-east, a hedge on the north-east, and so on; the children getting by degrees the idea that the boundaries of a given space are simply whatever touches it on every side. Thus one crop may touch another without any dividing line, and therefore one crop bounds the other. It is well that children should get clear notions on this subject, or, later, they will be vague when they learn that such a county is 'bounded' by so and so. In connection with bounded spaces whether they be villages, towns, ponds, fields, or what not, children should be led to notice the various crops raised in the district, why pasture-lands and why cornfields, what manner of rocks appear, and how many sorts of tree grow in the neighbourhood. For every field or other space that is examined, that they should draw a rude plan in the sand, giving the shape roughly and lettering the directions as N, S, W, etc.

Plans.—By-and-by, when they have learned to draw plans indoors, they will occasionally pace the length of a field and draw their plan according to scale, allowing an inch for five or for ten yards. The ground-plans of garden, stables, house, etc. might follow.

Local Geography.—It is probable that a child's own neighbourhood will give him opportunities to learn the meaning of hill and dale, pool and brook, watershed, the current, bed, banks, tributaries of a brook, the relative positions of villages and towns; and all this local geography he must be able to figure roughly on a plan done with chalk on a rock, or with walking stick in the gravel, perceiving the relative distances and situations of the places he marks.

X.—The Child And Mother-Nature

The Mother must refrain from too much Talk.—Does so wide a programme alarm the mother? Does she with dismay see herself talking through the whole of those five or six hours, and, even at that, not getting through a tithe of the teaching laid out for her? On the contrary, the less she says the better; and as for the quantity of educational work to be got through, it is the fable of the anxious pendulum over again: it is true there are countless 'ticks' to be ticked, but there will be always be a second of time to tick in, and no more than a single tick is to be delivered in any given second.

Making a New Acquaintance.—The rapid little people will have played their play, whether of 'sight-seeing' or 'picture-painting,' in a quarter of an hour or so; for the study of natural objects, an occasional 'Look!' an attentive examination of the object on the mother's own part, a name given, a remark—a dozen words long—made at the right moment, and the children have begun a new acquaintance which they will prosecute for themselves; and not more than one or two such presentations should occur in a single day.

Now, see how much leisure there is left! The mother's real difficulty will be to keep herself from much talk with the children, and to hinder them from occupying themselves with her. There are few things sweeter and more precious to the child than playful prattle with her mother; but one thing is better—the communing with the larger Mother, in order to which the child and she should be left to themselves. This is, truly, a delightful thing to watch: the mother reads her book or knits her sock, checking all attempts to make talk; the child stares up into a tree, or down into a flower—doing nothing, thinking of nothing; or leads a bird's life among the branches, or capers about in aimless ecstasy;—quite foolish, irrational doings, but, all the time a fashioning is going on: Nature is doing her part, with the vow—

"This child I to myself will take:

She shall be mine, and I will make

A lady of my own." [Wordsworth]

Two Things permissible to the Mother.—There is one thing the mother will allow herself to do as interpreter between Nature and the child, but that not oftener than once a week or once a month, and with look and gesture of delight rather than with flow of improving words—she will point out to the child some touch of especial loveliness in colouring or grouping in the landscape or the heavens. One other thing she will do, but very rarely, and with tender filial reverence (most likely she will say her prayers, and speak out of her prayer, for to touch on this ground with hard words is to wound the soul of the child): she will point to some lovely flower or gracious tree, not only as a beautiful, but a beautiful thought of God, in which we may believe He finds continual pleasure, and which He is pleased to see his human children rejoice in. Such a seed of sympathy with the Divine thought sown in the heart of the child is worth many of the sermons the man may listen to hereafter, much of the 'divinity' he may read.

XI.—Out-Of-Door Games, etc.

The bright hours fly by; and there is still at least one lesson on the programme, to say nothing of an hour or two for games in the afternoon. The thought of a lesson is uninviting after the discussion of much that is more interesting, and, truly, more important; but it need only be a little lesson, ten minutes long, and the slight break and the effort of attention will give the greater zest to the pleasure and leisure to follow.

The French Lesson.—The daily French lesson is that which should not be omitted. That children should learn French orally, by listening to and repeating French words and phrases; that they should begin so young that the difference of accent does not strike them, but they repeat the new French word all the same as if it were English and use it as freely; that they should learn a few—two or three, five or six—new French words daily, and that, at the same time, the old words should be kept in use—are points to be considered more fully hereafter: in the meantime, it is so important to keep tongue and ear familiar with French vocables, that not a lesson should be omitted. The French lesson may, however, be made to fit in with the spirit of the other out-of-door occupations; the half-dozen words may be the parts—leaves, branches, bark, trunk of a tree, or the colours of the flowers, or the movements of bird, cloud, lamb, child; in fact, the new French words should be but another form of expression for the ideas that for the time fill the child's mind.

Noisy Games.—The afternoon's games, after luncheon, are an important part of the day's doings for the elder children, though the younger have probably worn themselves out by this time with the ceaseless restlessness by means of which Nature provides for the due development of muscular tissue in them; let them sleep in the sweet air, and awake refreshed. Meanwhile, the elders play; the more they run, and shout, and toss their arms, the more healthful is the play. And this is one reason why mothers should carry their children off to lonely places, where they may use their lungs to their hearts' content without risk of annoying anybody. The muscular structure of the organs of voice is not enough considered; children love to indulge in cries and shouts and view-halloos, and this 'rude' and 'noisy' play, with which their elders have not much patience, is no more than Nature's way of providing for the due exercise of organs, upon whose working power the health and happiness of the child's future largely depend. People talk of 'weak lungs,' 'weak chest,' 'weak throat,' but perhaps it does not occur to everybody that strong lungs and strong throat are commonly to be had on the same terms as a strong arm or wrist—by exercise, training, use, work. Still, if the children can 'give voice' musically, and more rhythmically to the sound of their own voices, so much the better. In this respect French children are better off than English; they dance and sing through a hundred roundelays—just such games, no doubt, mimic marryings and buryings, as the children played at long ago in the market place of Jerusalem.

'Rondes.'—Before Puritan innovations made us a staid and circumspect people, English lads and lasses of all ages danced out little dramas on the village green, accompanying themselves with the words and airs of just such rondes as the French children sing to-day. We have a few of them left still—to be heard at Sunday-school treats and other gatherings of the children,—and they are well worth preserving: 'There came three dukes a-riding, a-riding, a-riding': 'Oranges and lemons, say the bells of St. Clement's'; 'Here we come gathering nuts in May'; 'What has my poor prisoner done?' and many more, all set to delightful sing-song airs that little feet trip to merrily, the more so for the pleasant titillation of the words—dukes, nuts, oranges,—who could not go to the tune of such ideas?

The promoters of the kindergarten system have done much to introduce games of this, or rather of a more educational kind; but is it not a fact that the singing games of the kindergarten are apt to be somewhat inane? Also, it is doubtful how far the prettiest plays, learnt at school and from a teacher, will take hold of the children as do the games which have been passed on from hand to hand through an endless chain of children, and are not be found in the print-books at all.

Skipping-rope and Shuttlecock.—Cricket, tennis, and rounders are the games par excellence if the children are old enough to play them, both as giving free harmonious play to the muscles, and also as serving the highest moral purpose of games in bringing the children under the discipline of rules; but the little family we have in view, all of them under nine, will hardly be up to scientific games. Races and chases, 'tag,' 'follow my leader,' and any romping game they may invent, will be more to their minds: still better are the hoop, the ball, the shuttlecock, and the invaluable skipping-rope. For the rope, the very best use is to skip with her own, throwing it backwards rather than forwards, so that the tendency of the movement is to expand the chest. Shuttlecock is a fine game, affording scope for ambition and emulation. Her biographer thinks it worth telling that Miss Austen could keep up in 'cup and ball' over a hundred times, to the admiration of nephews and nieces; in like manner, any feat in keeping up the shuttle-cock might be noted down as a family event, so that the children may be fired with ambition to excel in a game which affords most graceful and vigorous play to almost every muscle of the upper part of the body, and has this great recommendation, that it can be as well played within doors as without. Quite the best play is to keep up the shuttlecock with a bat-tledore in each hand, so that the muscles on either side are brought equally into play. But to 'ordain' about children's games is an idle waste of words, for here fashion is as supreme and as arbitrary as in questions of bonnet or crinoline.

Climbing.—Climbing is an amusement not much in favour with mothers; torn garments, bleeding knees, and boot-toes rubbed into holes, to say nothing of more serious risks, make a strong case against this form of delight. But, truly, the exercise is so admirable—the body being thrown into endless graceful postures which bring every muscle into play,—and the training in pluck, daring, and resource so invaluable that it is a pity trees and cliffs and walls should be forbidden even to little girls. The mother may do a good deal to avert serious mishaps by accustoming the younger children to small feats of leaping and climbing, so that they learn, at the same time, courage and caution from their own experiences, and are less likely to follow the lead of too-daring playmates. Later, the mother had best make up her mind to share the feelings of the hen that hatched a brood of ducklings, remembering that a little scream and sudden 'Come down instantly!' 'Tommy, you'll break your neck!' gives the child a nervous shock, and is likely to cause the fall it was meant to hinder by startling Tommy out of all presence of mind. Even boating and swimming are not without the reach of town-bred children, in days when everybody goes for a summer outing to the neighbourhood of the sea or of inland waters; and then, there are swimming baths in most towns. It would be well if most children of seven were taught to swim, not only for the possible usefulness of the art, but as giving them an added means of motion, and, therefore, of delight.

Clothing.—The havoc of clothes need not be great if the children are dressed for their little excursions, as they should be, in plainly made garments of some loosely woven woollen material, serge or flannel. Woollen has many advantages over cotton, and more over linen, as a clothing material; chiefly, that it is a bad conductor; that is to say, it does not allow the heat of the body too free an exit, nor the heat of the sun too free an entrance. Therefore the child in woollen, who has become heated in play, does not suffer a chill from the sudden loss of this heat, as does the child in linen garments; also, he is cooler in the sunshine, and warmer in the shade.

XII.—Walks In Bad Weather

Winter Walks as necessary as Summer Walks.—All we have said hitherto applies to the summer weather, which is, alas for us! a very limited and uncertain quantity in our part of the world. The question of out-of-door exercise in winter and in wet weather is really more important; for who that could would not be abroad in the summer time? If the children are to have what is quite the best thing for them, they should be two or three hours every day in the open air all through winter, say an hour and a half in the morning and as long in the afternoon.

Pleasures connected with Frost and Snow.—When frost and snow are on the ground children have very festive times, what with sliding, snow-balling, and snow-building. But even on the frequent days when it is dirty under foot and dull over head they should be kept interested and alert, so that the heart may do its work cheerfully, and a grateful glow be kept up throughout the body in spite of clouds and cold weather.

Winter Observations.—All that has been said about 'sight-seeing' and 'picture paint-ing,' the little French talk, and observations to be noted in the family diary, belongs just as much to winter weather as to summer; and there is no end to the things to be seen and noted. The party come across a big tree which they judge, from its build, to be an oak—down it goes in the diary; and when the leaves are out, the children come again to see if they are right. Many birds come into view the more freely in the cold weather that they are driven forth in search of food.

"The cattle mourn in corners where the fence screens them."

"The sun, with ruddy orb
Ascending, fires the horizon."

"Every herb and every spiry blade
Stretches a length of shadow o'er the field."

"The sparrows peep, and quit the sheltering eaves.

"The redbreast warbles still, but is content
With slender notes, and more than half suppress'd;
Pleased with his solitude, and flitting light
From spray to spray, wheree'er he rests he shakes
From many a twig the pendent drops of ice
That tinkle in the wither'd leaves below."

There is no reason why the child's winter walk should not be as fertile in observations as the poet's; indeed, in one way, it is possible to see the more in winter, because the things to be seen do not crowd each other out.

Habit of Attention.—Winter walks, too, whether in town or country, give great opportunities for cultivating the habit of attention. The famous conjurer, Robert Houdin, relates in his autobiography, that he and his son would pass rapidly before a shop window, that of a toy shop, for instance, and each cast an attentive glance upon it. A few steps further on each drew paper and pencil from his pocket, and tried which could enumerate the greater number of the objects momentarily seen in passing. The boy surprised his father in quickness of apprehension, being often able to write down forty objects, whilst his father could scarcely reach thirty; yet on their returning to verify his statement, the son was rarely found to have made a mistake. Here is a hint for a highly educational amusement for many a winter's walk.

Wet Weather Tramps.—But what about the wet days? The fact is, that rain, unless of the heaviest, does the children no harm at all if they are suitably clothed. But every sort of water proof garment should be tabooed, because the texture which will not admit rain will not allow of the escape of the insensible perspiration, and one secret of health for people who have no organic disease is the prompt carrying off of the decayed and harmful matters discharged by the skin.

Outer Garments for.—Children should have woollen rain-garments—made of coarse serge, for instance,—to be changed the moment they return from a walk, and then there is no risk of catching cold. This is the common-sense of the matter. Wet cloths are put upon the head of a fever patient; by-and-by the cloths dry, and are dipped again: what has become of the water? It has evaporated, and, in evaporating, has carried off much heat from the fevered head. Now, that which eases the hot skin of fever is just the one thing to be avoided in ordinary circumstances. To be wet to the skin may do a child no more harm than a bath would do him, if the wet clothes do not dry upon him—that is, if the water does not evaporate, carrying off much heat from his body in the process. It is the loss of animal heat which is followed by 'colds,' and not the 'wetting,' which mothers are ready to deplore. Keep an child active and happy in the rain, and he gets nothing but good from his walk. The case is altered if the child has a cold already; then active exercise might increase any inflammation already set up.

I do not know whether it is more than a pretty fancy of Richter's, that a spring shower is a sort of electric bath, and a very potent means of health; certainly rain clears the atmosphere—a fact of considerable importance in and about large towns. But it is enough for our purpose to prove that the rain need do no harm; for abundant daily exercise in the fresh air is of such vital importance to the children, that really nothing but sickness should keep them within doors. A mere time and distance tramp is sufficiently joyous for a wet day, for, taken good-humouredly, the beating rain itself is exhilarating. The 'long run' of the schoolboy, that is, a steady trot, breaking now and then into a run, is capital exercise; but regard must be had to the powers of the children, who must not be overdone.

Precautions.—At the same time, children should never be allowed to sit or stand about in damp clothes; and here is the use of waterproof rain-wraps—to keep them dry on short journeys to church, or school, or neighbour's house, where they cannot very well change their garments.

XIII.—'Red Indian' Life

Scouting.—Baden Powell's little book about Scouting set us upon a new track. Hundreds of families make joyous expeditions, far more educative than they dream, wherein scouting is the order of the day.

For example, one party of four or more lies in ambush,—the best ambush to be had, which is pitched upon after much consideration. The enemy scouts; first he finds the ambush, and then his skill is shown in getting within touch of the alert foe without being discovered. But every family should possess Scouting in default of the chance of going on the war-path with a Red Indian. The evil of the ready-made life we lead is that we do not discern the signs of the times. An alert intelligence towards what goes on in the open-air world is a great possession, and, strongly as we sympathise with the effort made to put down bird's-nesting, we shall lose, if we are not careful, one of the few bits of what we may call 'Red Indian' training still within our reach.

Bird-stalking.—But bird 'stalking,' to adapt a name, is a great deal more exciting and delightful than bird's nesting, and we get our joy at no cost of pain to other living things. All the skill of a good scout comes into play. Think, how exciting to creep noiselessy as shadows behind river-side bushes on hands and knees without disturbing a twig or pebble till you get within a yard of a pair of sandpipers, and then, lying low, to watch their dainty little runs, pretty tricks of head and tail, and to hear the music of their call. And here comes the real joy of bird-stalking. If in the winter months the children have become fairly familiar with the notes of our resident birds, they will be able in the early summer to 'stalk' to some purpose. The notes and songs in June are quite bewildering, but the plan is to single out those you are quite sure of, and then follow up the others. The key to a knowledge of birds is knowledge of their notes, and the only way to get this is to follow any note of which you are not sure. The joy of tracking a song or note to its source is the joy of a 'find,' a possession for life.

But bird-stalking is only to be done upon certain conditions. You must not only be 'most mousy-quiet,' but you must not even let a thought whisper, for if you let yourself think about anything else, the entirely delightful play of bird-life passes by you unobserved; nay, the very bird notes are unheard.

Here are two bird walks communicated by a bird lover:—

"We heard a note something like a chaffinch's, only slower, and we looked up in the boughs of the ash to try and track the bird by the sudden quiver of one twig here, another, there. We found a steep, rocky path which brought us almost level with the tree tops, and then we had a good view of the shy little willow wren busily seeking food. A note from the next tree like a bubbling of song drew us farther on, and then we found the wood wren and watched him as with up-turned head and bubbling throat he uttered his trill."

"A joyous burst of song came from a bush near by, and we crept on, to find a blackcap warbler with upraised crest turning excitedly round and round in the ecstasy of song. We waited, and traced him to his next station by his light touch on the branches. A hoarse screech from another tree announced a green-finch, and we had a long chase to get a glimpse of him; but he came to an outstanding twig, and then we heard his pretty song, which I should never have guessed to be his had we not seen him at it. A little squeaky note made us watch the tree trunks, and, sure enough, there was a tree-creeper running up and round and round an ash, uttering his note all the time.

"Another day we got behind a wall from which we could examine a field that lay beside the lake. There was the green plover with his jaunty crest, running and pecking, and, as he pecked, we caught sight of the rosy flash under his tail. We waited, hoping for more, for the plovers stand so still that they are lost in their surroundings. But someone coughed, and up went the plovers, a dozen of them, with their weary taunt, 'Why don't you let us alone?' Their distress roused other birds, and we saw a snipe rise from the water edge, a marshy place, with hasty zigzag flight; it made a long round and settled not much further than where it rose. The sandpipers rose, two flying close to the water's edge, whistling all the time. By the side of a little gully we watched a wagtail, and presently a turn in the sunshine showed us the yellow breast of the yellow wagtail. A loud 'tis-sic' near us drew our eyes to the wall, and there stood a pied wagtail with full beak, waiting to get rid of us before visiting his nest in the wall. We crept away and sheltered behind a tree, and after a few minutes' waiting we saw him go into his hole. An angry chatter near by (like a broom on Venetian blinds!) directed our eyes to a little brown wren on the wall with cocked-up tail, but in a minute he disappeared like a mouse over the side."

This from another bird-lover:—

"Now, they (the children) are beginning to care more for the birds than the eggs, and their first question, instead of being, 'What is the egg like?' is usually 'What is the bird like?' We have great searching through Morris's British Birds [John's British Birds, which costs as many shillings as Morris's does guineas, is better for beginners] to identify birds we have seen and to make quite sure of doubtful points.

"But now for the birds. Stonechats abound on the heaths. I pricked myself up to my knees standing in a gorse-patch watching and listening to the first I saw, but I was quite rewarded, and saw at least four pairs at one time. Do you know the birds? The cock-birds are such handsome little fellows, black head and mask, white collar, rufous breast and dark grey or brown back. They have a pretty little song, rather longer than a chaffinch's, besides the chit-chat cry when they are disturbed. They do not make a long flight, and will hover in the air like a flycatcher. The sandmartins have numbers of holes in the cliffs. We tried to see how deep they burrowed to build their nests, but though I put my arm in up to the elbows in several deserted holes, I could not reach the end. I think my favourites are the reed-warblers. I know of at least four pairs, and when I could induce the children to both stop talking for a few minutes, we were able to watch them boldly hopping up and down the reeds and singing in full view of us."

This is the sort of thing bird-stalkers come upon—and what a loss have those children who are not brought up to the gentle art wherein the eye is satisfied with seeing, and there is no greed of collecting, no play of the hunter's instinct to kill, and yet a lifelong joy of possession.

XIV.—The Children Require Country Air

The Essential Proportion of Oxygen.—Every one knows that the breathing of air which has lost little of its due proportion of oxygen is the essential condition of vigorous life and of a fine physique; also, that whatever produces heat, whether it be animal heat, or the heat of fire, candle, gas-lamp, produces that heat at the expense of the oxygen in the atmosphere—a bank which is drawn upon by every breathing and burning object; that in situations where much breathing and burning are going on, there is a terrible drain upon this vital gas; that the drain may be so excessive that there no longer sufficient oxygen in the air to support animal life, and death results; that where the drain is less excessive but still great, animal life may be supported, and people live in a flaccid, feeble life in a state of low vitality.

Excess of Carbonic Acid Gas.—Also we know that every breathing and every burning object expels a hurtful gas—carbonic acid. A very small proportion of this gas is present in the purest atmospheric air, and that small proportion is healthful; but increase that quantity by the action of furnaces, fires, living beings, gas-lamps, and the air is rendered unwholesome, just in proportion to the quantity of superfluous carbonic-acid gas it contains. If the quantity be excessive—as when many people are huddled together in a small unventilated room—speedy death by suffocation is the result.

Unvitiated, Unimpoverished Air.—For these reasons, it is not possible to enjoy fullness of life in a town. For grown-up people, the stimulus of town life does something to make up for the impurity of town air; as, on the other hand, country people too often forfeit their advantages through the habit of mental sluggishness they let themselves fall into: but, for the children—who not only breathe, but grow; who require, proportionately, more oxygen than adults need for their vital processes—it is absolutely cruel not to give them very frequent, if not daily, copious draughts of unvitiated, unimpoverished air, the sort of air that can be had only remote from towns.

Solar Light.—But this is only one of the reasons why, for health's sake alone, it is of the first importance to give children long days in the open country. They want light, solar light, as well as air. Country people are ruddier than town folk; miners are sallow, so are the dwellers in cellars and in sunless valleys. The reason is, that, to secure the ruddy glow of perfect health, certain changes must take place in the blood—the nature of which it would take too long to explain here—and that these changes in the blood, marked by free production of red corpuscles, appear to take place most favourably under the influence of abundant solar light. What is more, men of science are beginning to suspect that not only the coloured light rays of the solar spectrum, but the dark heat rays, and the chemical rays, minister to vitality in ways not yet fully understood.

A Physical Ideal for a Child.—There was a charming picture in Punch some time ago, of two little boys airing their English-French on their mother's new maid; two noble little fellows, each straight as a dart, with no superfluous flesh, eyes well opened, head erect, chest expanded, the whole body full of spring even in repose. It was worth looking at, if only as suggesting the sort of physique we delight to see in a child. No doubt the child inherits the most that he is in this respect as in all others; but this is what bringing-up may, with some limitations, effect:—The child is born with certain natural tendencies, and, according to his bringing-up, each such tendency may run into a blemish of person or character, or into a cognate grace. Therefore, it is worth while to have even a physical ideal for one's child; not, for instance, to be run away with by the notion that a fat child is necessarily a fine child. The fat child can easily be produced: but the bright eyes, the open regard, the springing step; the tones, clear as a bell; the agile, graceful movements that characterise the well-brought-up child, are the result, not of bodily well being only, but of 'mind and soul according well,' of a quick, trained intelligence, and of a moral nature habituated to the 'joy of self control.'

Part III:

'Habit Is Ten Natures'

I.—Education Based Upon Natural Law

A Healthy Brain.—What I desire to set before the reader is a method of education based upon natural law. In the first place, we have considered some of the conditions to be observed with a view to keep the brain in healthy working order; for it is upon the possession of an active, duly nourished brain that the possibility of a sound education depends.

Out-of-Door Life.—The consideration of out-of-door life, in developing a method of education, comes second in order; because my object is to show that the chief function of the child—his business in the world during the first six or seven years of his life—is to find out all he can, about whatever comes under his notice, by means of his five senses; that he has an insatiable appetite for knowledge got in this way; and that, therefore, the endeavour of his parents should be to put him in the way of making acquaintance freely with Nature and natural objects; that, in fact, the intellectual education of the young child should lie in the free exercise of perceptive power, because the first stages of mental effort are marked by the extreme activity of this power; and the wisdom of the educator is to follow the lead of Nature in the evolution of the complete human being.

The next subject for consideration—a rather dry psycho-physiological one—seems to me, all the same, to be very well worthy of attention as striking the keynote of a reasonable method of education.

Habit the Instrument by which Parents Work.—'Habit is ten natures!' If I could but make others see with my eyes how much this saying should mean to the educator! How habit, in the hands of the mother, is as his wheel to the potter, his knife to the carver—the instrument by means of which she turns out the design she has already conceived in her brain. Observe, the material is there to begin with; his wheel will not enable the potter to produce a porcelain cup out of coarse clay; but the instrument is as necessary as the material or the design. It is unpleasant to speak of one's self, but if the reader will allow me, I should like to run over the steps by which I have been brought to look upon habit as the means whereby the parent may make almost anything he chooses of his child. That which has become the dominant idea of one person's life, if it be launched suddenly at another, conveys no very great depth or weight of meaning to the second person—he wants to get at it by degrees, to see the steps by which the other has travelled. Therefore, I shall venture to show how I arrived at my present position, which is, from one of the three possible points of view—The formation of habits is education, and Education is the formation of habits.

II.—The Children Have No Self-Compelling Power

An Educational Cul-de-sac.—Some years ago I was accustomed to hear, 'Habit is ten natures,' delivered from the pulpit on at least one Sunday out of four. I had at the time just begun to teach, and was young and enthusiastic in my work. It was to my mind a great thing to be a teacher; it was impossible but that the teacher should leave his stamp on the children. His own was the fault if anything went wrong, if any child did badly in school or out of it. There was no degree of responsibility to which youthful ardour was not equal. But, all this zeal notwithstanding, the disappointing thing was, that nothing extraordinary happened. The children were good on the whole, because they were the children of parents who had themselves been brought up with some care; but it was plain that they behaved very much as twas their nature to.' The faults they had, they kept; the virtues they had were exercised just as fitfully as before. The good, meek little girl still told fibs. The bright, generous child was incurably idle. In lessons it was the same thing; the dawdling child went on dawdling, the dull child became no brighter. It was very disappointing. The children, no doubt, 'got on'—a little; but each one of them had the makings in her of a noble character, of a fine mind, and where was the lever to lift each of these little worlds? Such a lever there must be. This horse-in-a-mill round of geography and French, history and sums, was no more than playing at education; for who remembers the scraps of knowledge he laboured over as a child? and would not the application of a few hours in later life effect more than a year's drudgery at any one subject in childhood? If education is to secure the step-by-step progress of the individual and the race, it must mean something over and above the daily plodding at small tasks which goes by the name.

Love, Law, and Religion as Educational Forces.—Looking for guidance to the literature of education, I learned much from various sources, though I failed to find what seemed to me an authoritative guide, that is, one whose thought embraced the possibilities contained in the human nature of a child, and, at the same time, measured the scope of education. I saw how religious teaching helped the children, gave them power and motives for continuous effort, and raised their desires towards the best things. I saw in how far law restrained from evil, and love impelled towards good. But with these great aids from without and from above, there was still the depressing sense of labouring at education in the dark; the advance made by the young people in moral, and even in intellectual, power was like that of a door on its hinges—a swing forward to-day and back again to-morrow, with little sensible progress from year to year beyond that of being able to do harder sums and read harder books.

Why Children are incapable of Steady Effort.—Consideration made the reason of the failure plain: there was a warm glow of goodness at the heart of every one of the children, but they were all incapable of steady effort, because they had no strength of will, no power to make themselves do that which they knew they ought to do. Here, no doubt, come in the functions of parents and teachers; they should be able to make the child do that which he lacks the power to compel himself to. But it were poor training that should keep the child dependent upon personal influence. It is the business of education to find some way of supplementing that weakness of will which is the bane of most of us as well as of the children.

Children should be saved the Effort of Decision.—That the effort of decision is the most exhausting effort of life, has been well said from the pulpit; and if that remain true about ourselves, even when the decision is about trifling matters of going or coming, buying or not buying, it surely is not just to leave the children all the labour of an effort of will whenever they have to choose between the right and the wrong.

III.—What Is 'Nature'?

'Habit is ten natures,' went on being proclaimed in my ears; and at last it came home to me as a weighty saying, which might contain the educational 'Open, sesame!' I was in quest of. In the first place, what is Nature, and what, precisely, is Habit?

It is an astonishing thing, when we consider, what the child is, irrespective of race, country, or kindred, simply in right of his birth as a human being.

All Persons born with the same Primary Desires.—That we all have the same instincts and appetites, we are prepared to allow, but that the principles of action which govern all men everywhere are primarily the same, is a little startling; that, for instance, the same desires stir in the breasts of savage and of sage alike; that the desire of knowledge, which shows itself in the child's curiosity about things and his eager use of his eyes, is equally active everywhere; that the desire of society, which you may see in two babies presented to one another and all agog with glee and friendliness, is the cause, alike, of village communities amongst savage tribes and of the philosophical meeting of the learned; that everywhere is felt the desire of esteem—a wonderful power in the hands of the educator, making a word of praise or blame more powerful as a motive than any fear or hope of punishment or reward.

And Affections.—And it is not only the same desires; all people, everywhere, have the same affections and passions which act in the same way under similar provocation: joy and grief, love and resentment, benevolence, sympathy, fear, and much else, are common to all of us. So, too, of conscience, the sense of duty.

Content of the most Elemental Notion of Human Nature.—Dr Livingstone mentions that the only addition he felt called upon to make to the moral code of certain of the Zambesi tribes (however little they observed their own law) was, that a man should not have more than one wife. "Evil speaking, lying, hatred, disobedience to parents, neglect of them," were all known to be sin by these dark peoples whom civilised or Christian teaching had never before reached. Not only is a sense of duty common to mankind, but the deeper consciousness of God, however vague such consciousness may be. And all this and much more goes to make up the most elemental notion of human nature.

Nature plus Heredity.—Then, heredity comes in, and here, if you please, is ten natures: who is to deal with the child who is resentful, or stubborn, or reckless, because it is born in him, his mother's nature or his grandfather's? Think of the trick of the eye, the action of the hand, repeated from father to son; the peculiar character of the hand-writing, traceable, as Miss Power Cobbe tells us is the case in her family, for instance, through five generations; the artistic temperament, the taste for music or drawing, running in families: here you get Nature with a twist, confirmed, sealed, riveted, utterly proof, you would say, against any attempt to alter or modify it.

Plus Physical Conditions.—And, once more, physical conditions come into force. The puny, feeble child and the sturdy urchin who never ails must necessarily differ from one another in the strength of their desires and emotions.

Human Nature the Sum of certain Attributes.—What, then, with the natural desires, affections, and emotions common to the whole race, what with the tendencies which each family derives by descent, and those peculiarities which the individual owes to his own constitution of body and brain,—human nature, the sum of all these, makes out for itself a strong case; so much so, that we are inclined to think the best that can be done is to let it alone, to let every child develop unhindered according to the elements of character and disposition that are in him.

The Child must not be left to his Human Nature.—This is precisely what half the parents in the world, and three-fourths of the teachers, are content to do; and what is the consequence? That the world is making advances, but the progress is, for the most part, amongst the few whose parents have taken their education seriously in hand; while the rest, who have been allowed to stay where they were, be no more, or no better than Nature made them, act as a heavy drag: for, indeed, the fact is, that they do not stay where they were; it is unchangeably true that the child who is not being constantly raised to a higher and a higher platform will sink to a lower and a lower. Wherefore, it is as much the parent's duty to educate his child into moral strength and purpose and intellectual activity as it is to feed him and clothe him; and that in spite of his nature, if it must be so. It is true that here and there circumstances step in and 'make a man' of the boy whose parents have failed to bring him under discipline; but this is a fortuitous aid which the educator is no way warranted to count upon.

I was beginning to see my way—not yet out of the psychological difficulty, which, so far as I was concerned, blocked the way to any real education; but now I could put my finger on the place, and that was something. Thus: -

The will of the child is pitifully feeble, weaker in the children of the weak, stronger in the children of the strong, but hardly ever to be counted upon as a power in education.

The nature of the child—his human nature—being the sum of what he is as a human being, and what he is in right of the stock he comes of, and what he is as the result of his own physical and mental constitution—this nature is incalculably strong.

Problem before the Educator.—The problem before the educator is to give the child control over his own nature, to enable him to hold himself in hand as much in regard to the traits we call good, as to those we call evil:—many a man makes shipwreck on the rock of what he grew up to think his characteristic virtue—his open-handedness, for instance.

Divine Grace works on the Lines of Human Effort.—In looking for a solution of this problem, I do not undervalue the Divine grace—far otherwise; but we do not always make enough of the fact that Divine grace is exerted on the lines of enlightened human effort; that the parent, for instance, who takes the trouble to understand what he is about in educating his child, deserves, and assuredly gets, support from above; and that Rebecca, let us say, had no right to bring up her son to be "thou worm, Jacob," in the trust that Divine grace would, speaking reverently, pull him through. Being a pious man, the son of pious parents, he was pulled through, but his days, he complains at the end, were "few and evil."

The Trust of Parents must not be Supine.— And indeed this is what too many Christian parents expect: they let a child grow free as the wild bramble, putting forth unchecked whatever is in him—thorn, coarse flower, insipid fruit,—trusting, they will tell you, that the grace of God will prune and dig and prop the wayward branches lying prone. And their trust is not always misplaced; but the poor man endures anguish, is torn asunder in the process of recovery which his parents might have spared him had they trained the early shoots which should develop by-and-by into the character of their child.

Nature then, strong as she is, is not invincible; and, at her best, Nature is not to be permitted to ride rampant. Bit and bridle, hand and voice, will get the utmost of endeavour out of her if her training be taken in hand in time; but let Nature run wild, like the forest ponies, and not spur nor whip will break her in.

IV.—Habit May Supplant 'Nature'

'Habit is ten natures.' If that be true, strong as nature is, habit is not only as strong, but tenfold as strong. Here, then, have we a stronger than he, able to overcome this strong man armed.

Habit runs on the Lines of Nature.—But habit runs on the lines of nature: the cowardly child habitually lies that he may escape blame; the loving child has a hundred endearing habits; the good-natured child has a habit of giving; the selfish child, a habit of keeping. Habit, working thus according to nature, is simply nature in action, growing strong by exercise.

But Habit may be a Lever.—But habit, to be the lever to lift the child, must work contrary to nature, or at any rate, independently of her.

Directly we begin to look out for the working of habit on these lines, examples crowd upon us: there are the children trained in careful habits, who never soil their clothes; those trained in reticent habits, who never speak of what is done at home, and answer indiscreet questions with 'I don't know'; there are the children brought up in courteous habits, who make way for their elders with gentle grace, and more readily for the poor woman with the basket than for the well-dressed lady; and there are children trained in grudging habits, who never offer to yield, or go, or do.

A Mother forms her Children's Habits involuntarily.—Such habits as these, good, bad, or indifferent, are they natural to the children? No, but they are what their mothers have brought them up to; and as a matter of fact, there is nothing which a mother cannot bring her child up to, and there is hardly a mother anywhere who has not some two or three—crotchets sometimes, principles sometimes—which her children never violate. So that it comes to this—given, a mother with liberal views on the subject of education, and she simply cannot help working her own views into her children's habits; given, on the other hand, a mother whose final question is, 'What will people say? what will people think? how will it look?' and the children grow up with habits of seeming, and not of being; they are content to appear well-dressed, well-mannered, and well-intentioned to outsiders, with very little effort after beauty, order, and goodness at home, and in each other's eyes.

Habit forces Nature into New Channels.—The extraordinary power of habit in forcing nature into new channels hardly requires illustration; we have only to see a small boy at a circus riding two barebacked ponies with a foot on the back of each, or a pantomime fairy dancing on air, or a clown behaving like an indiarubber ball, or any of the thousand feats of skill and dexterity which we pay our shillings to see—mental feats as well as bodily, though, happily, these are the rarer—to be convinced that exactly anything may be accomplished by training, that is, the cultivation of persistent habits. And the power of habit is not seen in human beings alone. The cat goes in search of her dinner always at the same time and to the same place—that is, if it is usual to feed her in one spot. Indeed, the habit of place is so much to the cat, that she will often rather die of famine than forsake the house to which she is accustomed. As for the dog, he is still more a 'bundle of habits' than his master. Scatter the crumbs for the sparrows at nine o'clock every morning, and at nine o'clock they will come for their breakfast, crumbs or no crumbs. Darwin inclines to think that the terror and avoidance shown towards man by the wild birds and lesser animals is simply a matter of transmitted habit; he tells us how he landed upon certain of the Pacific islands where the birds had never seen man before, and they lighted upon him and flew about him with utter fearlessness. To come nearer home, what evidence of the mastery of habit is more sad and more overwhelming than the habits of the drunkard, for instance, persisted in, in spite of reason, conscience, purpose, religion, every motive which should influence a thinking being?

Parents and Teachers must lay down Lines of Habit.—All this is nothing new; we have always known that 'use is second nature,' and that 'man is a bundle of habits.' It was not the fact, but the application of the fact, and the physiology of habit, that were new and exceedingly valuable ideas to me, and I hope they may be of some use to the reader. It was new to me, for instance, to perceive that it rests with parents and teachers to lay down lines of habit on which the life of the child may run henceforth with little jolting or miscarriage, and may advance in the right direction with the minimum of effort.

V.—The Laying Down Of Lines Of Habit

'Begin it, and the thing will be completed!' is infallibly true of every mental and moral habitude: completed, not on the lines you foresee and intend, but on the lines appropriate and necessary to that particular habitude. In the phrase 'unconscious cerebration' we are brought face to face with the fact that, whatever seed of thought or feeling you implant in a child—whether through inheritance or by early training—grows, completes itself, and begets after its kind, even as does a corporeal organism. It is a marvellous and beautiful thing to perceive an idea when the idea itself is a fine one—developing within you of its own accord, to find your pen writing down sentences whose logical sequence delights you, and yet in the conception of which you have had no conscious part. When the experienced writer 'reels off' in this fashion, he knows that so far as the run of the words, the ordering of the ideas, go, his work will need no revision. So fine a thing is this, that the lingering fallacy of the infallible reason established itself thereupon. The philosopher, who takes pleasure in observing the ways of his own mind, is a thinker of high thoughts, and he is apt to forget that the thought which defiles a man behaves in precisely the same way as that which purifies: the one, as the other, develops, matures, and increases after its kind.

We Think, as we are accustomed to Think.— How does this bear on the practical work of bringing up children? In this way. We think, as we are accustomed to think; ideas come and go and carry on a ceaseless traffic in the rut—let us call it—you have made for them in the very nerve substance of the brain. You do not deliberately intend to think these thoughts; you may, indeed, object strongly to the line they are taking (two 'trains' of thought going on at one and the same time!), and objecting, you may be able to barricade the way, to put up 'No Road' in big letters, and to compel the busy populace of the brain-world to take another route. But who is able for these things? Not the child, immature of will, feeble in moral power, unused to the weapons of the spiritual warfare. He depends upon his parents; it rests with them to initiate the thoughts he shall think, the desires he shall cherish, the feelings he shall allow. Only to initiate; no more is permitted to them; but from this initiation will result the habits of thought and feeling which govern the man—his character, that is to say. But is not this assuming too much, seeing that, to sum up roughly all we understand by heredity, a child is born with his future in his hands? The child is born, doubtless, with the tendencies which should shape his future; but every tendency has its branch roads, its good or evil outcome; and to put the child on the right track for the fulfilment of the possibilities inherent in him, is the vocation of the parent.

Direction of Lines of Habit.—This relation of habit to human life—as the rails on which it runs to a locomotive—is perhaps the most suggestive and helpful to the educator; for just as it is on the whole easier for the locomotive to pursue its way on the rails than to take a disastrous run off them, so it is easier for the child to follow lines of habit carefully laid down than to run off these lines at his peril. It follows that this business of laying down lines towards the unexplored country of the child's future is a very serious and responsible one for the parent. It rests with him to consider well the tracks over which the child should travel with profit and pleasure; and, along these tracks, to lay down lines so invitingly smooth and easy that the little traveller is going upon them at full speed without stopping to consider whether or no he chooses to go that way. Habit and Free-will—But,—supposing that the doing of a certain action a score or two of times in unbroken sequence forms a habit which it is as easy to follow as not; that, persist still further in the habit without lapses, and it becomes second nature, quite difficult to shake off; continue it further, through a course of years, and the habit has the strength of ten natures, you cannot break through it without doing real violence to yourself;— grant all this, and also that it is possible to form in the child the habit of doing and saying, even of thinking and feeling, all that it is desirable he should do or say, think or feel,—and do you not take away the child's free-will, make a mere automaton of him by this excessive culture?

Habit rules ninety-nine in a hundred of our Thoughts and Acts.—In the first place, whether you choose or no to take any trouble about the formation of his habits, it is habit, all the same, which will govern ninety-nine one-hundredths of the child's life: he is the mere automaton you describe. As for the child's becoming the creature of habit, that is not left with the parent to determine. We are all mere creatures of habit. We think our accustomed thoughts, make our usual small talk, go through the trivial round, the common task, without any self-determining effort of will at all. If it were not so—if we had to think, to deliberate, about each operation of the bath or the table—life would not be worth having; the perpetually repeated effort of decision would wear us out. But, let us be thankful, life is not thus laborious. For a hundred times we act or think, it is not necessary to choose, to will, say, more than once. And the little emergencies, which compel an act of will, will fall in the children's lives just about as frequently as in our own. These we cannot save them from, nor is it desirable that we should. What we can do for them is to secure that they have habits which shall lead them in ways of order, propriety, and virtue, instead of leaving their wheel of life to make ugly ruts in miry places.

Habit powerful even where the Will decides.—And then, even in emergencies, in every sudden difficulty and temptation that requires an act of will, why, conduct is still apt to run on the lines of the familiar habit. The boy who has been accustomed to find both profit and pleasure in his books does not fall easily into idle ways because he is attracted by an idle schoolfellow. The girl who has been carefully trained to speak the exact truth simply does not think of a lie as a ready means of getting out of a scrape, coward as she may be.

But this doctrine of habit, is it, after all, any more than an empirical treatment of the child's symptoms? Why should the doing of an act or the thinking of a thought, say, a score of times in unbroken succession, have any tendency to make the doing of that act or the thinking of that thought a part of the child's nature? We may accept the doctrine as an act of faith resting on experience; but if we could discover the raison d'être of this enormous force of habit it would be possible to go to work on the laying down of habits with real purpose and method.

VI.—The Physiology Of Habit

A work of Dr. Carpenter's was perhaps the first which gave me the clue I was in search of. In his Mental Physiology—a most interesting book, by the way—he works out the analogy between mental and physical activity, and shows that the correspondence in effect is due to a correspondence in cause.

Growing Tissues form themselves to Modes of Action.—To state roughly the doctrine of the school Dr. Carpenter represents—the tissues, as muscular tissue, for instance, undergo constant waste and as constant reparation. Even those modes of muscular action which we regard as natural to us, as walking and standing erect, are in reality the results of a laborious education; quite as much so as many modes of action which we consciously acquire, as writing or dancing; but the acquired modes become perfectly easy and natural. Why? Because it is the law of the constantly growing tissues that they should form themselves according to the modes of action required of them. In a case where the brain is repeatedly sending down to the muscles, under nervous control as they are, the message to have a certain action done, that action becomes automatic in the lower centre, and the faintest suggestion from outside comes to produce it without the intervention of the brain. Thus, the joints and muscles of the child's hand very soon accommodate themselves to the mode of action required of them in holding and guiding the pen. Observe, it is not that the child learns with his mind how to use his pen, in spite of his muscles; but that the newly growing muscles themselves take form according to the action required of them. And here is the explanation of all the mountebank feats which appear simply impossible to the untrained looker-on. They are impossible to him, because his joints and muscles have not the same powers which have been produced in the mountebank by a process of early training.

Therefore Children should learn Dancing, Swimming, etc., at an Early Age.—So much for mere bodily activities. And here we have the reason why children should learn dancing, riding, swimming, calisthenics, every form of activity which requires a training of the muscles, at an early age: the fact being, that muscles and joints have not merely to conform themselves to new uses, but to grow to a modified pattern; and this growth and adaptation take place with the greatest facility in early youth. Of course, the man whose muscles have kept the habit of adaptation picks up new games, new muscular exercises, without very great labour. But teach a ploughman to write, and you see the enormous physical difficulty which unaccustomed muscles have in growing to any new sort of effort. Here we see how important it is to keep watch over the habits of enunciation, carriage of the head, and so on, which the child is forming hour by hour. The poke, the stoop, the indistinct utterance, is not a mere trick to be left off at pleasure 'when he is older and knows better,' but is all the time growing into him becoming a part of himself, because it is registered in the very substance of his spinal cord. The part of his nervous system where consciousness resides (the brain) has long ago given a standing order, and such are the complications of the administration, that to recall the order would mean the absolute re-making of the parts concerned. And to correct bad habits of speaking, for instance, it will not be enough for the child to intend to speak plainly and to try to speak plainly; he will not be able, to do so habitually until some degree of new growth has taken place in the organs of voice whilst he is making efforts to form the new habit.

Moral and Mental Habits make their Mark upon Physical Tissues.—But, practically, everybody knows that the body, and every part of the body, accommodates itself very readily to the uses it is put to: we know that if a child accustom herself to stand on one foot, thus pushing up one shoulder, the habit will probably end in curvature of the spine; that to permit drooping shoulders, and, consequently, contracted chest, is to prepare the way for lung disease. The physical consequences of bad habits of this sort are so evident, that we cannot blind ourselves to the relation of cause and effect. What we are less prepared to admit is, that habits which do not appear to be in any sense physical—a flippant habit, a truthful habit, an orderly habit—should also make their mark upon a physical tissue, and that it is to this physical effect the enormous strength of habit is probably due. Yet when we consider that the brain, the physical brain, is the exceedingly delicate organ by means of which we think and feel and desire, love and hate and worship, it is not surprising that that organ should be modified by the work it has to do; to put the matter picturesquely, it is as if every familiar train of thought made a rut in the nervous substance of the brain into which the thoughts run lightly of their own accord, and out of which they can only be got by an effort of will.

Persistent Trains of Thought.—Thus, the mistress of the house knows that when her thoughts are free to take their own course, they run to cares of the house or the larder, to to-morrow's dinner or the winter's clothing; that is, thought runs into the rut which has been, so to speak, worn for it by constant repetition. The mother's thoughts run on her children, the painter's on pictures, the poet's on poems; those of the anxious head of the house on money cares, it may be, until in times of unusual pressure the thoughts beat, beat, beat in that well-worn rut of ways and means, and decline to run in any other channel, till the poor man loses his reason, simply because he cannot get his thoughts out of that one channel made in the substance of his brain. And, indeed, "that way madness lies" for every one of us, in the persistent preying of any one train of thought upon the brain tissue. Pride, resentment, jealousy, an invention that a man has laboured over, an opinion he has conceived, any line of thought which he has no longer the power to divert, will endanger a man's sanity.

Incessant Regeneration of Brain Tissue.—If we love, hate, think, feel, worship, at the expense of actual physical effort on the part of the brain, and consequent waste of tissue, how enormous must be the labour of that organ with which we, in fact, do everything, even many of those acts whose final execution falls to the hands or feet! It is true: and to repair this excessive waste, the brain consumes the lion's share of the nourishment provided for the body. As we have already seen, fully a sixth or a fifth of all the blood in the body goes to repair the waste in the king's house; in other words, new brain tissue is being constantly formed at a startlingly rapid rate: one wonders at what age the child has no longer any part left of that brain with which he was born.

The new tissue repeats the old, but not quite exactly, just as a new muscular growth adapts itself to any now exercise required of it, so the new brain tissue is supposed to 'grow to' any habit of thought in force during the time of growth—'thought' here including, of course, every exercise of mind and soul. "The cerebrum of man grows to the modes of thought in which it is habitually exercised," says an able physiologist; or, in the words of Dr Carpenter, "Any sequence of mental action which has been frequently repeated, tends to perpetuate itself; so that we find ourselves automatically prompted to think, feel, or do what we have been before accustomed to think, feel, or do, under like circumstances, without any consciously formed purpose or anticipation of results. For there is no reason to regard the cerebrum as an exception to the general principle, that whilst each part of the organism tends to form itself in accordance with the mode in which it is habitually exercised, this tendency will be specially strong in the nervous apparatus, in virtue of that incessant regeneration which is the very condition of its functional activity. It scarcely, indeed, admits of a doubt, that every state of ideational consciousness which is either very strong or is habitually repeated, leaves an organic impression on the cerebrum, in virtue of which the same state may be reproduced at any future time in correspondence to a suggestion fitted to excite it."

Artificial Reflex Actions may be Acquired.—Or, to take Huxley's way of putting the case:

"By the help of the brain we may acquire an infinity of artificial reflex actions; that is to say, an action may require all our attention and all our volition for its first, second, or third performance, but by frequent repetition it becomes, in a manner, part of our organization, and is performed without volition or even consciousness.

"As every one knows, it takes a soldier a long time to learn his drill—for instance, to put himself into the attitude of 'attention' at the instant the word of command is heard. But after a time the sound of the word gives rise to the act, whether the soldier be thinking of it or not. There is a story, which is credible enough, though it may not be true, of a practical joker who, seeing a discharged veteran carrying home his dinner, suddenly called out 'Attention!' whereupon the man instantly brought his hands down, and lost his mutton and potatoes in the gutter. The drill had been thorough, and its effects had become embodied in the man's nervous structure.

"The possibility of all education (of which military drill is only one particular form) is based upon the existence of this power which the nervous system possesses, of organizing conscious actions into more or less unconscious, or reflex, operations. It may be down laid as a rule, that if any two mental states be called up together, or in succession, with due frequency and vividness, the subsequent production of the one of them will suffice to call up the other, and that whether we desire it or not.

Intellectual and Moral Education.—"The object of intellectual education is to create such indissoluble associations of our ideas of things, in the order and relation in which they occur in nature; that of a moral education is to unite as fixedly, the ideas of evil deeds with those of pain and degradation, and of good actions with those of pleasure and nobleness."

But it is the intimate interlocking of mind and matter which is more directly important to the educator—the idea which we have put broadly under the (by no means scientifically accurate) figure of a rut. Given, that the constant direction of the thoughts produces a certain set in the tissues of the brain, this set is the first trace of the rut or path, a line of least resistance, along which the same impression, made another time, will find it easier to travel than to take another path. So arises a right-of-way for any given habit of action or thought.

Character affected by Acquired Modification of Brain Tissue.—What follows? Why, that the actual conformation of the child's brain depends upon the habits which the parents permit or encourage; and that the habits of the child produce the character of the man, because certain mental habitudes once set up, their nature is to go on for ever unless they should be displaced by other habits. Here is an end to the easy philosophy of, 'It doesn't matter,' 'Oh, he'll grow out of it,' 'He'll know better by-and-by,' 'He's so young, what can we expect?' and so on. Every day, every hour, the parents are either passively or actively forming those habits in their children upon which, more than upon anything else, future character and conduct depend.

Outside Influence.—And here comes in the consideration of outside influence. Nine times out of ten we begin to do a thing because we see some one else do it; we go on doing it, and—there is the habit! If it is so easy for ourselves to take up a new habit, it is tenfold as easy for the children; and this is the real difficulty in the matter of the education of habit. It is necessary that the mother be always on the alert to nip in the bud the bad habit her children may be in the act of picking up from servants or from other children.

VII.—The Forming Of A Habit—'Shut The Door After You'

"Do Ye Next Thinge."

"Lose this day loitering, and 'twill be the same story

To-morrow; and the next, more dilatory:

The indecision brings its own delays,

And days are lost, lamenting o'er lost days,"

says Marlowe, who, like many of us, knew the misery of the intellectual indolence which cannot brace itself to "Do ye next thinge." No question concerning the bringing up of children can, conceivably, be trivial, but this, of dilatoriness, is very important. The effort of decision, we have seen, is the greatest effort of life; not the doing of the thing, but the making up of one's mind as to which thing to do first. It is commonly this sort of mental indolence, born of indecision, which leads to dawdling habits. How is the dilatory child to be cured? Time? She will know better as she grows older? Not a bit of it: "And the next, more dilatory" will be the story of her days, except for occasional spurts. Punishments? No; your dilatory person is a fatalist. 'What can't be cured must be endured,' he says, but he will endure without any effort to cure. Rewards? No; to him a reward is a punishment presented under another aspect: the possible reward he realizes as actual; there it is, within his grasp, so to say; in foregoing the reward he is punished; and he bears the punishment. What remains to be tried when neither time, reward, nor punishment is effectual? That panacea of the educationist: 'One custom overcometh another.' This inveterate dawdling is a habit to be supplanted only by the contrary habit, and the mother must devote herself for a few weeks to this cure as steadily and untiringly as she would to the nursing of her child through measles. Having in a few—the fewer the better—earnest words pointed out the miseries that must arise from this fault, and the duty of overcoming it, and having so got the (sadly feeble) will of the child on the side of right-doing, she simply sees that for weeks together the fault does not recur. The child goes to dress for a walk; she dreams over the lacing of her boots—the tag in her fingers poised in mid air—but her conscience is awake; she is constrained to look up, and her mother's eye is upon her, hopeful and expectant. She answers to the rein and goes on; midway, in the lacing of the second boot, there is another pause, shorter this time; again she looks up, and again she goes on. The pauses become fewer day by day, the efforts steadier, the immature young will is being strengthened, the habit of prompt action acquired. After that first talk, the mother would do well to refrain from one more word on the subject; the eye (expectant, not reproachful), and, where the child is far gone in a dream, the lightest possible touch, are the only effectual instruments. By-and-by, 'Do you think you can get ready in five minutes to-day without me?' 'Oh yes, mother.' 'Do not say "yes" unless you are quite sure.' 'I will try.' And she tries, and succeeds. Now, the mother will be tempted to relax her efforts—to overlook a little dawdling because the dear child has been trying so hard. This is absolutely fatal. The fact is, that the dawdling habit has made an appreciable record in the very substance of the child's brain. During the weeks of cure new growth has been obliterating the old track, and the track of a new habit is being formed. To permit any reversion to the old bad habit is to let go all this gain. To form a good habit is the work of a few weeks; to guard it is a work of incessant, but by no means anxious care. One word more,—prompt action on the child's part should have the reward of absolute leisure, time in which to do exactly as she pleases, not granted as a favour, but accruing (without any words) as a right.

Habit a Delight in itself.—Except for this one drawback, the forming of habits in the children is no laborious task, for the reward goes hand in hand with the labour; so much so, that it is like the laying out of a penny with the certainty of the immediate return of a pound. For a habit is a delight in itself; poor human nature is conscious of the

ease that it is to repeat the doing of anything without effort; and, therefore, the formation of a habit, the gradually lessening sense of effort in a given act, is pleasurable. This
is one of the rocks that mothers sometimes split upon: they lose sight of the fact that a
habit, even a good habit, becomes a real pleasure; and when the child has really formed
the habit of doing a certain thing, his mother imagines that the effort is as great to him
as at first, that it is virtue in him to go on making this effort, and that he deserves, by
way of reward, a little relaxation—she will let him break through the new habit a few
times, and then go on again. But it is not going on; it is beginning again, and beginning
in the face of obstacles. The 'little relaxation' she allowed her child meant the forming
of another contrary habit, which must be overcome before the child gets back to where
he was before.

As a matter of fact, this misguided sympathy on the part of mothers is the one thing
that makes it a laborious undertaking to train a child in good habits; for it is the nature
of the child to take to habits as kindly as the infant takes to his mother's milk.

Tact, Watchfulness, and Persistence.—For example, and to choose a habit of no great
consequence except as a matter of consideration for others: the mother wishes her child
to acquire the habit of shutting the door after him when he enters or leaves a room.
Tact, watchfulness, and persistence are the qualities she must cultivate in herself; and,
with these, she will be astonished at the readiness with which the child picks up the
new habit.

Stages in the Formation of a Habit.—'Johnny,' she says, in a bright, friendly voice, 'I
want you to remember something with all your might: never go into or out of a room in
which anybody is sitting without shutting the door.' 'But if I forget, mother?' 'I will try
to remind you.' 'But perhaps I shall be in a great hurry.' 'You must always make time to
do that.' 'But why, mother?' 'Because it is not polite to the people in the room to make
them uncomfortable.' 'But if I am going out again that very minute?' 'Still, shut the door,
when you come in; you can open it again to go out. Do you think you can remember?'
'I'll try, mother.'

'Very well; I shall watch to see how few "forgets" you make.'

For two or three times Johnny remembers; and then, he is off like a shot and half-way
downstairs before his mother has time to call him back. She does not cry out, 'Johnny,
come back and shut the door!' because she knows that a summons of that kind is exas-
perating to big or little. She goes to the door, and calls pleasantly, 'Johnny!' Johnny has
forgotten all about the door; he wonders what his mother wants, and, stirred by curiosity, comes back, to find her seated and employed as before. She looks up, glances at the
door, and says, 'I said I should try to remind you.' 'Oh, I forgot,' says Johnny, put upon
his honour; and he shuts the door that time, and the next, and the next.

But the little fellow has really not much power to recollect, and the mother will have to
adopt various little devices to remind him; but of two things she will be careful—that he
never slips off without shutting the door, and that she never lets the matter be a cause
of friction between herself and the child, taking the line of his friendly ally to help him

against that bad memory of his. By and by, after, say, twenty shuttings of the door with never an omission, the habit begins to be formed; Johnny shuts the door as a matter of course, and his mother watches him with delight come into a room, shut the door, take something off the table, and go out, again shutting the door.

The Dangerous Stage.—Now that Johnny always shuts the door, his mother's joy and triumph begin to be mixed with unreasonable pity. 'Poor child,' she says to herself, 'it is very good of him to take so much pains about a little thing, just because he is bid!' She thinks that, all the time, the child is making an effort for her sake; losing sight of the fact that the habit has become easy and natural, that, in fact, Johnny shuts the door without knowing that he does so. Now comes the critical moment. Some day Johnny is so taken up with a new delight that the habit, not yet fully formed, loses its hold, and he is half-way downstairs before he thinks of the door. Then he does think of it, with a little prick of conscience, strong enough, not to send him back, but to make him pause a moment to see if his mother will call him back. She has noticed the omission, and is saying to herself, 'Poor little fellow, he has been very good about it this long time; I'll let him off this once.' He, outside, fails to hear his mother's call, says, to himself—fatal sentence!—'Oh, it doesn't matter,' and trots off.

Next time he leaves the door open, but it is not a 'forget.' His mother calls him back in a rather feeble way. His quick ear catches the weakness of her tone, and, without coming back, he cries, 'Oh, mother, I'm in such a hurry,' and she says no more, but lets him off. Again he rushes in, leaving the door wide open. 'Johnny!'—in a warning voice. 'I'm going out again just in a minute, mother,' and after ten minutes' rummaging he does go out, and forgets to shut the door. The mother's mis-timed easiness has lost for her every foot of the ground she had gained.

VIII.—Infant 'Habits'

The whole group of habitudes, half physical and half moral, on which the propriety and comfort of everyday life depend, are received passively by the child; that is, he does very little to form these habits himself, but his brain receives impressions from what he sees about him; and these impressions take form as his own very strongest and most lasting habits.

Some Branches of Infant Education.—Cleanliness, order, neatness, regularity, punctuality, are all 'branches' of infant education. They should be about the child like the air he breathes, and he will take them in as unconsciously. It is hardly necessary to say a word about the necessity for delicate cleanliness in the nursery. The babies get their share of tubbing, and unlimited washing is done on their behalf; but, indeed, scrupulous as mothers of the cultured class are, a great deal rests with the nurses, and it needs much watchfulness to secure that there shall not be the faintest odour about the infant or anything belonging to him, and that the nurseries be kept sweet and thoroughly aired. One great difficulty is, that there are still some nurses who belong to a class to which an open window is an abomination; and another is, they do not all know the meaning of odours: they cannot see 'a smell,' and, therefore, it is not easy to persuade them that a smell is matter, microscopic particles which the child takes into him with every breath he draws.

A Sensitive Nose.—By the way, a very important bit of physical education for a child is to train in him a sensitive nose—nostrils which sniff out the least 'stuffiness' in a room, or the faintest odour attached to clothes or furniture. The sense of smell appears to have been given us not only as an avenue of pleasure, but as a sort of danger-signal to warn us of the presence of noxious matters: yet many people appear to go through the world without a nose at all; and the fact tends to show that a quick sense of smell is a matter of education and habit. The habit is easily formed. Encourage the children to notice whether the room they enter 'smells' quite fresh when they come in out of the open air, to observe the difference between the air of the town and the fresher air beyond; and train them to perceive the faintest trace of pleasant or harmless odours.

The Baby is Ubiquitous.—To return to the nursery. It would be a great thing if the nurse could be impressed with the notion that the baby is ubiquitous, and that he not only sees and knows everything, but will keep, for all his life, the mark of all he sees:—

"If there's a hole in a' your coats,

I pray ye, tent it;

A chiel's amang ye takin' notes,

And, faith, he'll prent it":—

'prent it' on his own active brain, as a type for his future habits. Such a notion on the nurse's part might do something to secure cleanliness that goes beyond that of clean aprons. One or two little bits of tidiness that nurses affect are not to be commended on the score of cleanliness—the making up of the nursery beds early in the morning, and the folding up of the children's garments when they take them off at night. It is well to stretch a line across the day nursery at night, and hang the little garments out for an airing, to get rid of the insensible perspiration with which they have been laden during the day. For the same reason, the beds and bedclothes should be turned down to air for a couple of hours before they are made up.

Personal Cleanliness as an Early Habit.— The nursery table, if there be one, should be kept as scrupulously nice as that of the dining-room. The child who sits down to a crumpled or spotted tablecloth, or uses a discoloured metal spoon, is degraded—by so much. The children, too, should be encouraged to nice cleanliness in their own persons. We have all seen the dainty baby-hand stretched out to be washed; it has got a smudge, and the child does not like it. May they be as particular when they are big enough to wash their own hands! Not that they should be always clean and presentable; children love to 'mess about' and should have big pinafores for the purpose. They are all like that little French prince who scorned his birthday gifts, and entreated to be allowed to make dear little mud-pies with the boy in the gutter. Let them make their mud-pies freely; but that over, they should be impatient to remove every trace of soil, and should do it themselves. Young children may be taught to take care of their fingernails, and to cleanse the corners of eyes and ears. As for sitting down to table with unwashed hands and unbrushed hair, that, of course, no decent child is allowed to do. Children should be early provided with their own washing materials, and accustomed to find real pleasure in the bath, and in attending to themselves. There is no reason why a child of five or six should not make himself thoroughly clean without all that torture of soap in the eyes and general pulling about and poking which children hate, and no wonder. Besides, the child is not getting the habit of the daily bath until he can take it for himself, and it is important that this habit should be formed before the reckless era of school-life begins.

Modesty and Purity.—The operations of the bath afford the mother opportunities to give necessary teaching and training in habits of decency, and a sense of modesty. To let her young child live and grow in Eden-like simplicity is, perhaps, the most tempting and natural course to the mother. But alas! we do not live in the Garden, and it may be well that the child should be trained from the first to the conditions under which he is to live. To the youngest child, as to our first parents, there is that which is forbidden. In the age of unquestioning obedience, let him know that not all of his body does Almighty God allow him to speak of, think of, display, handle, except for purposes of cleanliness. This will be the easier to the mother if she speak of heart, lungs, etc., which, also, we are not allowed to look at or handle, but which have been so enclosed in walls of flesh and bone that we cannot get at them. That which is left open to us is so left, like that tree in the Garden of Eden, as a test of obedience; and in the one case, as in the other, disobedience is attended with certain loss and ruin.

The Habit of Obedience and the Sense of Honour.—The sense of prohibition, of sin in disobedience, will be a wonderful safeguard against knowledge of evil to the child brought up in habits of obedience; and still more effective will be the sense of honour, of a charge to keep—the motive of the apostolic injunctions on this subject. Let the mother renew this charge with earnestness on the eve, say, of each birthday, giving the child to feel that by obedience in this matter he may glorify God with his body; let her keep watch against every approach of evil; and let her pray daily that each one of her children may be kept in purity for that day. To ignore the possibilities of evil in this kind is to expose the child to frightful risks. At the same time, be it remembered that words which were meant to hinder may themselves be the cause of evil, and that a life full of healthy interests and activities is amongst the surest preventives of secret vice.

Order Essential.—What has been said about cleanliness applies as much to order—order in the nursery, and orderly habits in the nurse. One thing under this head: the nursery should not be made the hospital for the disabled or worn-out furniture of the house; cracked cups, chipped plates, jugs and teapots with fractured spouts, should be banished. The children should be brought up to think that when once an article is made unsightly by soil or fracture it is spoiled, and must be replaced; and this rule will prove really economical, for when children and servants find that things no longer 'do,' after some careless injury, they learn to be careful. But, in any case, it is a real detriment to the children to grow up using imperfect and unsightly makeshifts.

The pleasure grown-up people take in waiting on children is really a fruitful source of mischief;—for instance, in this matter of orderly habits. Who does not know the litter the children leave to be cleared up after them a dozen times a day, in the nursery, garden, drawing-room, wherever their restless little feet carry them? We are a bit sentimental about scattered toys and faded nosegays, and all the tokens of the children's presence; but the fact is, that the lawless habit of scattering should not be allowed to grow upon children. Everybody condemns the mother of a family whose drawers are chaotic, whose possessions are flung about heedlessly; but at least some of the blame should be carried back to her mother. It is not as a woman that she has picked up a miserable habit which destroys the comfort, if not the happiness, of her home; the habit of disorder was allowed to grow upon her as a child, and her share of the blame is, that she has failed to cure herself.

The Child of Two should put away his Playthings.—The child of two should be taught to get and to replace his playthings. Begin early. Let it be a pleasure to him, part of his play, to open his cupboard, and put back the doll or the horse each in its own place. Let him always put away his things as a matter of course, and it is surprising how soon a habit of order is formed, which will make it pleasant to the child to put away his toys, and irritating to him to see things in the wrong place. If parents would only see the morality of order, that order in the nursery becomes scrupulousness in after life, and that the training necessary to form the habit is no more, comparatively, than the occasional winding of a clock, which ticks away then of its own accord and without trouble to itself, more pains would be taken to cultivate this important habit.

Neatness Akin to Order.—Neatness is akin to order, but is not quite the same thing: it implies not only 'a place for everything, and everything in its place,' but everything in a suitable place, so as to produce a good effect; in fact, taste comes into play. The little girl must not only put her flowers in water but arrange them prettily, and must not be put off with some rude kitchen mug or jug for them, or some hideous pink vase, but must have jar or vase graceful in form and harmonious in hue, though it be but a cheap trifle. In the same way, everything in the nursery should be 'neat'—that is, pleasing and suitable; and children should be encouraged to make neat and effective arrangements of their own little properties. Nothing vulgar in the way of print, picture-book, or toy should be admitted—nothing to vitiate a child's taste or introduce a strain of commonness into his nature. On the other hand, it would be hard to estimate the refining, elevating influence of one or two well-chosen works of art, in however cheap a reproduction.

Regularity.—The importance of Regularity in infant education is beginning to be pretty generally acknowledged. The young mother knows that she must put her baby to bed at a proper time, regardless of his cries, even if she leave him to cry two or three times, in order that, for the rest of his baby life, he may put himself sweetly to sleep in the dark without protest. But a good deal of nonsense is talked about the reason of the child's cries—he is supposed to want his mother, or his nurse, or his bottle, or the light, and to be 'a knowing little fellow,' according to his nurse, quite up to the fact that if he cries for these things he will get them.

Habits of Time and Place.—The fact is, the child has already formed a habit of wakefulness or of feeding at improper times, and he is as uneasy at his habits being broken in upon as the cat is at a change of habitation; when he submits happily to the new regulation, it is because the new habit is formed, and is, in its turn, the source of satisfaction. According to Dr. Carpenter, "Regularity should begin even with infant life, as to times of feeding, repose, etc. The bodily habit thus formed greatly helps to shape the mental habit at a later period. On the other hand, nothing tends more to generate a habit of self-indulgence than to feed a child, or to allow it to remain out of bed, at unseasonable times, merely because it cries. It is wonderful how soon the actions of a young infant (like those of a young dog or horse) come into harmony with systematic 'training' judiciously exercised." The habit of regularity is as attractive to older children as to the infant. The days when the usual programme falls through are, we know, the days when the children are apt to be naughty.

IX.—Physical Exercises

Importance of Daily.—The subject of the natural training of eye and muscles was taken up pretty fully in treating of 'Out-of-door Life.' I will only add, that to give the child pleasure in light and easy motion—the sort of delight in the management of his own body that a good rider finds in managing his horse—dancing, drill, calisthenics, some sort of judicious physical exercise, should make part of every day's routine. Swedish drill is especially valuable, and many of the exercises are quite suitable for the nursery. Certain moral qualities come into play in alert movements, eye-to-eye attention, prompt and intelligent replies; but it often happens that good children fail in these points for want of physical training.

Drill of Good Manners.—Just let them go through the drill of good manners: let them rehearse little scenes in play,—Mary, the lady asking the way to the market; Harry, the boy who directs her, and so on. Let them go through a position drill—eyes right, hands still, heads up. They will invent a hundred situations, and the behaviour proper to each, and will treasure hints thrown in for their guidance; but this sort of drill should be attempted while children are young, before the tyranny of mauvaise honte sets in. Encourage them to admire and take pride in light springing movements, and to eschew a heavy gait and clownish action of the limbs.

Training of the Ear and Voice.—The training of the ear and voice is an exceedingly important part of physical culture. Drill the children in pure vowel sounds, in the enunciation of final consonants; do not let them speak of 'walkin and 'talkin',' of a 'fi-ine da-ay,' 'ni-ice boy-oys.' Drill them in pronouncing difficult words —'imperturbability,' 'ipecacuanha,' 'Antananarivo,'—with sharp precision after a single hearing; in producing the several sounds of each vowel and the sounds of the consonants without attendant vowels. French, taught orally, is exceedingly valuable as affording training for both ear and voice.

The Habit of Music.—As for a musical training, it would be hard to say how much that passes for inherited musical taste and ability is the result of the constant hearing and producing of musical sounds, the habit of music, that the child of musical people grows up with. Mr. Hullah maintained that the art of singing is entirely a trained habit—that every child may be, and should be, trained to sing. Of course, transmitted habit must be taken into account. It is a pity that the musical training most children get is of a random character; that they are not trained, for instance, by carefully graduated ear and voice exercises, to produce and distinguish musical tones and intervals.

Let Children Alone.—In conclusion, let me say that the education of habit is successful in so far as it enables the mother to let her children alone, not teasing them with perpetual commands and directions—a running fire of Do and Don't; but letting them go their own way and grow, having first secured that they will go the right way, and grow to fruitful purpose. The gardener, it is true, 'digs about and dungs,' prunes and trains, his peach tree; but that occupies a small fraction of the tree's life: all the rest of the time the sweet airs and sunshine, the rains and dews, play about it and breathe upon it, get into its substance, and the result is—peaches. But let the gardener neglect his part, and the peaches will be no better than sloes.

Part IV
Some Habits Of Mind — Some Moral Habits

Science of Education.—Allow me to say once more, that I venture to write upon subjects bearing on home education with the greatest deference to mothers; believing, that in virtue of their peculiar insight into the dispositions of their own children, they are blest with both knowledge and power in the management of them which lookers on can only admire from afar. At the same time, there is such a thing as a science of education, that does not come by intuition, in the knowledge of which it is possible to bring up a child entirely according to natural law, which is also Divine law, in the keeping of which there is great reward.

Education in Habit favours an Easy Life.—We have seen why Habit, for instance, is such a marvellous force in human life. I find this view of habit very encouraging, as giving a scientific reasonableness to the conclusions already reached by common experience. It is pleasant to know that, even in mature life, it is possible by a little persistent effort to acquire a desirable habit. It is good, if not pleasant, to know, also, with what fatal ease we can slip into bad habits. But the most comfortable thing in this view of habit is, that it falls in with our natural love of an easy life. We are not unwilling to make efforts in the beginning with the assurance that by-and-by things will go smoothly; and this is just what habit is, in an extraordinary degree, pledged to effect. The mother who takes pains to endow her children with good habits secures for herself smooth and easy days; while she who lets their habits take care of themselves has a weary life of endless friction with the children. All day she is crying out, 'Do this!' and they do it not; 'Do that!' and they do the other. 'But,' you say, 'if habit is so powerful, whether to hinder or to help the child, it is fatiguing to think of all the habits the poor mother must attend to. Is she never to be at ease with her children?'

Training in Habit Becomes a Habit.—Here, again, is an illustration of that fable of the anxious pendulum, overwhelmed with the thought of the number of ticks it must tick. But the ticks are to be delivered tick by tick, and there will always be a second of time to tick in. The mother devotes herself to the formation of one habit at a time, doing no more than keep watch over those already formed. If she be appalled by the thought of overmuch labour, let her limit the number of good habits she will lay herself out to form. The child who starts life with, say, twenty good habits, begins with a certain capital which he will lay out to endless profit as the years go on. The mother who is distrustful of her own power of steady effort may well take comfort in two facts. In the first place, she herself acquires the habit of training her children in a given habit, so that by-and-by it becomes, not only no trouble, but a pleasure to her. In the second place, the child's most fixed and dominant habits are those which the mother takes no pains about, but which the child picks up for himself through his close observation of all that is said and done, felt and thought, in his home.

Habits inspired in the Home Atmosphere.—We have already considered a group of half physical habits—order, regularity, neatness—which the child imbibes, so to speak, in a way. But this is not all: habits of gentleness, courtesy, kindness, candour, respect for other people, or—habits quite other than these, are inspired by the child as the very atmosphere of his home, the air he lives in and must grow by.

I. The Habit of Attention

Let us pass on, now, to the consideration of a group of mental habits which are affected by direct training rather than by example.

First, we put the habit of Attention, because the highest intellectual gifts depend for their value upon the measure in which their owner has cultivated the habit of attention. To explain why this habit is of such supreme importance, we must consider the operation of one or two of the laws of thought. But just recall, in the meantime, the fixity of attention with which the trained professional man—the lawyer, the doctor, the man of letters—listens to a roundabout story, throws out the padding, seizes the facts, sees the bearing of every circumstance, and puts the case with new clearness and method; and contrast this with the wandering eye and random replies of the uneducated;—and you see that to differentiate people according to their power of attention is to employ a legitimate test.

A Mind at the Mercy of Associations.—We will consider, then, the nature and the functions of attention. The mind—with the possible exception of the state of coma—is never idle; ideas are for ever passing through the brain, by day and by night, sleeping or walking, mad or sane. We take a great deal too much upon ourselves when we suppose that we are the authors and intenders of the thoughts we think. The most we can do is to give direction to these trains of thought in the comparatively few moments when we are regulating the thoughts of our hearts. We see in dreams—the rapid dance of ideas through the brain during lighter sleep—how ideas follow one another in a general way. In the wanderings of delirium, in the fancies of the mad, the inconsequent prattle of the child, and the babble of the old man, we see the same thing, i.e.—the law according to which ideas course through the mind when they are left to themselves. You talk to a child about glass—you wish to provoke a proper curiosity as to how glass is made, and what are its uses. Not a bit of it; he wanders off to Cinderella's glass slipper; then he tells you about his godmother who gave him a boat; then about the ship in which Uncle Harry went to America; then he wonders why you do not wear spectacles, leaving you to guess that Uncle Harry does so. But the child's ramblings are not whimsical; they follow a law, the law of association of ideas, by which any idea presented to the mind recalls some other idea which has been at any time associated with it—as glass and Cinderella's slipper; and that, again some idea associated with it. Now this law of association of ideas is a good servant and a bad master. To have this aid in recalling the events of the past, the engagements of the present, is an infinite boon; but to be at the mercy of associations, to have no power to think what we choose when we choose, but only as something 'puts it into our head,' is to be no better than an imbecile.

Wandering Attention.—A vigorous effort of will should enable us at any time to fix our thoughts. Yes; but a vigorous self-compelling will is the flower of a developed character; and while the child has no character to speak of, but only natural disposition, who is to keep humming-tops out of a geography lesson, or a doll's sofa out of a French verb? Here is the secret of the weariness of the home schoolroom—the children are thinking all the time about something else than their lessons; or rather, they are at the mercy of the thousand fancies that flit through their brains, each in the train of the last. "Oh, Miss Smith," said a little girl to her governess, "there are so many things more interesting than lessons to think about!"

Where is the harm? In this: not merely that the children are wasting time, though that is a pity; but that they are forming a desultory habit of mind, and reducing their own capacity for mental effort.

The Habit of Attention to be Cultivated in the Infant.—The help, then, is not the will of the child but in the habit of attention, a habit to be cultivated even in the infant. A baby, notwithstanding his wonderful powers of observation, has no power of attention; in a minute, the covered plaything drops from listless little fingers, and the wandering glance lights upon some new joy. But even at this stage the habit of attention may be trained: the discarded plaything is picked up, and, with 'Pretty!' and dumb show, the mother keeps the infant's eyes fixed for fully a couple of minutes—and this is her first lesson in attention. Later, as we have seen, the child is eager to see and handle every object that comes in his way. But watch him at his investigations: he flits from thing to thing with less purpose than a butterfly amongst the flowers, staying at nothing long enough to get the good out of it. It is the mother's part to supplement the child's quick observing faculty with the habit of attention. She must see to it that he does not flit from this to that, but looks long enough at one thing to get a real acquaintance with it.

Is little Margaret fixing round eyes on a daisy she has plucked? In a second, the daisy will be thrown away, and a pebble or buttercup will charm the little maid. But the mother seizes the happy moment. She makes Margaret see that the daisy is a bright yellow eye with white eyelashes round it; that all the day long it lies there in the grass and looks up at the great sun, never blinking as Margaret would do, but keeping its eyes wide open. And that is why it is called daisy, 'day's eye,' because its eye is always looking at the sun which makes the day. And what does Margaret think it does at night, when there is no sun? It does what little boys and girls do; it just shuts up its eye with its white lashes tipped with pink, and goes to sleep till the sun comes again in the morning. By this time the daisy has become interesting to Margaret; she looks at it with big eyes after her mother has finished speaking, and then, very likely, cuddles it up to her breast or gives it a soft little kiss. Thus the mother will contrive ways to invest every object in the child's world with interest and delight.

Attention to 'Things'; Words a Weariness.—But the tug of war begins with the lessons of the schoolroom. Even the child who has gained the habit of attention to things, finds words a weariness. This is a turning point in the child's life, and the moment for mother's tact and vigilance. In the first place, never let the child dawdle over copybook or sum, sit dreaming with his book before him. When a child grows stupid over a lesson, it is time to put it away. Let him do another lesson as unlike the last as possible, and then go back with freshened wits to his unfinished task. If mother or governess have been unwary enough to let the child 'moon' over a lesson, she must just exert her wits to pull him through; the lesson must be done, of course, but must be made bright and pleasant to the child.

Lessons Attractive.—The teacher should have some knowledge of the principles of education; should know what subjects are best fitted for the child considering his age, and how to make these subjects attractive; should know, too, how to vary the lessons, so that each power of the child's mind should rest after effort, and some other power be called into play. She should know how to incite the child to effort through his desire of approbation, of excelling, of advancing, his desire of knowledge, his love of his parents, his sense of duty, in such a way that no one set of motives be called unduly into play to the injury of the child's character. But the danger she must be especially alive to, is the substitution of any other natural desire for that of knowledge, which is equally natural, and is adequate for all the purposes of education.

Time-table; Definite Work in a Given Time.—I shall have opportunities to enter into some of these points later; meantime, let us look in at a home schoolroom managed on sound principles. In the first place, there is a time-table, written out fairly, so that the child knows what he has to do and how long each lesson is to last. This idea of definite work to be finished in a given time is valuable to the child, not only as training him in habits of order, but in diligence; he learns that one time is not 'as good as another'; that there is no right time left for what is not done in its own time; and this knowledge alone does a great deal to secure the child's attention to his work. Again, the lessons are short, seldom more than twenty minutes in length for children under eight; and this, for two or three reasons. The sense that there is not much time for his sums or his reading, keeps the child's wits on the alert and helps to fix his attention; he has time to learn just so much of any one subject as it is good for him to take in at once: and if the lessons be judiciously alternated—sums first, say, while the brain is quite fresh; then writing, or reading—some more or less mechanical exercise, by way of a rest; and so on, the program varying a little from day to day, but the same principle throughout—a 'thinking' lesson first, and a 'painstaking' lesson to follow,—the child gets through his morning lessons without any sign of weariness.

Even with regular lessons and short lessons, a further stimulus may be occasionally necessary to secure the attention of the child. His desire of approbation may ask the stimulus, not only of a word of praise, but of something in the shape of a reward to secure his utmost efforts. Now, rewards should be dealt out to the child upon principle: they should be the natural consequences of his good conduct.

A Natural Reward.—What is the natural consequence of work well and quickly done? Is it not the enjoyment of ampler leisure? The boy is expected to do two right sums in twenty minutes: he does them in ten minutes; the remaining ten minutes are his own, fairly earned, in which he should be free for a scamper in the garden, or any delight he chooses. His writing task is to produce six perfect m's: he writes six lines with only one good m in each line, the time for the writing lesson is over and he has none for himself; or, he is able to point out six good m's in his first line, and he has the rest of the time to draw steamboats and railway trains. This possibility of letting the children occupy themselves variously in the few minutes they may gain at the end of each lesson, is compensation which the home schoolroom offers for the zest which the sympathy of numbers, and emulation, are supposed to give to schoolwork.

Emulation.—As for emulation, a very potent means of exciting and holding the attention of children, it is often objected that a desire to excel, to do better than others, implies an unloving temper, which the educator should rather repress than cultivate. Good marks of some kind are usually the rewards of those who do best, and it is urged that these good marks are often the cause of ungenerous rivalry. Now, the fact is, the children are being trained to live in the world, and in the world we all do get good marks of one kind or another, prize, or praise, or both, according as we excel others, whether in football or tennis, or in picture painting or poem-making. There are envyings and heart burnings amongst those who come in second best; so it has been from beginning, and doubtless will be to the end. If the child is go out into an emulous world, why, it may be possibly be well that he should brought up in an emulous school. But here is where the mother's work comes in. She can teach her child to be first without vanity, and to be last without bitterness; that is, she can bring him up in such a hearty outgoing of love and sympathy that joy in his brother's success takes the sting out of his own failure, and regret for his brother's failure leaves no room for self glorification. Again, if a system of marks be used as a stimulus to attention and effort, the good marks should be given for conduct rather than for cleverness—that is, they should be within everybody's reach: every child may get his mark for punctuality, order, attention, diligence, obedience, gentleness; and therefore, marks of this kind may be given without danger of leaving a rankling sense of injustice in the breast of the child who fails. Emulation becomes suicidal when it is used as the incentive to intellectual effort, because the desire for knowledge subsides in proportion as the desire to excel becomes active. As a matter of fact, marks of any sort, even for conduct, distract the attention of children from their proper work, which is in itself interesting enough to secure good behaviour as well as attention.

Affection as a Motive.—That he ought to work hard to please his parents who do so much for him, is a proper motive to bring before the child from time to time, but not too often: if the mother trade on her child's feelings, if, 'Do this or that to please mother,' 'Do not grieve poor mother,' etc., be brought too frequently before the child as the reason for right doing, a sentimental relation is set up which both parent and child will find embarrassing, the true motives of action will be obscured, and the child unwilling to appear unloving, will end in being untrue.

Attractiveness of Knowledge.—Of course, the most obvious means of quickening and holding the attention of children lies in the attractiveness of knowledge itself, and in the real appetite for knowledge with which they are endowed. But how successful faulty teachers are in curing children of any desire to know, is to be seen in many a school room. I shall later, however, have an opportunity for a few words on this subject.

What is Attention?—It is evident that attention is no 'faculty' of the mind; indeed, it is very doubtful how far the various operations of the mind should be described as 'faculties' at all. Attention is hardly even an operation of the mind, but is simply the act by which the whole mental force is applied to the subject in hand. This act, of bringing the whole mind to bear, may be trained into a habit at the will of the parent or teacher, who attracts and holds the child's attention by means of a sufficient motive.

Self-Compelled.—As the child gets older, he is taught to bring his own will to bear; to make himself attend in spite of the most inviting suggestions from without. He should be taught to feel a certain triumph in compelling himself to fix his thoughts. Let him know what the real difficulty is, how it is the nature of his mind to be incessantly thinking, but how the thoughts, if left to themselves, will always run off from one thing to another, and that the struggle and the victory required of him is to fix his thoughts upon the task in hand. 'You have done your duty,' with a look of sympathy from his mother, is a reward for the child who has made this effort in the strength of his growing will. But it cannot be too much borne in mind that attention is, to a great extent, the product of the educated mind; that is, one can only attend in proportion as one has the intellectual power of developing the topic.

It is impossible to overstate the importance of this habit of attention. It is, to quote words of weight, "within the reach of everyone, and should be made the primary object of all mental discipline"; for whatever the natural gifts of the child, it is only so far as the habit of attention is cultivated in him that he is able to make use of them.

The Secret of Overpressure.—If it were only as it saves wear and tear, a perpetual tussle between duty and inclination, it is worth while for the mother to lay herself out to secure that her child never does a lesson into which he does not put his heart. And that is no difficult undertaking; the thing is, to be on the watch from the beginning against the formation of the contrary habit of inattention. A great deal has been said lately about overpressure, and we have glanced at one or two of the causes whose effects go by this name. But truly, one of the most fertile causes of an overdone brain is a failure in the habit of attention. I suppose we are all ready to admit that it is not the things we do, but the things we fail to do, which fatigue us, with the sense of omission, with the worry of hurry in overtaking our tasks. And this is almost the only cause of failure in the work in the case of the healthy schoolboy or schoolgirl: wandering wits hinder a lesson from being fully taken in at the right moment; that lesson becomes a bugbear, continually wanted henceforth and never there; and the sense of loss tries the young scholar more than would the attentive reception of a dozen such lessons.

The Schoolboy's Home Work.—In the matter of home work, the parents may still be of great use to their boys and girls after they begin to go to day-school; not in helping them, that should not be necessary; but let us suppose a case: 'Poor Annie does not her finish her lessons till half past nine, she really has so much to do'; 'Poor Tom is at his books till ten o'clock; we never see anything of the children in the evening,' say the distressed parents; and they let their children go on in a course which is absolutely ruinous both to bodily health and brain power.

Wholesome Home Treatment for Mooning.—Now, the fault is very seldom in the lessons, but in the children; they moon over their books, and a little wholesome home treatment should cure them of that ailment. Allow them, at the utmost, an hour and a half for their home-work; treat them tacitly as defaulters if they do not appear at the end of that time; do not be betrayed into word or look of sympathy; and the moment the time for lessons is over, let some delightful game or storybook be begun in the drawing room. By-and-by they will find that it is possible to finish lessons in time to secure a pleasant evening afterwards, and the lessons will be much the better done for the fact that concentrated attention has been bestowed upon them. At the same time the custom of giving home-work, at any rate to children under fourteen, is greatly to be deprecated. The gain of a combination of home and school life is lost to the children; and a very full scheme of school work may be carried through in the morning hours.

Rewards and Punishments should be relative Consequences of Conduct.—In considering the means of securing attention, it has been necessary to refer to discipline—the dealing out of rewards and punishments,—a subject which every tyro of a nursery maid or nursery governess feels herself very competent to handle. But this, too, has its scientific aspect: there is a law by which all rewards and punishments should be regulated: they should be natural, or, at any rate, the relative consequences of conduct; should imitate, as nearly as may be without injury to the child, the treatment which such and such conduct deserves and receives in after life. Miss Edgeworth, in her story of Rosamond and the Purple Jar, hits the right principle, though the incident is rather extravagant. Little girls do not often pine for purple jars in chemists' windows; but that we should suffer for our wilfulness in getting what is unnecessary by going without what is necessary, is precisely one of the lessons of life we all have to learn, and therefore is the right sort of lesson to teach a child.

Natural and Elective Consequences.—It is evident that to administer rewards and punishments on this principle requires patient consideration and steady determination on the mother's part. She must consider with herself what fault of disposition the child's misbehaviour springs from; she must aim her punishment at that fault, and must brace herself to see her child suffer present loss for his lasting gain. Indeed, exceedingly little actual punishment is necessary where children are brought up with care. But this happens continually—the child who has done well gains some natural reward (like that ten minutes in the garden), which the child forfeits who has done less well; and the mother must brace herself and her child to bear this loss; if she equalise the two children she commits a serious wrong, not against the child who has done well, but against the defaulter, whom she deliberately encourages to repeat his shortcoming. In placing her child under the discipline of consequences, the mother must use much tact and discretion. In many cases, the natural consequence of the child's fault is precisely that which it is her business to avert, while, at the same time, she looks about for some consequence related to the fault which shall have an educative bearing on the child: for instance, if a boy neglects his studies, the natural consequences is that he remains ignorant; but to allow him to do so would be criminal neglect on the part of the parent.

II. The Habits of Application, Etc.

Rapid Mental Effort—The habits of mental activity and of application are trained by the very means employed to cultivate that of attention. The child may plod diligently through his work who might be trained to rapid mental effort. The teacher herself must be alert, must expect instant answers, quick thought, rapid work. The tortoise will lag behind the hare, but the tortoise must be trained to move, every day, a trifle quicker. Aim steadily at securing quickness of apprehension and execution, and that goes far towards getting it.

Zeal must be Stimulated.—So of application. The child must not be allowed to get into the mood in which he says, 'Oh, I am so tired of sums,' or 'of history.' His zeal must be stimulated; and there must be always a pleasing vista before him; and the steady, untiring application to work should be held up as honourable, while fitful, flagging attention and effort are scouted.

III. The Habit of Thinking

'A Lion' Operations included in Thinking.—The actual labour of the brain is known to psychologists under various names, and divided into various operations: let us call it thinking, which, for educational purposes, is sufficiently exact; but, by 'thinking,' let us mean a real conscious effort of mind, and not the fancies that flit without effort through the brain. This sort of thing, for instance, an example quoted by Archbishop Thompson in his Laws of Thought [This example, offered by so able a psychologist, is so admirable that I venture to quote it more than once]:—"when Captain Head was travelling across the pampas of South America, his guide one day suddenly stopped him, and pointing high into the air, cried out 'A lion!' Surprised at such an exclamation, accompanied with such an act, he turned up his eyes, and with difficulty perceived, at an immeasurable height, a flight of condors, soaring in circles in a particular spot. Beneath this spot, far out of sight of himself of himself or guide, lay the carcass of a horse, and over that carcass stood, as the guide well knew, a lion, whom the condors were eyeing with envy from their airy height. The signal of the birds was to him what the sight of the lion alone would have been to the traveller—a full assurance of its existence.

Here was an act of thought which cost the thinker no trouble, which was easy to him as to cast his eyes upward, yet which from us, unaccustomed to the subject, would re-quire many steps and some labour. The sight of the condors convinced him that there was some carcass or other; but as they kept wheeling far above it, instead of swooping down to their feast, he guessed that some beast had anticipated them. Was it a dog, or a jackal? No; the condors would not fear to drive away, or share with, either: it must be some large beast, and as there were lions in the neighbourhood, he concluded that one was here." And all these steps of thought are summed in the words 'A lion.'

This is the sort of thing that the children should go through, more or less, in every lesson—a tracing of effect from cause, or of cause from effect; a comparing of things to find out wherein they are alike, and wherein they differ; a conclusion as to causes or consequences from certain premises.

IV. The Habit of Imagining

The Sense of Incongruous.—All their lessons will afford some scope for some slight exercise of the children's thinking power, some more and some less, and the lessons must be judiciously alternated, so that the more mechanical efforts succeed the more strictly intellectual, and that the pleasing exercise of the imagination, again, succeed efforts of reason. By the way, it is a pity when the sense of the ludicrous is cultivated in children's books at the expense of better things. Alice in Wonderland is a delicious feast of absurdities, which none of us, old or young, could afford to spare; but it is doubtful whether the child who reads it has the delightful imaginings, the realizing of the unknown, with which he reads The Swiss Family Robinson.

This point is worth considering in connection with Christmas books for the little people. Books of 'comicalities' cultivate no power but the sense of the incongruous; and though life is the more amusing for the possession of such a sense, when cultivated to excess it is apt to show itself a flippant habit. Diogenes and the Naughty Boys of Troy is irresistible, but it is not the sort of thing the children will live over and over, and 'play at' by the hour, as we have all played at Robinson Crusoe finding the footprints. They must have 'funny books,' but do not give the children too much nonsense reading.

Commonplace Tales: Tales of Imagination—Stories, again, of the Christmas holidays, of George and Lucy, of the amusements, foibles, and virtues of children in their own condition of life, leave nothing to the imagination. The children know all about everything so well that it never occurs to them to play at the situations in any one of these tales, or even to read it twice over. But let them have tales of the imagination, scenes laid in other lands and other times, heroic adventures, hairbreadth escapes, delicious fairy tales in which they are never roughly pulled up by the impossible—even where all is impossible, and they know it, and yet believe.

Imagination and Great Conceptions.—And this, not for the children's amusement merely: it is not impossible that posterity may write us down a generation blest with little imagination, and, by so far, the less capable of great conceptions and heroic efforts, for it is only as we have it in us to let a person or a cause fill the whole stage of the mind, to the exclusion of self occupation, that we are capable of large hearted action on behalf of that person or cause. Our novelists say there is nothing left to imagine; and that, therefore, a realistic description of things as they are is all that is open to them. But imagination is nothing if not creative, unless it see, not only what is apparent, but what is conceivable, and what is poetically fit in given circumstances.

Imagination Grows.—Now imagination does not descend, full grown, to take possession of an empty house; like every other power of the mind, it is the merest germ of a power to begin with, and grows by what it gets; and childhood, the age of faith, is the time for its nourishing. The children should have the joy of living in far lands, in other persons, in other times—a delightful double existence; and this joy they will find, for the most part, in their story books. Their lessons, too, history and geography, should cultivate their conceptive powers. If the child do not live in the times of his history lesson, be not at home in the climes of his geography book describes, why, these lessons will fail of their purpose. But let lessons do their best, and the picture gallery of the imagination is poorly hung if the child have not found his way into the realms of fancy.

Thinking comes by Practice.—How the children's various lessons should be handled so as to induce habits of thinking, we shall consider later; but this for the present: thinking, like writing or skating, comes by practice. The child who has never thought, never does think, and probably never will think; for are there not people enough who go through the world without any deliberate exercise of their own wits? The child must think, get at the reason why of things for himself, every day of his life, and more each day than the day before. Children and parents both are given to invert this educational process. The child asks 'Why?' and the parent answers, rather proud of this evidence of thought in his child. There is some slight show of speculation even in wondering 'Why?' but it is the slightest and most superficial effort the thinking brain produces. Let the parent ask 'Why?' and the child produce the answer, if he can. After he has turned the matter over and over in his mind, there is no harm in telling him—and he will remember it—the reason why. Every walk should offer some knotty problem for the children to think out—"Why does that leaf float on the water, and this pebble sink?" and so on.

V. The Habit of Remembering

Remembering and Recollecting.—Memory is the storehouse of whatever knowledge we possess; and it is upon the fact of the stores lodged in the memory that we take rank as intelligent beings. The children learn in order that they may remember. Much of what we have learned and experienced in childhood, and later, we cannot reproduce, and yet it has formed the groundwork of after knowledge; later notions and opinions have grown out of what we once learned and knew. That is our sunk capital, of which we enjoy the interest though we are unable to realize. Again, much that we have learned and experienced is not only retained in the storehouse of memory, but is our available capital, we can reproduce, recollect upon demand. This memory which may be drawn upon by the act of recollection is our most valuable endowment.

A 'Spurious' Memory.—There is a third kind of (spurious) memory—facts and ideas floating in the brain which yet make no part of it, and are exuded at a single effort; as when a barrister produces all his knowledge of a case in his brief, and then forgets to tell about it; or when the schoolboy 'crams' for an examination, writes down what he has thus learned, and behold, it is gone from his gaze for ever: as Ruskin puts it, "They cram to pass, and not to know, they do pass, and they don't know." That this barrister, the physician, should be able thus to dismiss the case on which he has ceased to be occupied, the publisher the book he has rejected, is well for him, and this art of forgetting is not without its uses: but what of the schoolboy who has little left after a year's work but his place in a class list?

Memory a Record in the Brain Substance.—To say anything adequate on the subject of memory is impossible here; but let us try to answer two or three queries which present themselves on the surface. How do we come to 'remember' at all? How do we gain the power to utilise remembered facts—that is, to recollect? And under what conditions is knowledge acquired that neither goes to the growth of brain and mind, nor is available on demand, but is lightly lodged in the brain for some short period, and is then evacuated at a single throw? We are interested in a wonderful invention—an instrument which records spoken words, and will deliver, say a century hence, speech or lecture on the very words and in the very tones of the speaker. Such an instrument is that function of the brain called memory, whereby the impressions received by the brain are recorded mechanically—at least, such is the theory pretty generally received now by physiologists. That is, the mind takes cognizance of certain facts, and the nerve substance of the brain records that cognizance.

Made under what Conditions.—Now, the questions arise, Under what conditions is such an imprint of fact or event made upon the substance of the brain? Is the record permanent? And is the brain capable of receiving an indefinite number of such impressions? It appears, both from common experience and from an infinite number of examples quoted by psychologists, that any object or idea which is regarded with attention makes the sort of impression on the brain which is said to fix it in the memory. In other words, give an instant's undivided attention to anything whatsoever, and that thing will be remembered. In describing this effect, the common expression is accurate beyond its intention. We say, "Such and such a sight or sound, or sensation, made a strong impression on me." And that is precisely what has happened: arrest the attention upon any fact or incident, that fact or incident is remembered; it is impressed, imprinted upon the brain substance. The inference is plain. You want a child to remember? Then secure his whole attention, the fixed gaze of his mind, as it were, upon the fact to be remembered; then he will have it: by a sort of photographic (!) process, that fact or idea is 'taken' by his brain, and when he is an old man, perhaps, the memory of it will flash across him.

Recollection and the Law of Association.—But it is not enough to have a recollection flash across one incidentally; we want to have the power of recalling at will: and for this, something more is necessary than an occasional act of attention producing a solitary impression. Supposing, for instance, that by good teaching you secure the child's attention to the verb avoir, he will remember it; that is to say, some infinitely slight growth of brain tissue will record and retain that one French verb. But one verb is nothing; you want the child to learn French, and for this you must not only fix his attention upon each new lesson, but each must be so linked into the last that it is impossible for him to recall one without the other following in its train. The physical effect of such a method appears to be that each new growth of the brain tissue is, so to speak, laid upon the last; that is, to put it figuratively, a certain tract of the brain may be conceived of as being overlaid with French. This is to make a practical use of that law of association of ideas of which one would not willingly become the sport; and it is the neglect of this law which invalidates much good teaching. The teacher is content to produce a solitary impression which is only recalled as it is acted upon by a chance suggestion; whereas he should forge the links of a chain to draw his bucket out of the well. Probably the reader may have heard, or heard of, a Dr. Pick, who grounded a really philosophical system of mnemonics on these two principles of attention and association. Whatever we may think of his application of it, the principle he asserted is the right one.

Every Lesson must recall the Last.—Let every lesson gain the child's entire attention, and let each new lesson be so interlaced with the last that the one must recall the other; that again, recalls the one before it, and so on to the beginning.

No Limit to the Recording Power of the Brain.—But the 'lightly come, lightly go' of a mere verbal memory follows no such rules. The child gets his exercise 'by heart,' says it off like a parrot, and behold, it is gone; there is no record of it upon the brain at all. To secure such a record, there must be time; time for that full gaze of the mind we call attention, and for the growth of the brain tissue to the new idea. Given these conditions, there appears to be no limit of quantity to the recording power of the brain. Except in this way: a girl learns French, and speaks it fairly well; by the time she is a grandmother she has forgotten it entirely, has not a word left. When this is the case, her French has been disused; she has not been in the habit of reading, hearing, or speaking French from youth to age. Whereby it is evident that, to secure right-of-way to that record of French imprinted on her brain, the path should have been kept open by frequent goings and comings.

But Links of Association a Condition of Recollection.—To acquire any knowledge or power whatsoever, and then to leave it to grow rusty in a neglected corner of the brain, is practically useless. Where there is no chain of association to draw the bucket out of the well, it is all the same as if there were no water there. As to how to form these links, every subject will suggest a suitable method. The child has a lesson about Switzerland to-day, and one about Holland to-morrow, and the one is linked to the other by the very fact that the two countries have hardly anything in common; what the one has, the other has not. Again, the association will be of similarity, and not of contrast. In our own experience we find that colours, places, sounds, odors recall persons or events; but links of this sensuous order can hardly be employed in education. The link between any two things must be found in the nature of the things associated.

VI. The Habit of Perfect Execution

The Habit of turning out Imperfect Work.—'Throw perfection into all you do' is a counsel upon which a family may be brought up with great advantage. We English, as a nation, think too much of persons, and too little of things, work, execution. Our children are allowed to make their figures or their letters, their stitches, their dolls' clothes, their small carpentry, anyhow, with the notion that they will do better by-and-by. Other nations—the Germans and the French, for instance—look at the question philosophically, and know that if children get the habit of turning out imperfect work, the men and women will undoubtedly keep that habit up. I remember being delighted with the work of a class of about forty children, of six and seven, in an elementary school at Heidelberg. They were doing a writing lesson, accompanied by a good deal of oral teaching from a master, who wrote each word on the blackboard. By-and-by the slates were shown, and I did not observe one faulty or irregular letter on the whole forty slates. The same principle of 'perfection' was to be discerned in a recent exhibition of school-work held throughout France. No faulty work was shown, to be excused on the plea that it was the work of children.

A Child should Execute Perfectly. No work should be given to a child that he cannot execute perfectly, and then perfection should be required from him as a matter of course. For instance, he is set to do a copy of strokes, and is allowed to show a slateful at all sorts of slopes and all sorts of intervals; his moral sense is vitiated, his eye is injured. Set him six strokes to copy; let him, not bring a slateful, but six perfect strokes, at regular distances and at regular slopes. If he produces a faulty pair, get him to point out the fault, and persevere until he has produced his task; if he does not do it to-day, let him go on to-morrow and the next day, and when the six perfect strokes appear, let it be an occasion of triumph. So with the little tasks of painting, drawing, or construction he sets himself—let everything he does be well done. An unsteady house of cards is a thing to be ashamed of. Closely connected with this habit of 'perfect work' is that of finishing whatever is taken in hand. The child should rarely be allowed to set his hand to a new undertaking until the last is finished.

VII. Some Moral Habits—Obedience

It is disappointing that, in order to cover the ground at all, we must treat those moral habits, which the mother owes it to her children to cultivate in them, in a slight and inadequate way; but the point to be borne in mind is, that all has been already said about the cultivation of habit applies with the greatest possible force to each of these habits.

The Whole Duty of a Child—First and infinitely the most important, is the habit of obedience. Indeed, obedience is the whole duty of the child, and for this reason—every other duty of the child is fulfilled as a matter of obedience to his parents. Not only so: obedience is the whole duty of man; obedience to conscience, to law, to Divine direction.

It has been well observed that each of the three recorded temptations of our Lord in the wilderness is a suggestion, not of an act of overt sin, but of an act of wilfulness, that state directly opposed to obedience, and out of which springs all that foolishness which is bound up in the heart of a child.

Obedience no Accidental Duty.—Now, if the parent realize that obedience is no mere accidental duty, the fulfilling of which is a matter that lies between himself and the child, but that he is the appointed agent to train the child up to the intelligent obedience of the self compelling, law-abiding human being, he will see that he has no right to forego the obedience of his child, and that every act of disobedience in the child is a direct condemnation of the parent. Also, he will see that the motive of the child's obedience is not the arbitrary one of, 'Do this, or that, because I have said so,' but the motive of the apostolic injunction, "Children, obey your parents in the Lord, for this is right."

Children must have the Desire to Obey.—It is only in proportion as the will of the child is in the act of obedience, and he obeys because his sense of right makes him desire to obey in spite of temptations to disobedience—not of constraint, but willingly—that the habit has been formed which will, hereafter, enable the child to use the strength of his will against his inclinations when these prompt him to lawless courses. It is said that the children of parents who are most strict in exacting obedience often turn out ill; and that orphans and other poor waifs brought up under strict discipline only wait their opportunity to break into license. Exactly so; because, in these cases, there is no gradual training of the child in the habit of obedience; no gradual enlisting of his will on the side of sweet service and a free will offering of submission to the highest law: the poor children are simply bullied into submission to the will, that is, the wilfulness, of another; not at all, 'for it is right'; only because it is convenient.

Expect Obedience.—The mother has no more sacred duty than that of training her infant to instant obedience. To do so is no difficult task; the child is still "trailing clouds of glory...from God, who is his home"; the principle of obedience is within him, waiting to be called into exercise. There is no need to rate the child, or threaten him, or use any manner of violence, because the parent is invested with authority which the child intuitively recognizes. It is enough to say, 'Do this,' in a quiet, authoritative tone, and expect it to be done. The mother often loses her hold over children because they detect in the tone of her voice that she does not expect them obey her behests; she does not think enough of her position; has not sufficient confidence in her own authority. The mother's great stronghold is in the habit of obedience. If she begin by requiring that her children always obey her, why, they will always do so as a matter of course; but let them once get the thin end of the wedge in, let them discover that they can do otherwise than obey, and a woeful struggle begins, which commonly ends in the children doing that which is right in their own eyes.

This is the sort of thing which is fatal: The children are in the drawing room, and a caller is announced. 'You must go upstairs now.' 'Oh, mother dear, do let us stay in the window-corner; we will be as quiet as mice!' The mother is rather proud of her children's pretty manners, and they stay. They are not quiet, of course; but that is the least of the evils; they have succeeded in doing as they chose and not as they were bid, and they will not put their necks under the yoke again without a struggle. It is in little matters that the mother is worsted. 'Bedtime, Willie!' 'Oh, mamma, just let me finish this'; and the mother yields, forgetting that the case in point is of no consequence; the thing that matters is that the child should be daily confirming a habit of obedience by the unbroken repetition of acts of obedience. It is astonishing how clever the child is in finding ways of evading the spirit while he observes the letter. 'Mary, come in.' 'Yes, mother'; but her mother calls four times before Mary comes. 'Put away your bricks'; and the bricks are put away with slow reluctant fingers. 'You must always wash your hands when you hear the first bell.' The child obeys for that once, and no more.

To avoid these displays of wilfulness, the mother will insist from the first on an obedience which is prompt, cheerful, and lasting—save for lapses of memory on the child's part. Tardy, unwilling, occasional obedience is hardly worth the having; and it is greatly easier to give the child the habit of perfect obedience by never allowing him in anything else, than it is to obtain this mere formal obedience by a constant exercise of authority. By-and-by, when he is old enough, take the child into confidence; let him know what a noble thing it is to be able to make himself do, in a minute, and brightly, the very thing he would rather not do. To secure this habit of obedience, the mother must exercise great self-restraint; she must never give a command which she does not intend to see carried out to the full. And she must not lay upon her children burdens, grievous to be borne, of command heaped upon command.

Law Ensures Liberty.—The children who are trained to perfect obedience may be trusted with a good deal of liberty: they receive a few directions which they know they must not disobey; and for the rest, they are left to learn how to direct their own actions, even at the cost of some small mishaps; and are not pestered with a perpetual fire of 'Do this' and 'Don't do that!'

VIII.—Truthfulness

It is unnecessary to say a word of the duty of Truthfulness; but the training of the child in the habit of strict veracity is another matter, and one which requires delicate care and scrupulosity on the part of the mother.

Three Causes of Lying—All Vicious.—The vice of lying causes: carelessness in ascertaining the truth, carelessness in stating the truth, and a deliberate intention to deceive. That all three are vicious, is evident from the fact that a man's character may be ruined by what is no more than a careless mis-statement on the part of another; the speaker repeats a damaging remark without taking the trouble to sift it; or he repeats what he has heard or seen with so little care to deliver the truth that his statement becomes no better than a lie.

Only One Kind visited on Children.—Now, of the three kinds of lying, it is only, as a matter of fact, the third which is severely visited upon the child; the first and the second he is allowed in. He tells you he has seen 'lots' of spotted dogs in the town—he has really seen two; that 'all the boys' are collecting crests—he knows of three who are doing so; that 'everybody' says Jones is a 'sneak'—the fact is he has heard Brown say so. These departures from strict veracity are on matters of such slight importance that the mother is apt to let them pass as the 'children's chatter'; but, indeed, ever such lapse is damaging to the child's sense of truth—a blade which easily loses its keenness of edge.

Accuracy of Statement.—The mother who trains her child to strict accuracy of statement about things small and great fortifies him against temptations to the grosser forms of lying; he will not readily colour a tale to his own advantage, suppress facts, equivocate, when the statement of the simple fact has become a binding habit, and when he has not been allowed to form the contrary vicious habit of playing fast and loose with words.

Exaggeration and Ludicrous Embellishments.—Two forms of prevarication, very tempting to the child, will require great vigilance on the mother's part—that of exaggeration and that of clothing a story with ludicrous embellishments. However funny a circumstance may be as described by the child, the ruthless mother must strip the tale of everything over and above the naked truth: for, indeed, a reputation for facetiousness is dearly purchased by the loss of that dignity of character, in child or man, which accompanies the habit of strict veracity; it is possible, happily, to be humorous, without any sacrifice of truth.

Reverence, etc.—As for reverence, consideration for others, respect for persons and property, I can only urge the importance of a sedulous cultivation of these moral qualities—the distinguishing marks of a refined nature—until they become the daily habits of the child's life; and the more, because a self assertive, aggressive, self seeking temper is but too characteristic of the times we live in.

Temper—Born in a Child.—I am anxious, however, to a say a few words on the habit of sweet temper. It is very customary to regard temper as constitutional, that which is born in you and is neither to be helped nor hindered. 'Oh, she is a good tempered little soul; nothing puts her out!' 'Oh, he has his father's temper; the least thing that goes contrary makes him fly into a passion,' are the sorts of remarks we hear constantly.

Not Temper, but Tendency.—It is no doubt true that children inherit a certain tendency to irascibility or to amiability, to fretfulness, discontentment, peevishness, sullenness, murmuring, and impatience; or to cheerfulness, trustfulness, good-humour, patience, and humility. It is also true that upon the preponderance of any of these qualities—upon temper, that is—the happiness or wretchedness of child and man depends, as well as the comfort or misery of the people who live with him. We all know people possessed of integrity and of many excellent virtues who make themselves intolerable to their belongings. The root of evil is, not that these people were born sullen, or peevish, or envious—that might have been mended; but that they were permitted to grow up in these dispositions. Here, if anywhere, the power of habit is invaluable: it rests with the parents to correct the original twist, all the more so if it is from them the child gets it, and to send their child into the world best with an even, happy temper, inclined to make the best of things, to look on the bright side, to impute the best and kindest motives to others, and to make no extravagant claims on his own account—fertile source of ugly tempers. And this, because the child is born with no more than certain tendencies.

Parents must correct Tendency by New Habit of Temper.—It is by force of habit that a tendency becomes a temper; and it rests with the mother to hinder the formation of ill tempers, to force that of good tempers. Nor is it difficult to do this while the child's countenance is as an open book to his mother, and she reads the thoughts of his heart before he is aware of them himself. Remembering that every envious, murmuring, discontented thought leaves a track in the very substance of the child's brain for such thoughts to run in again and again—that this track, this rut, so to speak, is ever widening and deepening with the traffic in ugly thoughts—the mother's care is to hinder at the outset the formation of any such track. She sees into her child's soul—sees the evil temper in the act of rising: now is her opportunity.

Change the Child's Thoughts.—Let her change the child's thoughts before ever the bad temper has had time to develop into conscious feeling, much less act: take him out of doors, send him to fetch or carry, tell him or show him something of interest,—in a word, give him something else to think about; but all in a natural way, and without letting the child perceive that he is being treated. As every fit of sullenness leaves place in the child's mind for another fit of sullenness to succeed it, so every such fit averted by the mother's tact tends to obliterate the evil traces of former sullen tempers. At the same time, the mother is careful to lay down a highway for the free course of all sweet and genial thoughts and feelings.

I have been offering suggestions, not for a course of intellectual and moral training, but only for the formation of certain habits which should be, as it were, the outworks of character. Even with this limited programme, I have left unnoticed many matters fully as important as those touched upon. In the presence of an embarrassment of riches, it has been necessary to adopt some principle of selection; and I have thought it well to dwell upon considerations which do not appear to me to have their full weight with educated parents, rather than upon those of which every thoughtful person recognizes the force.

Part V
Lessons as Instruments of Education

I. The Matter and Method of Lessons

It seems to me that we live in an age of pedagogy; that we of the teaching profession are inclined to take too much upon ourselves, and that parents are ready to yield the responsibility of direction, as well as of actual instruction, more than is wholesome for the children.

Parents must reflect on the Subject-matter of Instruction.—I am about to invite your attention to a subject that parents are accustomed to leave very much in the hands of the schoolmaster or governess when they do not instruct their children themselves—I mean the choice of subjects of instruction, and the ways of handling those subjects. Teachers are the people who have, more than others, given themselves to the consideration of what what a child should learn and how he should learn it; but the parent, also, should have thought on this subject, and even when he does not profess ot teach his children, should have his own carefully formed opinions as to the subject-matter and the method of their intellectual education: and this for the sake of the teacher as well as for that of the children. Nothing does more to give vitality and purpose to the work of the teacher than the certainty that the parents of his pupils go with him.

Even when children go to schools taught by qualified persons, some insight on the part of fathers and mothers is useful as hindering the teacher from dropping into professional grooves, valuing proficiency in this or that subject for its own sake, and not as it affects the children. But in the early days of the home schoolroom, it is iniquitous to leave the young governess, with little qualification beyond her native French or German, or scanty English, to chalk out a course for herself and her charges. That the children waste their time is the least of the evils that accrue: they are forming habits dead against intellectual effort; and by-and-by, when they go to school, the lessons go over their heads, the work slips through their fingers, and their powers of passive resistance baffle the most strenuous teachers.

Home the best Growing-ground for Young Children.—All the same, whatever be the advantages of Kindergarten or other schools for little children, the home schoolroom ought to be the best growing-ground for them. And doubtless it would be so, were the mother at liberty to devote herself to the instruction of her children; but this she is seldom free to do. If she can live in a town, she can send them to school when they are six; if in the country, she must have a governess; and the difficulty is to get a woman who is not only acquainted with the subjects she undertakes to teach, but who understands in some measure the nature of the child and the art and objects of education; a woman capable of making the very most of the children without waste of power or of time. Such a rara avis does not present herself in answer to every advertisement; and in default of a trained teacher, the mother must undertake to train the governess—that is, she may supplement with her own insight the scanty knowledge and experience of the young teacher. 'I wish the children to be taught to read, thus and thus, because_____': or, 'to learn and history in such a way that the lessons may have such and such effects.' Half an hour's talk of this kind with a sensible governess will secure a whole month's work for the children, so well directed that much is done in little time, and the widest possible margin secured for play and open-air exercise.

Three Questions for the Mother.—But if the mother is to inoculate the governess with her views as to the teaching of writing, French, geography, she must, herself, have definite views. She must ask herself seriously, Why must the children learn at all? What should they learn? And, How should they learn it? If she take the trouble to fiind a definite and thoughtful answer to each of these three queries, she will be in a position to direct her children's studies; and will, at the same time, be surprised to find that three-fourths of the time and labour ordinarily spent by the child at his lessons is lost time and wasted energy.

Children learn, to Grow.—Why must the child learn? Why do we eat? Is it not in order that the body may live and grow and be able to fulfil its functions? Precisely so must the mind be sustained and developed by means of the food convenient for it, the mental pabulum of assimilated knowledge. Again, the body is developed not only by means of proper sustenance, but by the appropriate exercise of each of its members. A young mother remarked to me the other day, that before her marriage she had such slender arms she never liked to exhibit them; but a strong five-months-old baby had cured her of that; she could toss and lift him with ease, and could now show well-rounded arms with anybody: and just as the limbs grow strong with exercise, so does intellectual effort with a given power of the mind make that power effective. People are apt to overlook the fact that mind must have its aliment—we learn that we may know, not that we may grow; hence the parrot-like saying of lessons, the cramming of ill-digested facts for examinations, all the ways of taking in knowledge which the mind does not assimilate.

Doctoring of the Material of Knowledge.—Specialists, on the other hand, are apt to attach too much importance to the several exercise of the mental 'faculties.' We come across books on teaching, with lessons elaborately drawn up, in which certain work is assigned to the perspective faculties, certain work to the imagination, to the judgment, and so on. Now this doctrine of the faculties, which rests on a false analogy between the mind and the body, is on its way to the limbo where the phrenologist's 'bumps' now rest in peace. The mind would appear to be one and indivisible, and endowed with manifold powers; and this sort of doctoring of the material of knowledge is unnecessary for the healthy child, whose mind is capable of self-direction, and of applying itself to its proper work upon the parcel of knowledge delivered to it. Almost any subject which common sense points out as suitable for the instruction of children will afford exercise for all their powers, if properly presented.

Children learn, to get Ideas.—The child must learn, in the second place, in order that ideas may be freely sown in the fruitful soil of his mind. 'Idea, the image or picture formed by the mind of anything external, whether sensible or spiritual.'—so, the dictionary; therefore, if the business of teaching be to furnish the child with ideas, any teaching which does not leave him possessed of a new mental image has, by so far, missed its mark. Now, just think of the listless way in which the children too often drag through reading and tables, geography and sums, and you will see that it is a rare thing for any part of any lesson to flash upon them with the vividness which leaves a mental picture behind. It is not too much to say that a morning in which a child receives no new idea is a morning wasted, however closely the little student has been kept at his books.

Ideas Grow and Produce after their Kind.—For the dictionary appears to me to fall short of the truth in its definition of the term 'idea.' An idea is more than an image or picture; it is, so to speak, a spiritual germ endowed with vital force—with power, that is, to grow, and to produce after its kind. It is the very nature of an idea to grow: as the vegetable germ secretes that it lives by, so, fairly implant an idea in the child's mind, and it will secrete its own food, grow, and bear fruit in the form of a succession of kindred ideas. We know from our own experience that, let our attention be forcibly drawn to some public character, some startling theory, and for days after we are continually hearing or reading matter which bears on this one subject, just as if all the world were thinking about what occupies our thoughts: the fact being, that the new idea we have received is in the act of growth, and is reaching out after its appropriate food. This process of feeding goes on with peculiar avidity in childhood, and the growth of an idea in the child is proportionably rapid.

Scott and Stephenson worked with Ideas.—Scott got an idea, a whole group of ideas, out of the Border tales and ballads, the folklore of the country-side, on which his boyhood was nourished: his ideas grew and brought forth, and the Waverley novels are the fruit they bore. George Stephenson made little clay engines with his playmate, Thomas Tholoway; by-and-by, when he was an engineman, he was always watching his engine, cleaning it, studying it; an engine was his dominant idea, and it developed into no less a thing than the locomotive.

Value of Dominant Ideas.—But how does this theory of the vital and fruitful character of ideas bear upon the education of the child? In this way: give your a child a single valuable idea, and you have done more for his education than if you had laid upon his mind the burden of bushels of information; for the child who grows up with a few dominant ideas has his self-education provided for, his career marked out.

Lessons must furnish Ideas.—In order for the reception of an idea, the mind must be in an attitude of eager attention, and how to secure that state we have considered elsewhere. One thing more: a single idea may be a possession so precious in itself, so fruitful, that the parent cannot fitly allow the child's selection of ideas to be a matter of chance; his lessons should furnish him with such ideas as shall make for his further education.

Children learn to get Knowledge.—But it is not only to secure due intellectual growth and the furnishing his mind with ideas, that the child must learn: the common notion, that he learns for the sake of getting knowledge, is also a true one so much so, that no knowledge should be so precious as that gained in childhood, no later knowledge should be so clearly chronicled on the brain, nor so useful as the foundation of that to follow. At the same time, the child's capacity for knowledge is very limited; his mind is, in this respect at least, but a little phial with a narrow neck; and, therefore, it behooves the parent or teacher to pour in only of the best.

Diluted Knowledge.—But, poor children, they are too often badly used by their best friends in the matter of the knowledge offered them. Grown-up people who are not mothers talk and think far more childishly than the child does in their efforts to approach his mind. If a child talk twaddle, it is because his elders are in the habit of talking twaddle to him; leave him to himself, and his remarks are wise and sensible so far as his small experience guides him. Mothers seldom talk down to their children; they are too intimate with the little people, and have, therefore, too much respect for them: but professional teachers, whether the writers of books or the givers of lessons are too apt to present a single grain of pure knowledge in a whole gallon of talk, imposing upon the child the labour of discerning the grain and of extracting it from the worthless flood.

Dr. Arnold's Knowledge as a Child.—On the whole, the children who grow up amongst their elders and are not provided with what are called children's books at all, fare the better on what they are able to glean for themselves from the literature of grown-up people. Thus it is told of Dr. Arnold that when he was three years old he received as a present from his father of Smollett's History of England as a reward for the accuracy with which he went through the stories connected with the portraits and pictures the successive reigns—an amusement which probably laid the foundation of the great love for history which distinguished him in after life. When occupying the professorial chair at Oxford, he made quotations, we are told, from Dr. Priestley's Lectures on History—verbally accurate quotations, we may believe, for such was the habit of his mind; besides, a child has little skill in recasting his matter—and that, though he had not had the book in his hands since he was a child of eight. No doubt he was an exceptional child; and all I maintain is, that had his reading been the sort of diluted twaddle which is commonly thrust upon children, it would have been impossible for him to cite passages a week, much less some two score years, after the reading.

Literature Proper for Children.—This sort of weak literature for the children, both in any story and lesson books, is the result of a reactionary process. Not so long ago the current impression was that the children had little understanding, but prodigious memory for facts; dates, numbers, rules, catechisms of knowledge, much information in small parcels, was supposed to be the fitting material for a child's education. We have changed all that, and put into the children's hands lesson-books with pretty pictures and easy talk, almost as good as story-books; but we do not see that, after all, we are but giving the same little pills of knowledge in the form of a weak and copious diluent. Teachers, and even parents, who are careful enough about their children's diet, are so reckless as to the sort of mental aliment offered to them, that I am exceedingly anxious to secure consideration for this question, of the lessons and literature proper for the little people.

Four Tests which should be applied to Children's Lessons.—We see, then, that the children's lessons should provide material for their mental growth, should exercise the several powers of their minds, should furnish them with fruitful ideas, and should afford them knowledge, really valuable for its own sake, accurate, and interesting, of the kind that the child may recall as a man with profit and pleasure. Before applying these tests to the various subjects in which children are commonly instructed, may I remind you of two or three points which I have endeavoured to establish in the preceding pages:—

Resume of Six Points already considered.—

(a) That the knowledge most valuable to the child is that which he gets with his own eyes and ears and fingers (under direction) in the open air.

(b) That the claims of the schoolroom should not be allowed to encroach on the child's right to long hours daily for exercise and investigation.

(c) That the child should be taken daily, if possible, to scenes—moor or meadow, park, common, or shore—where he may find new things to examine, and so add to his store of real knowledge. That the child's observation should be directed to flower or boulder, bird or tree; that, in fact, he should be employed in gathering the common information which is the basis of scientific knowledge.

(d) That play, vigorous healthful play, is, in its turn, fully as important as lessons, as regards both bodily health and brain-power.

(e) That the child, though under supervision, should be left much to himself—both that he may go to work in his own way on the ideas that he receives, and also that he may be the more open to natural influences.

(f) That the happiness of the child is the condition of his progress; that his lessons should be joyous, and that occasions of friction in the schoolroom are greatly to be deprecated.

Promising so much, let us now consider—What the child should learn, and how they should be taught.

II. The Kindergarten As A Place of Education

The Mother the best Kindergartnerin.—It is hardly necessary, here, to discuss the merits of the Kindergarten school. The success of such a school demands rare qualities in the teacher—high culture, some knowledge of psychology and of the art of education; intense sympathy with the children, much tact, much common sense, much common information, much 'joyousness of nature,' and much governing power;—in a word, the Kindergarten method is nicely contrived to bring the child en rapport with a superior intelligence. Given such a superior being to conduct it, and the Kindergarten is beautiful—'tis like a little heaven below'; but put a commonplace woman in charge of such a school, and the charmingly devised gifts and games and occupations become so many instruments of wooden teaching. If the very essence of the Kindergarten method is personal influence, a sort of spiritual mesmerism, it follows that the mother is naturally the best Kindergartnerin; for who so likely as she to have the needful tact, sympathy, common sense, culture?

The Nursery need not therefore be a Kindergarten.—Though every mother should be a Kindergartnerin, in the sense in which Froebel would employ the term, it does not follow that every nursery should be a regularly organized Kindergarten. Indeed, the machinery of the Kindergarten is no more than a device to ensure the carrying out of certain educational principles, and some of these it is the mother's business to get at, and work out according to Froebel's methods—or her own. For instance, in the Kindergarten the child's senses are carefully and progressively trained: he looks, listens, learns by touch; gets ideas of size, colour, form, number; is taught to copy faithfully, express exactly. And in this training of the senses, the child is made to pursue the method the infant shapes for himself in his early studies of ring or ball.

Field of Knowledge too circumscribed.—But it is possible that the child's marvellous power of obtaining knowledge by means of his senses may be undervalued; that the field may be too circumscribed; and that, during the first six or seven years in which he might have become intimately acquainted with the properties and history of every natural object within his reach, he has obtained, exact ideas, it is true—can distinguish a rhomboid from a pentagon, a primary from a secondary colour, has learned to see so truly that he can copy what he sees in folded paper or woven straw,—but this at the expense of much of that real knowledge of the external world which at no time of his life will he be so fitted to acquire. Therefore, while the exact nicely graduated training of the Kindergarten may be of value, the mother will endeavour to give it by the way, and will by no means let it stand for that wider training of the senses, to secure which for her children is a primary duty.

Again, the child in the Kindergarten is set to such tasks only as he is competent to perform, and then, whatever he has to do, he is expected to do perfectly. I have seen a four-years-old child blush and look as self-condemend, because he had folded a slip of a paper irregularly, as if found out in a falsehood. But mother or nurse is quite able to secure that the child's small offices are perfectly executed; and, here is an important point, without that slight strain of distressful anxiety which may be observed in children labouring to please that smiling goddess, their 'Kindergarnerin.'

Training of a Just Eye and Faithful Hand.—The Kindergarten 'Occupations' afford opportunities for training in this kind of faithfulness; but in the home a thousand such opportunities occur; if only in such trifles as the straightening of a tablecloth or of a picture, the hanging of a towel, the packing of a parcel—every thoughtful mother invents a thousand ways of training in her child a just eye and a faithful hand. Nevertheless, as a means of methodical training, as well as of happy employment, the introduction of some of the games and occupations of the Kindergarten into the nursery may be allowed; provided that the mother does not depend upon these, but makes all the child's occupations subserve the purposes of his education.

'Sweetness and Light' in the Kindergarten—The child breathes an atmosphere of 'sweetness and light' in the Kindergarten. You see the sturdy urchin of five stiffen his back and decline to be a jumping frog, and the Kindergartnerin comes with unruffled gentleness, takes him by the hand, and leads him out of the circle,—he is not treated as an offender, only he does not choose to do as the others do, therefore he is not wanted there: the next time, he is quite content to be a frog. Here we have the principle for the discipline of the nursery. Do not treat the child's small contumacy too seriously; do not assume that he is being naughty: just leave him out when he is not prepared to act in harmony with the rest. Avoid friction; and above all, do not let him disturb the moral atmosphere in all gentleness and serenity, remove him from the company of others, when he is being what nurses call 'tiresome.'

Once more, the Kindergarten professes to take account of the joyousness of the child's nature: to allow him full and free expression for the glee that is in him, without the 'rampaging' which follows if he is left to himself to find an outlet for his exuberant life. This union of joy and gentleness is the very temper to be cultivated in the nursery. The boisterous behaviour sometimes allowed in children is unnecessary—within doors, at any rate: but even a momentary absence of sunshine on the faces of her children will be a graver cause of uneasiness to the mother. On the whole, we may say that some of the principles which should govern Kindergarten training are precisely those in which every thoughtful mother endeavours to bring up her family; while the practices of the Kindergarten, being only ways, amongst others, of carrying out these principles, and being apt to become stereotyped and wooden, are unnecessary, but may be adopted so far as they fit in conveniently with the mother's general scheme for the education of her family.

III. Further Consideration Of The Kindergarten

The Childhood of Tolstoi—There is possibly no known field of research in which so little available work has been done as in that covered by the word 'children.' The 'fair lande' lies under our very eyes, but whoso would map it out must write 'Unexplored' across vast tracts. Thoughtful persons begin to suspect that the mistakes we make through this ignorance are grievous and injurious. For example, are not all our schemes of education founded on the presumption that a child's mind—his 'thinking, feeling man'—begins 'very small,' and grows great with the growth of his body? We cannot tell if this is indeed the case. The children keep themselves to themselves in a general way, their winning ways and frank confidences notwithstanding; but if one of us do, by chance, get a child revealed to him, he is startled to find that the child has by far the keener intelligence, the wiser thoughts, the larger soul of the two. When genius is able to lift the veil and show us a child, it does a service which, in our present state of thought, we are hardly able to appraise; and when genius or simplicity, or both, shall have given us enough such studies to generalize upon, we shall doubtless reconsider the whole subject, and shall be dismayed at the slights we have been putting upon children in the name of education. Count Tolstoi gives us, in Childhood, Boyhood, Youth [see Appendix], unmistakable child-portraiture, a miniature in which a mother may see her child and recognise what and how much there is in him:—

"Like our own dear mother," the little fellow writes, in the verses he makes for his grandmother's birthday; and then, when the verses come to be read, ah! The humiliation of the soul he goes through, and how surely he expects father and grandmother to find him out for a hypocrite. "Why did I write it? She's not here, and it was not necessary to mention her; I love grandma, it's true; I reverence her, but still she is not the same. Why did I write it? Why have I lied?" This is the sort of thing there is in children. We recognise it as we read, and remember the dim, childish days when we, too, had an 'organ of truth' just so exquisitely delicate; and the recollection should quicken our reverence of the tender consciences of children.

"The Story of a Child."—I should like while speaking of this subject to mention another book which contains the self-revelation of a child,—a child that once was summoned, to give evidence, out of the dark abysm of time. This is the sort of study of a child that is really precious, because it is to be had on no other terms than by harking back to our own childhood, vivifying it, reproducing it, by mere force of imaginative power. This is absolutely the only way to get into sympathy with a child, for children, with all their frank confidences and ready chatter, are quite inscrutable little persons, who never tell anyone the sort of things that read in this 'Story.' There is no need to tell each other, for other children know, and, as for telling the grown-ups, children are fully persuaded that no grown-up, not even mother, could understand; Otto might, perhaps, and confidences will be poured into the ear of a dog which the loving mother lays herself out for in vain.

"Each in his hidden sphere of joy or woe,

Our hermit spirits dwell, and range apart,

Our eyes see all around in gloom or glow—

Hues of their own, fresh borrow'd from the heart."

And this is even more notably the case with children than with ourselves. It is a law of our nature with which it is absolutely useless to contend, and our only means of true intimacy with a child is the power of recovering our own childhood—a power which we are apt to let slip as of no vital importance. This, Miss Margaret Deland helps us to do: we recognise our old selves, with a difference, in Ellen. Just so irrational, inconsequent, loving and heroic, and generally tiresome to the grown-up world were our own impulses that long ago, on which we look back with tenderness, but seldom with complacency. If we rise, after reading, The Story of a Child [See Appendix], a little more humble, a little more diffident, ready to believe more than we see, why, it will do us no harm, and should bless and help the children. From one word of the author's we should like to differ. Miss

Deland thinks that it may be wholesome for the elders to understand children better, but for the children, why, she thinks that most of us grow up wonderfully well in spite of this and all other difficulties. In a sense this is true, but, in another sense, one of the saddest things in life is the issue of splendid child-material into common place, uninteresting maturity, of a kind that the world seems to be neither the best nor the worse for.

Tolstoi's childhood and that of Miss Deland's little heroine would appear to be a far cry from the 'Kindergarten'; but as a matter of fact these two revelations of what children are bring our contention to a point.

We are told that, "but yesterday, in the University of Edinburgh, the greatest figure in the Faculty was Sir James Simpson, the discoverer of chloroform. The other day his successor and nephew, Professor Simpson, was asked by the librarian of the University to go to the library and pick out the books on his subject that were no longer needed. And his reply to the librarian was this: 'Take every text-book that is more than ten years old, and put it down in the cellar.'" So far as education is a science, the truth of even ten—much more, a hundred—years ago is not the whole truth of to-day.

"Thought beyond their thoughts to those high seers were given"; and, in proportion as the urgency of educational effort presses upon us, will be the ardour of our appreciation, the diligence of our employment, of those truths which the great pioneers, Froebel and the rest, have won for us by no less than prophetic insight. But, alas, and alas, for the cravings of lazy human nature—we may not have an educational pope; we must think out for ourselves, as well as work out, those things that belong to the perfect bringing-up of our children.

What we Owe to Froebel.—We reverence Froebel. Many of his great thoughts we share; we cannot say borrow, because some, like the child's relations to the universe, are at least as old as Plato; others belong to universal practice and experience, and this shows their psychological rightness. Froebel gathered diffused thought and practice into a system, but he did a greater thing than this. He raised an altar to the enthusiasm of childhood upon which the flame has never since gone out. The true Kindergartnerin is the artist amongst teachers; she is filled with the inspiration of her work, and probably most sincere teachers have caught something from her fervour, some sense of the beauty of childhood, and of the enthralling delight of truly educational work.

Requirements of a Person.—And yet I enter a caveat. Our first care should be to preserve the individuality, to give play to the personality, of children. Now persons do not grow in a garden, much less in a greenhouse. It is a doubtful boon to a person to have conditions too carefully adapted to his needs. The exactly due sunshine and shade, pruning and training, are good for a plant whose uses are subordinate, so to say, to the needs and pleasures of its owner. But a person who has other uses in the world, and mother or teacher who regards him as a plant and herself as the gardener, will only be saved from grave mistakes by the force of human nature in herself and in her child.

Nature as an Educator.—The notion of supplementing Nature from the cradle is a dangerous one. A little guiding, a little restraining, much reverent watching, Nature asks of us; but beyond that, it is the wisdom of parents to leave children as much as may be to Nature, and "to a higher Power than Nature itself."

Danger of undervaluing Children's Intelligence.—Those of us who have watched an urchin of seven making Catherine-wheels down the length of a street, or a group of little girls dancing to a barrel organ, or small boys and girls on a door-step giving what Dickens calls 'dry nourishment' to their babies, or a small girl sent by her mother to make four careful purchases out of sixpence and bring home the change—are not ready to believe that physical, mental, and moral development waits, so to speak, upon Kindergarten teaching. Indeed, I am inclined to question whether, in the interest of carrying out a system, the charming Kindergartnerin is not in danger sometimes of greatly undervaluing the intelligence of her children. I know a person of three who happened to be found by a caller alone in the drawing room. It was spring, and the caller thought to make himself entertaining with talk about the pretty 'baa-lambs.' But a pair of big blue eyes were fixed upon him and a solemn person made this solemn remark, "Isn't it a dwefful howid thing to see a pig killed!" We hope she had never seen or even heard of the killing of a pig, but she made as effective a protest against twaddle as would any woman of Society. Boers and kopjes, Russians and Japs, Treasure Island, Robinson Crusoe and his man Friday, the fight of Thermopylae, Ulysses and the Suitors—these are the sorts of things that children play at by the month together; even the toddlers of three and four will hold their own manfully with their brothers and sisters. And, if the little people were in the habit of telling how they feel, we should learn perhaps that they are a good deal bored by the nice little games in which they frisk like lambs, flap their fins, and twiddle their fingers like butterflies.

We all like to be Humoured.—'But,' says the reader, 'children do all these things so pleasantly and happily in the Kindergarten!' It is a curious thing about human nature that we all like to be managed by persons who take the pains to play on our amiabilities. Even a dog can be made foolishly sentimental; and, if we who are older have our foibles in this kind, it is little wonder that children can be wooed to do anything by persons whose approaches to them are always charming. It is true that 'W.V.,' the child whom the world has been taught to love, sang her Kindergarten songs with little hands waving in the 'air so blue'! but that was for the delectation and delusion of the elders when bedtime came. 'W.V.' had greater thoughts at other times.

Teachers mediate too much.—There are still, probably, Kindergartens where a great deal of twaddle is talked in song and story, where the teacher conceives that to make poems for the children herself and to compose tunes for their singing and to draw pictures for their admiration, is to fulfil her function to the uttermost. The children might echo Wordsworth's complaint of 'the world,' and say, the teacher is too much with us, late and soon. Everything is directed, expected, suggested. No other personality out of book, picture, or song, no, not even that of Nature herself, can get at the children without the mediation of the teacher. No room is left for spontaneity or personal initiation on their part.

Danger of Personal Magnetism.—Most of us are misled by our virtues, and the entire zeal and enthusiasm of the Kindergartnerin is perhaps her stone of stumbling. 'But the children are so happy and good!' Precisely; the home-nursery is by no means such a scene of peace, but I venture to think it a better growing place. I am delighted to see that an eminent Froebelian protests against the element of personal magnetism in the teacher; but there is, or has been, a good deal of this element in the successful Kindergartner, and we all know how we lose vigour and individuality under this sort of influence. Even apart from this element of charm, I doubt if the self-adjusting property of life in the Kindergarten is good for the children.

'Kindergarten' a False Analogy.—The world suffered that morning when the happy name of 'Kindergarten' suggested itself to the greatest among educational 'Fathers.' No doubt it was simple and fit in its first intention as meaning an out-of-door garden life for the children; but, a false analogy has hampered, or killed, more than one philosophic system—the child became a plant in a well-ordered garden. The analogy appealed to the orderly, scientific German mind, which does not much approve of irregular, spontaneous movement in any sort. Culture, due stimulus, sweetness and light, became the chief features of a great educational code. From the potting-shed to the frame and thence to the flower-bed, the little plant gets in due proportion what is good for him. He grows in a seemly way, in ordered ranks; and in fit season puts forth his flower.

Now, to a figure a person by any analogy whatsoever is dangerous and misleading; there is nothing in nature commensurable with a person. Because the analogy of the garden plant is very attractive, it is the more misleading; manifestations of purpose in a plant are wonderful and delightful, but in a person such manifestations are simply normal. The outcome of any thought is necessarily moulded by that thought, and to have a cultivated garden as the ground-plan of our educational thought, either means nothing at all, which it would be wronging the Master to suppose, or it means undue interference with the spontaneous development of a human being.

Mother-games too strenuous for a Child.—To begin with the 'Mother-games,' a sweet conception, most lovingly worked out. But let us consider; the infant is exquisitely aware of every mood of his mother, the little face clouds with grief or beams with joy in response to the expression of hers. The two left to themselves have rare games. He jumps and pulls, crows and chuckles, crawls and kicks and gurgle with joy; and, amid all the play, is taught what he may not do. Hands and feet, legs and arms, fingers and toes, are continually going while he is awake; mouth, eyes and ears are agog. All is play without intention, and mother plays with baby as glad as he. Nature sits quietly by and sees to it that all the play is really work; and development of every sort is going on at a greater rate during the first two years of life than at any like period of after life—enough development and not too much, for baby is an inordinate sleeper. Then comes in the educator and offers a little more. The new games are so pretty and taking that baby might as well be doing these as his own meaningless and clumsy jumpings and pattings. But a real labour is being put upon the child in addition to the heaviest two years' work that his life will know. His sympathy with his mother is so acute that he perceives something strenuous in the new play, notwithstanding all the smiles and pretty talk; he answers by endeavour, great in proportion as he is small. His nerve centres and brain power have been unduly taxed, some of the joy of living has been taken from him, and though his baby response to direct education is very charming, he has less latent power left for the future calls of life.

The Society of his Equals too stimulating for a child.—Let us follow the little person to the Kindergarten, where he has the stimulus of classmates of his own age. It certainly is stimulating. For ourselves, no society is so much so as that of a number of persons of our own age and standing; this is the great joy of college life; a wholesome joy for all young people for a limited time. But persons of twenty have, or should have, some command over their inhibitory centres. They should not permit the dissipation of nerve power caused by too much social stimulus; yet even persons of twenty are not always equal to the task of self-management in exciting circumstances. What then, is to be expected of persons of two, three, four, five? That the little person looks rather stolid than otherwise is no guarantee against excitement within. The clash and sparkle of our equals now and then stirs up to health; but for everyday life, the mixed society of elders, juniors and equals, which we get in a family, gives at the same time the most repose and the most room for individual development. We have all wondered at the good sense, reasonableness, fun and resourcefulness shown by a child in his own home as compared with the same child in school life.

Danger of supplanting Nature.—Danger lurks in the Kindergarten, just in proportion to the completeness and beauty of its organization. It is possible to supplement Nature so skillfully that we run some risk of supplanting her, depriving her of space and time to do her own work in her own way. 'Go and see what Tommy is doing and tell him he mustn't,' is not sound doctrine. Tommy should be free to do what he likes with his limbs and his mind through all the hours of the day when he is not sitting up nicely at meals. He should run and jump, leap and tumble, lie on his face watching a worm, or on his back watching the bees in a lime tree. Nature will look after him and give him promptings of desire to know many things; and somebody must tell as he wants to know; and to do many things, and somebody should be handy just to put him in the way; and to be many things, naughty and good, and somebody should give direction.

Importance of Personal Initiative.—Here we come to the real crux of the Kindergarten question. The busy mother says she has no leisure to be that somebody, and the child will run wild and get into bad habits; but we must not make a fetish of habit; education is a life as well as a discipline. Health, strength, and agility, bright eyes and alert movements, come of a free life, out-of-doors, if it may be and as for habits, there is no habit or power so useful to man or woman as that of personal initiative. The resourcefulness which will enable a family of children to invent their own games and occupations through the length of a summer's day is worth more in after life than a good deal of knowledge about cubes and hexagons, and this comes, not of continual intervention on the mother's part, but of much masterly inactivity.

Parents and Teachers must sow Opportunities.—The educational error of our day is that we believe too much in mediators. Now, Nature is her own mediator, undertakes, herself, to find work for eyes and ears, taste and touch; she will prick the brain with problems and the heart with feelings; and the part of the mother or teacher in the early years (indeed, all through life) is to sow opportunities, and then to keep in the background, ready with a guiding or restraining hand only when these are badly wanted. Mothers shirk their work and put it, as they would say, into better hands than their own, because they do not recognise that wise letting alone is the chief thing asked of them, seeing that every mother has in Nature an all-sufficient handmaid, who arranges for due work and due rest of mind, muscles, and senses.

In one way the children of the poor have better chances than those of the rich. Poor children get education out of household ways; but there is a great deal of teaching to be got out of a wisely ordered nursery, and their own small persons and possessions should, as I have said, afford much 'Kindergarten' training to the little family at home. At six or seven, definite lessons should begin, and these need not be watered down or served with jam for the acute intelligences that will in this way be brought to bear on them.

'Only' Children.—But what of only children, or the child too old to play with her baby brother? Surely the Kindergarten is a great boon for these! Perhaps so; but a cottage-child as a companion, or a lively young nursemaid, might be better. A child will have taught himself to paint, paste, cut paper, knit, weave, hammer and saw, make lovely things in clay and sand, build castles with his bricks; possibly, too, will have taught himself to read, write, and do sums, besides acquiring no end of knowledge and notions about the world he lives in, by the time he is six or seven. What I contend for is that he shall do these things because he chooses (provided that the standard of perfection in his small works be kept before him).

The Child should be allowed some Ordering of his Life.—The details of family living will give him the repose of an ordered life; but, for the rest, he should have more free-growing time than is possible in the most charming school. The fact that lessons look like play is no recommendation: they just want the freedom of play and the sense of his own ordering that belongs to play. Most of us have little enough opportunity for the ordering of our own lives, so it is well to make much of the years that can be given to children to gain this joyous experience.

Helen Keller.—I think what I have said of natural development as opposed to any too carefully organized system is supported by a recent contribution, of unique value, to the science of education—I mean the autobiography of Helen Keller.

When she was nineteen months old, Helen had a severe illness, in which she lost sight and hearing, and consequently speech. She never recovered the lost senses and here, we should say, was a soul almost inviolably sealed, to which there was no approach but through the single sense of touch; yet, this lady's book, written with her own unaided hands (she used a typewriter), with hardly any revision, should rank as a classic for the purity and pregnancy of the style, independently of the vital interest of the matter. How was the miracle accomplished? Of her childhood Helen says herself that, save for a few impressions, "the shadows of the prison-house" enveloped it. But there were always roses, and she had the sense of smell; and there was love—but she was not loving then. When she was seven Miss Sullivan came to her. This lady herself had been blind for some years, and had been at the Perkins Institute, founded by that Dr Howe who liberated the intelligence of Laura Bridgman. But Miss Sullivan is no mere output of any institution. She is a person of fine sanity and wholesomeness, trusting to her personal initiative, and aware from the first that her work was to liberate the personality of her little pupil and by no means to superimpose her own. "Thus I came up out of Egypt," says Miss Keller of the arrival of her teacher, and the voice which she heard from Sinai said, "Knowledge is love and light and vision"; and then follows that amazing and enthralling epic which tells how it was all done, how the one word water was the key which opened the doors of the child's mind, while the word love opened those of the closed heart. Thenceforth, many new words came every day with crowds of ideas; and it is not too much to say that this imprisoned and desolate child entered upon such a large inheritance of thought and knowledge, of gladness and vision, as few of us of the seeing and hearing world attain to. The instrument in this great liberation was nothing more than the familiar manual alphabet, followed in course of time by raised books and 'Braille.'

Miss Sullivan on Systems of Education.—Like all great discoveries, this, of a soul, was, in all its steps, marked by simplicity. Miss Sullivan had little love for psychologists and all their ways; would have no experiments; would not have her pupil treated as a phenomenon, but as a person. "No," she says, "I don't want any more Kindergarten materials . . . I am beginning to suspect all elaborate and special systems of education. They seem to me to be built up on the supposition that every child is a kind of idiot who must be taught to think, whereas if the child is left to himself he will think more and better, if less showily. Let him go and come freely, let him touch real things, and combine his impressions for himself, instead of sitting indoors at a little round table, while a sweet-voiced teacher suggests that he build a stone wall with his wooden blocks, or make a rainbow out of strips of coloured paper, plant straw trees in bead flower-pots. Such teaching fills the mind with artificial associations that must be got rid of before the child can develop independent ideas out of actual experiences." It is a great thing to have a study of education as it were de novo, in which we see the triumph of mind, not only over apparently insuperable natural obstacles, but over the dead wall of systematized education—a more complete hindrance to any poor child than her grievous defects proved to Helen Keller.

The Kindergarten in the United States.—This question of the Kindergarten, as the proper place for the education of young children, is so important that I should like to recommend to parents and teachers the examination of the subject contained in the Special Reports published by the Board of Education. [See Appendix]

We must go to the United States to witness the apotheosis of educational theory; I say theory rather than practice, because the American mind, like the French, seems to me severely logical as well as generously impulsive. A theory arrives, is liberally entertained, and is set to work with due appliances on a magnificent scale to do that which in it lies for the education of a great people. To say, educational science in America appears to be deductive rather than inductive; theories are translated into experiments with truly imposing zeal and generosity. An inductive theory of education is, on the other hand, arrived at by means of long, slow, various, and laborious experiments which disclose, here a little, and there a little, of universal truth. The Americans have chosen, perhaps, the easier way, and in the end, they too experiment upon their theory. The Kindergarten system illustrates what I mean; notwithstanding its German name, the Kindergarten is not a common product in the Fatherland; it is in America that the ideas of Froebel have received their greatest development, that the Kindergarten has become a cult, and the great teacher a prophet. But the impulse has worn itself out; any way, it is waxing weak.

Mr. Thistleton Mark on the Kindergarten.—According to Mr. Thistleton Mark—whose able paper on 'Moral Education in American Schools' offers matter for much profitable reflection—"Even a stationary Froeblian is driven to have some better holdfast than the ipse dixit of the great reformer. The word Kindergarten is no longer a proper noun signifying always and everywhere the one, sole, original, and identical thing. It is a common noun, and as such is assured of a more permanent place in American speech." That is to say, educational thought in America is tending towards the broad and natural conception expressed in the phrase 'education is a life.' But I wish that educationalists would give up the name Kindergarten. I cannot help thinking that it is somewhat of a strain to conscientous minds to draw the cover of Froeblian doctrine and practice over the broader and more living conceptions that are abroad to-day. Even revolutionized Kindergarten practice must suffer from the memory and habit of weaknesses such as are pointed out by Dr Stanley Hall in the following words:—

Dr. Stanley Hall on the Kindergarten.—"The most decadent intellectual new departure of the American Froebelists is the emphasis now laid upon the mother-plays as the acme of Kindergarten wisdom. These are represented by very crude poems, indifferent music and pictures, illustrating certain incidents of child life believed to be of fundamental and typical significance. I have read these in German and in English, have strummed the music, and have given a brief course of lectures from the sympathetic standpoint, trying to put all the new wine of meaning I could think of into them. But I am driven to the conclusion that, if they are not positively unwholesome and harmful for the child, and productive of anti-scientific and unphilosphical intellectual habits in the teacher, they should nevertheless be superseded by the far better things now available." [quoted by Mr. Thistleton Mark].

"Another cardinal error of the Kindergarten is the intensity of its devotion to gifts and occupations. In devising these Froebel showed great sagacity; but the scheme as it left his own hands was a very inadequate expression of his educational ideas, even for his time. He thought it a perfect grammar of play and an alphabet of industries; and in this opinion he was utterly mistaken. Play and industry were then relatively undeveloped; and while his devices were beneficent for the peasant children in the country, they lead in the interests of the modern city a child a very pallid and unreal life." With these important utterances I must conclude a superficial examination of the very important question,—Is the Kindergarten the best training-ground for a child?

IV.—Reading

Time of Teaching to Read, an Open Question.—Reading presents itself first amongst the lessons to be used as instruments of education, although it is open to discussion whether the child should acquire the art unconsciously, from his infancy upwards, or whether the effort should be deferred until he is, say, six or seven, and then made with vigour. In a valuable letter, addressed to her son John, we have the way of teaching to read adopted by that pattern mother, the mother of the Wesleys:—

Mrs. Wesley's Plan.—"None of them was taught to read till five years old, except Kezzy, in whose case I was overruled; and she was more years in learning than any of the rest had been months. The way of teaching was this: the day before a child began to learn, the house was set in order, every one's work appointed them, and a charge given that no one should come into the room from nine to twelve, or from two to five, which were our school hours. One day was allowed the child wherein to learn its letters, and each of them did in that time know all its letters, great and small, except Molly and Nancy, who were a day and a half before they knew them perfectly, for which I thought them then very dull; but the reason I thought them so was because the rest learned them so readily; and your brother Samuel, who was the first child I ever taught, learned the alphabet in a few hours. He was five years old the tenth of February; the next day we began to learn, and as soon as he knew the letters, began at the first chapter of Genesis. He was taught to spell the first verse, then to read it over and over until he could read it off-hand without hesitation; so on, to the second verse, etc., 'till he took ten verses for a lesson, which he quickly did. Easter fell low that year, and by Whitsuntide he could read a chapter very well; for he read continually, and had such a prodigious memory, that I cannot remember to have told him the same word twice. What was yet stranger, any word he had learnt in his lesson he knew wherever he saw it, either in his Bible or any other book, by which means he learned very soon to read an English author well." [Southey's Life of Wesley].

It is much to be wished that thoughtful mothers would more often keep account of the methods they employ with their children, with some definite note of the success of this or that plan.

Many persons consider that to learn to read a language so full of anomalies and difficulties as our own is a task which should not be imposed too soon on the childish mind. But, as a matter of fact, few of us can recollect how or when we learned to read: for all we know, it came by nature, like the art of running; and not only so, but often mothers of the educated classes do not know how their children learned to read. 'Oh, he taught himself,' is all the account his mother can give of little Dick's proficiency. Whereby it is plain, that this notion of the extreme difficulty of learning to read is begotten by the elders rather than by the children. There would be no little books entitled Reading Without Tears, if tears were not sometimes shed over the reading lesson; but, really, when that is the case, the fault rests with the teacher.

The Alphabet.—As for his letters, the child usually teaches himself. He has his box of ivory letters and picks out p for pudding, b for blackbird, h for horse, big and little, and knows them both. But the learning of the alphabet should be made a means of cultivating the child's observation: he should be made to see what he looks at. Make big B in the air, and let him name it; then let him make round O, and crooked S, and T for Tommy, and you name the letters as the little finger forms them with unsteady strokes in the air. To make the small letters thus from memory is a work of more art, and requires more careful observation on the child's part. A tray of sand is useful at this stage. The child draws his finger boldly through the sand, and then puts a back to his D; and behold, his first essay in making a straight line and a curve. But the devices for making the learning of the 'A B C' interesting are endless. There is no occasion to hurry the child: let him learn one form at a time, and know it so well that he can pick out the d's, say, big and little, in a page of large print. Let him say d for duck, dog, doll, thus: d-uck, d-og, prolonging the sound of the initial consonant, and at last sounding d alone, not dee, but d', the mere sound of the consonant separated as far as possible from the following vowel.

Let the child alone, and he will learn the alphabet for himself: but few mothers can resist the pleasure of teaching it; and there is no reason why they should, for this kind of learning is no more than play to the child, and if the alphabet be taught to the little student, his appreciation of both form and sound will be cultivated. When should he begin? Whenever his box of letters begins to interest him. The baby of two will often be able to name half a dozen letters; and there is nothing against it so long as the finding and naming of letters is a game to him. But he must not be urged, required to show off, teased to find letters when his heart is set on other play.

Word-making. The first exercises in the making of words will be just as pleasant to the child. Exercises treated as a game, which yet teach the powers of the letters, will be better to begin with than actual sentences. Take up two of his letters and make the syllable 'at': tell him it is the word we use when we say 'at home,' 'at school.' Then put b to 'at'— bat; c to 'at'—cat; fat, hat, mat, sat, rat, and so on. First, let the child say what the word becomes with each initial consonant to 'at,' in order to make hat, pat, cat. Let the syllables all be actual words which he knows. Set the words in a row, and let him read them off. Do this with the short vowel sounds in combination with each of the consonants, and the child will learn to read off dozens of words of three letters, and will master the short-vowel sounds with initial and final consonants without effort. Before long he will do the lesson for himself. 'How many words can you make with "en" and another letter, with "od" and another letter?' etc. Do not hurry him.

Word-making with Long Vowels, etc.—When this sort of exercise becomes so easy that it is no longer interesting, let the long sounds of the vowels be learnt in the same way: use the same syllables as before with a final e; thus 'at' becomes 'ate,' and we get late, pate, rate, etc. The child may be told that a in 'rate' is long a; a in 'rat' is short a. He will make the new sets of words with much facility, helped by the experience he gained in the former lessons.

Then the same sort of thing with final 'ng'—'ing,' 'ang,' 'ong,' 'ung'; as in ring, fang, long, sung: initial 'th,' as then, that: final 'th,' as with, pith, hath, lath, and so on, through endless combinations which will suggest themselves. This is not reading, but it preparing the ground for reading; words will be no longer unfamiliar, perplexing objects, when the child meets with them in a line of print. Require him to pronounce the words he makes with such finish and distinctness that he can himself hear and count the sounds in given way.

Early Spelling.—Accustom him from the first to shut his eyes and spell the word he has made. This is important. Reading is not spelling, nor is it necessary to spell in order to read well; but the good speller is the child whose eye is quick enough to take in the letters which compose it, in the act of reading off a word, and this is a habit to be acquired from the first: accustom him to see the letters in the word, and he will do without effort.

If words were always made on a given pattern in English, if the same letter always represented the same sounds, learning to read would be an easy matter; for the child would soon acquire the few elements of which all words would, in that case, be composed. But many of our English words are, each, a law unto itself: there is nothing for it, but the child must learn to know them at sight; he must recognise 'which,' precisely as he recognizes 'B,' because he has seen it before, been made to look at it with interest, so that the pattern of the word is stamped upon his retentive brain. This process should go on side by side with the other—the learning of the powers of the letters; for the more variety you can throw into his reading lessons, the more will the child enjoy them. Lessons in word-making help him to take intelligent interest in words; but his progress in the art of reading depends chiefly on the 'reading at sight' lessons.

Reading at Sight.—The teacher must be content to proceed very slowly, securing the ground under her feet as she goes. Say—

> "Twinkle, twinkle, little star,
>
> How I wonder what you are,"

is the first lesson; just those two lines. Read the passage for the child, very slowly, sweetly, with just expression, so that it is pleasant to him to listen. Point to each word as you read. Then point to 'twinkle,' 'wonder,' 'star,' 'what,'—and expect the child to pronounce each word in the verse taken promiscuously; then, when he shows that he knows each word by itself, and not before, let him read the two lines with clear enunciation and expression: insist from the first on clear, beautiful reading, and do not let the child fall into a dreary monotone, no more pleasant to himself than to his listener. Of course, by this time he is able to say the two lines; and let him say them clearly and beautifully. In his after lesson he will learn the rest of the little poem.

The Reading of Prose.—At this stage, his reading lessons must advance so slowly that he may just as well learn his reading exercises, both prose and poetry, as recitation lessons. Little poems suitable to be learned in this way will suggest themselves at once; but perhaps prose is better, on the whole, as offering more of the words in everyday use, of Saxon origin, and of anomalous spelling. Short fables, and such graceful, simple prose as we have in Mrs Gatty's Parables from Nature, and, still better, in Mrs Barbauld's prose poems, are very suitable. Even for their earliest reading lessons, it is unnecessary to put twaddle into the hands of children.

But we have not yet finished the reading lesson on 'Twinkle, twinkle little star.' The child should hunt through two or three pages of good clear type for 'little,' star,' you,' are,' each of the words he has learned, until the word he knows looks out upon him like the face of a friend in a crowd of strangers, and he is able to pounce upon it anywhere. Lest he grow weary of the search, the teacher should guide him, unawares, to the line or paragraph where the word he wants occurs. Already the child has accumulated a little capital; he knows eight or ten words so well that he will recognise them anywhere, and the lesson has occupied probably ten minutes.

The next 'reading at sight' lesson will begin with a hunt for the familiar words, and then—

"Up above the world so high,

Like a diamond in the sky,"

should be gone through in the same way. As spelling is simply the art of seeing, seeing the letters in a word as we see the features of a face—say to the child, 'Can you spell sky?'—or any of the shorter words. He is put on his mettle, and if he fails this time, be sure he will be able to spell the word when you ask him next; but do not let him learn to spell or even say the letters aloud with the word before him.

As for understanding what they read, the children will be full of bright, intelligent remarks and questions, and will take this part of the lesson into their own hands; indeed, the teacher will have to be on her guard not to let them carry her away from the subject.

Careful Pronunciation.—The little people will probably have to be pulled up on the score of pronunciation. They must render 'high,' sky,' 'like,' 'world,' with delicate precision; 'diamond,' they will no doubt wish to hurry over, and say as 'di'mond,' just as they will reduce 'history' to 'hist'ry.' But here is another advantage of slow and steady progress—the saying of each word receives due attention, and the child is trained in the habit of careful enunciation. Every day increases the number of words he is able to read at sight, and the more words he knows already, the longer his reading lesson becomes in order to afford the ten or dozen new words which he should master every day.

A Year's Work.—'But what a snail's progress!' you are inclined to say. Not so slow, after all: a child will thus learn, without appreciable labour, from two to three thousand words in the course of a year; in other words, he will learn to read, for the mastery of this number of words will carry him with comfort through most of the books that fall in his way.

Ordinary Method.—Now, compare the steady progress and constant interest and liveliness of such lessons with the deadly weariness of the ordinary reading lesson. The child blunders through a page or two in a dreary monotone without expression, with imperfect enunciation. He comes to a word he does not know, and he spells it; that throws no light on the subject, and he is told the word: he repeats it, but as he has made no mental effort to secure the word, the next time he meets with it the same process is gone through. The reading lesson for that day comes to an end. The pupil has been miserably bored, and has not acquired one new word. Eventually, he learns to read, somehow, by mere dint of repetition; but consider what an abuse of his intelligence is a system of teaching which makes him undergo daily labour with little or no result, and gives him a distaste for books before he has learned to use them.

V.—The First Reading Lesson

[It is so important that children should be taught to read in a rational way, that I introduce two papers—by the writer—which have appeared in Parents' Review, in the hope that they will make the suggested method fairly clear & familiar.]

(Two Mothers Confer)

"You don't mean to say you would go plump into words of three or four syllables before a child knows his letters?"

"It is possible to read words without knowing the alphabet, as you know a face without singling out its features; but we learn not only the names but the sounds of the letters before we begin to read words."

"Our children learn their letters without any teaching. We always keep by us a shallow table drawer, the bottom covered half an inch deep with sand. Before they are two, the babies make round O and crooked S, and T for Tommy, and so on, with dumpy, uncertain little fingers. The elder children teach the little ones by way of a game."

"The sand is capital! We have various devices, but none so good as that. Children love to be doing. The funny, shaky lines the little finger makes in the sand will be ten times as interesting as the shapes the eye sees."

"But the reading! I can't get over three syllables in the first lesson. Why, it's like teaching a twelve-months old child to waltz."

"You say that because we forget that a group of letters is no more than the sign of a word, while a word is only the vocal sign of a thing or an act. This is how the child learns. First, he gets the notion of the table; he sees several tables; he finds they have legs, by which you can scramble up; very often covers which you may pull off; and on them many things lie, good and pleasant for a baby to enjoy; sometimes, too, you can pull these things off the table, and they go down with a bang, which is nice. The grown-up people call this pleasant thing, full of many interests, 'table,' and, by-and-by, baby says 'table' too; and the word 'table' comes to mean, in a vague way, all this to him. 'Around table,' 'on the table,' and so on, form part of the idea of 'table' to him. In the same way baby chimes in when his mother sings. She says, 'Baby, sing,' and, by-and-by, notions of 'sing,' 'kiss,' 'love,' dawn on his brain."

"Yes, the darlings! and it's surprising how many words a child knows even before he can speak them; 'pussy,' 'dolly,' 'carriage,' soon convey interesting ideas to him."

"That's just it. Interest the child in the thing, and he soon learns the sound-sign for it—that is, its name. Now, I maintain that, when he is a little older, he should learn the form-sign—that is, the printed word—on the same principle. It is far easier for a child to read plum-pudding than to read 'to, to,' because 'plum-pudding' conveys a far more interesting idea."

"That may be, but when he gets into words of three or four syllables; but what would you do while he's in words of one syllable—indeed, of two or three letters?"

"I should never put him into words of one syllable at all. The bigger the word, the more striking the look of it, and, therefore, the easier it is to read, provided always that the idea it conveys is interesting to a child. It is sad to see an intelligent child toiling over a reading lesson infinitely below his capacity—ath, eth, ith, oth, uth—or, at the very best, 'The cat sat on the mat.' How should we like to begin to read German, for example, by toiling over all conceivable combinations of letters, arranged on no principle but similarity of sound; or, worse still, that our readings should be graduated according to the number of letters each word contains? We should be lost in a hopeless fog before a page of words of three letters all drearily like one another, with no distinctive features for the eye to seize upon; but the child? 'oh, well—children are different; no doubt it is good for the child to grind in this mill!' But this is only one of many ways in which children are needlessly and cruelly oppressed!"

"You are taking high moral ground! All the same, I don't think I am convinced. It is far easier for a child to spell cat, cat, than to spell plum-pudding, plum-pudding."

"But spelling and reading are two things. You must learn to spell in order to write words, not to read them. A child is droning over a reading-lesson, spells c o u g h; you say 'cough,' and she repeats. By dint of repetition, she learns at last to associate the look of the word with the sound, and says 'cough' without spelling it; and you think she has arrived at 'cough' through c o u g h. Not a bit of it; c o f spells cough!"

"Yes; but 'cough' has a silent u, and a gh with the sound of f. There, I grant, is a great difficulty. If only there were no silent letters, and if all letters had always the same sound, we should, indeed, have reading made easy. The phonetic people have something to say for themselves."

"You would agree with the writer of an article in a number of a leading review: 'Plough ought to be written and printed plow; through, thru; enough, enuf; ought, aut or ort';

and so on. All this goes on the mistaken idea that in reading we look at the letters which compose a word, think of their sounds, combine these, and form the word. We do nothing of the kind; we accept a word, written or printed, simply as the symbol of a word we are accustomed to say. If the word is new to us we may try to make something of the letters, but we know so well that this is a shot in the dark, that we are careful not to say the new word until we have heard someone else say it."

"Yes, but children are different."

"Children are the same, 'only more so.' We could, if we liked, break up a word into its sounds, or put certain sounds together to make a word. But these are efforts beyond the range of children. First, as last, they learn to know a word by the look of it, and the more striking it looks the easier it is to recognise; provided always that the printed word is one which they already know very well by sound and by sense."

"It is not clear yet; suppose you tell me, step by step, how you would give your first reading lesson. An illustration helps so much."

"Very well: Bobbie had his first lesson yesterday—on his sixth birthday. The lesson was part of the celebration. By the way, I think it's rather a good idea to begin a new study with a child on his birthday, or some great day; he begins by thinking the new study a privilege."

"That is a hit. But go on; did Bobbie know his letters?"

"Yes, he had picked them up, as you say; but I had been careful not to allow any small readings. You know how Susanna Wesley used to retire to her room with the child who was to have his first reading-lesson, and not to appear again for some hours, when the boy came out able to read a good part of the first chapter of Genesis? Well, Bobbie's first reading-lesson was a solemn occasion, too, for which we had been preparing for a week or two. First, I bought a dozen penny copies of the 'History of Cock Robin'—good bold type, bad pictures, that we cut out.

Then we had a nursery pasting day—pasting the sheets on common drawing-paper, six one side down, and six the other; so that now we had six complete copies, and not twelve.

Then we cut up the first page only, of all six copies, line by line, and word by word. We gathered up the words and put them in a box, and our preparations were complete.

Now for the lesson. Bobbie and I are shut in by ourselves in the morning room. I always use a black-board in teaching the children. I write up, in good clear 'print' hand, Cock Robin. Bobbie watches with more interest because he knows his letters. I say, pointing to the word, 'cock robin,' which he repeats.

"Then the words in the box are scattered on the table, and he finds half a dozen 'cock robins' with great ease.

We do the same thing with 'sparrow,' 'arrow,' 'said,' 'killed,' 'who,' and so on, till all the words in the verse have been learned. The words on the black-board grow into a column, which Bob reads backwards and forwards, and every way, except as the words run in the verse.

Then Bobbie arranges the loose words into columns like that on the board.

Then into columns of his own devising, which he reads off.

Lastly, culminating joy (the whole lesson has been a delight!), he finds among the loose words, at my dictation,

> 'Who killed Cock Robin
> I said the sparrow
> With my bow and arrow
> I killed Cock Robin,'

Arranging the words in verse form. Then I had still one unmutilated copy, out of which Bob had the pleasure of reading the verse, and he read it forwards and backwards. So long as he lives he will know those twelve words."

"No doubt it was a pleasant lesson; but, think of all the pasting and cutting!"

"Yes, that is troublesome. I wish some publisher would provide us with what we want—nursery rhymes, in good bold type, with boxes of loose words to match, a separate box, or division, for each page, so that the child may not be confused by having too many words to hunt amongst. The point is that he should see, and look at, the new word many times, so that its shape becomes impressed upon his brain."

"I see; but he is only able to read 'Cock Robin'; he has no general power of reading."

"On the contrary, he will read those twelve words wherever he meets with them. Suppose he learns ten words a day, in half a year he will have at least six hundred words; he will know how to read a little."

"Excellent, supposing your children remember all they learn. At the end of a week, mine would remember 'Cock Robin,' perhaps, but it the rest would be gone!"

"Oh, but we keep what we get! When we have mastered the words of the second verse, Bob runs through the first in the book, naming words here and there as I point to them. It takes less than a minute, and the ground is secured."

"The first lesson must have been long?"

"I'm sorry to say it lasted half an hour. The child's interest tempted me to do more than I should."

"It all sounds very attractive—a sort of game—but I cannot be satisfied that a child should learn to read without knowing the powers of the letters. You constantly see a child spell a word over to himself, and then pronounce it; the more so, if he has been carefully taught the sounds of the letters—not merely their names."

"Naturally; for though many of our English words are each a law unto itself, others offer a key to a whole group, as arrow gives us sp arrow, m arrow, h arrow; but we have alternate days—one for reading, the other for word-building—and that is one way to secure variety, and, so, the joyous interest which is the real secret of success."

VI—Reading By Sight And Sound

Learning to read is Hard Work.—Probably that vague whole which we call 'Education' offers no more difficult and repellent task than that to which every little child is (or ought to be) set down—the task of learning to read. We realize the labour of it when some grown man makes a heroic effort to remedy shameful ignorance, but we forget how contrary to Nature it is for a little child to occupy himself with dreary hieroglyphics—all so dreadfully alike!—when the world is teeming with interesting objects which he is agog to know. But we cannot excuse our volatile Tommy, nor is it good for him that we should. It is quite necessary he should know how to read; and not only so—the discipline of the task is altogether wholesome for the little man. At the same time, let us recognise that learning to read is to many children hard work, and let us do what we can to make the task easy and inviting.

Knowledge of Arbitrary Symbols—In the first place, let us bear in mind that reading is not a science nor an art. Even if it were, the children must still be the first consideration with the educator; but it is not. Learning to read is no more than picking up, how we can, a knowledge of certain arbitrary symbols for objects and ideas. There are absolutely no right and necessary 'steps' to reading, each of which leads to the next; there is no true beginning, middle, or end. For the arbitrary symbols we must know in order to read are not letters, but words. By way of illustration, consider the delicate differences of sound represented by the letter 'o' in the last sentence; to analyze and classify the sounds of 'o' in 'for,' 'symbols,' 'know,' 'order,' 'to,' 'not,' and 'words,' is a curious, not especially useful, study for a philologist, but a laborious and inappropriate one for a child. It is time we faced the fact that the letters which compose an English word are full of philological interest, and that their study will be a valuable part of education by-and-by; but meantime, sound and letter-sign are so loosely wedded in English, that to base the teaching of reading on the sounds of the letters only, is to lay up for the child much analytic labour, much mental confusion, due to the irregularities of the language; and some little moral strain in making the sound of a letter in a given word fall under any of the 'sounds' he has been taught.

Definitely, what is it we propose in teaching a child to read? (a) that he shall know at sight, say, some thousand words; (b) That he shall be able to build up new words with the elements of these. Let him learn ten new words a day, and in twenty weeks he will be to some extent able to read, without any question as to the number of letters in a word. For the second, and less important, part of our task, the child must know the sounds of the letters, and acquire power to throw given sounds into new combinations.

What we want is a bridge between the child's natural interests and those arbitrary symbols with which he must become acquainted, and which, as we have seen, are words, and not letters.

These Symbols should be Interesting.—The child cares for things, not words; his analytic power is very small, his observing faculty is exceedingly quick and keen; nothing is too small for him; he will spy out the eye of a fly; nothing is too intricate, he delights in puzzles. But the thing he learns to know by looking at it, is a thing which interests him. Here we have the key to reading. No meaningless combinations of letters, no cla, cle, cli, clo, clu, no ath, eth, ith, oth, uth, should be presented to him. The child should be taught from the first to regard the printed word as he already regards the spoken word, as the symbol of fact or idea of full of interest. How easy to read 'robin redbreast,' 'buttercups and daisies'; the number of letters in the words is no matter; the words themselves convey such interesting ideas that the general form and look of them fixes itself on the child's brain by the same law of association of ideas which makes it easy to couple the objects with their spoken names. Having got a word fixed on the sure peg of the idea it conveys, the child will use his knowledge of the sounds of the letters to make up other words containing the same elements with great interest. When he knows 'butter' he is quite ready to make 'mutter' by changing the b for an m.

Tommy's First Lesson—But example is better than precept, and more convincing than the soundest reasoning. This is the sort of reading lesson we have in view. Tommy knows his letters by name and sound, but he knows no more. To-day he is to be launched into the very middle of reading, without any 'steps' at all, because reading is neither an art nor a science, and has, probably, no beginning. Tommy is to learn to read to-day—

> "I like little pussy,
>
> Her coat is so warm" -

And he is to know those nine words so well that he will be able to read them wherever they may occur henceforth and for evermore.

"Oh, yes," says a reader, "as in the 'Cock Robin' lesson; grant that the principle is sound—and there is much to be said on both sides of that question—but grant it, who in the world could get through all the pasting and cutting and general messing preparatory to the great lesson? No; the method of the books may be only second-best, but ready-made books must do for me. I have no time to make my own apparatus."

I must own that the cutting and pasting was very clumsy, but the lesson served its purpose because it induced a good friend to education [Miss Miller, founder of a Training College at Oxford] to have a delightful 'Little Pussy' box prepared for us, loose words, nice big type, two lines in a bag. Whoso learns "Little Pussy' as it should be learned will know at least one hundred words—not a bad stock-in-trade for a beginner—all of them good useful words that we want every day. There is one objection; such contractions as 'I'll' are ugly at the best, and I hope that in the word-lessons based upon 'Little Pussy,' pieces will be chosen in which this fault is avoided.

Steps.—And now, we begin. Material: Tommy's box of loose letters, the new 'Little Pussy' box, pencil and paper, or much better, blackboard and chalk. We write up in good big print hand 'Pussy.' Tommy watches with interest: he knows the letters, and probably says them as we write. Besides, he is prepared for the great event of his life; he knows he is going to begin to learn to read to-day. But we do not ask anything yet of his previous knowledge. We simply tell him that the word is 'pussy.' Interest at once; he knows the thing, pussy, and the written symbol is pleasant in his eyes because it is associated with an existing idea in his mind. He is told to look at the word 'pussy' until he is sure he would know it again. Then he makes 'pussy' from memory with his own loose letters. Then the little bag containing our two lines in loose words is turned out, and he finds the word 'pussy'; and, lastly, the little sheet with the poem printed on it is shown to him, and he finds 'pussy,' but is not allowed yet to find out the run of the rhyme. 'Coat, little, like, is, her, warm, I, so,' are taught in the same way, in less time than it takes to describe the lesson. When each new word is learned, Tommy makes a column of the old ones, and reads up and down and cris-cras, the column on the blackboard.

Reading Sentences—He knows words now, but he cannot yet read sentences. Now for the delight of reading. He finds at our dictation, amongst his loose words, 'pussy—is—warm,' places them in 'reading' order, one after the other, and then reads off the sentence. Joy, as of one who has found a new planet! And Tommy has indeed found a new poet. Then, 'her-little-coat-is-warm,' 'Pussy-is-so-little,' 'I-like-pussy,' 'Pussy-is-little-like-her-coat,' and so on through a dozen more little arrangements. If the rhyme can be kept a secret till the whole is worked out, so much the better. To make the verses up with his own loose words will give Tommy such a delicious sense that knowledge is power, as few occasions in after life will afford. Anyway, reading is to him a delight henceforth, and it will require very bad management indeed to make him hate it.

Tommy's Second Lesson.—Tommy promises himself another reading lesson next day, but he has instead a spelling lesson, conducted somewhat in this way:

He makes the word 'coat' with his letters, from memory if he can; if not, with the pattern word. Say 'coat' slowly; give the sound of the c. 'Take away c, and what have we left?' A little help will get 'oat' from him. How would you make 'boat' (say the word very slowly, bringing out the sound of b). He knows the sounds of the letters, and says b-oat readily; fl-oat, two added sounds, which you lead him to find out; g-oat, he will give you the g, and find goat a charming new word to know; m-oat, he easily decides on the sound of m; a little talk about moat; the other words are too familiar to need explanation. Tommy will, no doubt, offer 'note' and we must make a clean breast of it and say, 'No, note is spelt with other letters'; but what other letters we do not tell him now. Thus he comes to learn incidentally and very gradually that different groups of letters may stand for the same sounds. But we do not ask him to generalize; we only let him have the fact that n-oat does not spell the symbol we express by 'note.' 'Stoat'—he will be able to give the sounds of the initial letters, and stoat again calls for a little talk—another interesting word. He has made a group of words with his letters, and there they are on the black-board in a column, thus

     c-oat

     m-oat

     g-oat

     fl-oat

     st-oat

     b-oat

He reads the column up and down and cris-cras; every word has a meaning and carries an idea. Then the loose words he knows are turned out, and we dictate new sentences, which he arranges: 'I-like-her-goat'; 'her-little-stoat-is-warm,' and so on, making the new words with loose letters.

Unknown Words—Now for a new experience. We dictate 'pussy in the boat.' Consternation! Tommy does not know 'in' nor 'the.' 'Put counters for the words you don't know; they may soon come in our lessons,' and Tommy has a desire and a need—that is, an appetite for learning.

Like Combinations have Different Sounds.—We deal with the remaining words in the same way—'little' gives brittle, tittle, skittle: pussy, is, I, and her, give no new words. 'Like' gives mike and pike. 'so' gives no, do (the musical 'do'), and lo! From 'warm' we get arm, harm, charm, barm, alarm; we pronounced warm as arm. Tommy perceives that such a pronunciation is wrong and vulgar, and sees that all these words are sounded like 'arm,' but not one of them like 'warm'—that is, he sees that the same group of letters need not always have the same sound. But we do not ask him to make a note of this new piece of knowledge; we let it grow into him gradually, after many experiences.

By this time he has eighteen new words on the blackboard of which to make sentences with the nine loose words of 'pussy.' Her skittle is little, her charm is brittle, her arm is warm, and so on. But we take care that the sentences make sense. Her goat is brittle, is 'silly,' and not to be thought of at all. Tommy's new words are written in his 'note-book' in print hand, so that he can take stock of his possessions in the way of words.

Moral Training in Reading Lessons—The next day we do the last two lines of the stanza, as at first. These lines afford hardly any material for a spelling lesson, so in our next lesson we go on with the second verse. But our stock of words is growing; we are able, as we go on, to make an almost unlimited number of little sentences. If we have to use counters now and then, why, that only whets our appetite for knowledge. By the time Tommy has worked 'Little Pussy' through he has quite a large stock of words; has considerable power to attack new words with familiar combinations; what is more, he has achieved; he has courage to attack all 'learning,' and has a sense that delightful results are quite within reach. Moreover, he learns to read in a way that affords him some moral training. There is no stumbling, no hesitation from the first, but bright attention and perfect achievement. His reading lesson is a delight, of which he is deprived when he comes to his lesson in a lazy, drawling mood. Perfect enunciation and precision are insisted on, and when he comes to arrange the whole of the little rhyme in his loose words and read it off (most delightful of all the lessons) his reading must be a perfect and finished recitation. [Spirited nursery rhymes form the best material for such reading lessons. A 'Delightful Reading Box' has been issued on similar plan to the 'Pussy' Box, whose one fault is that the verses are a little dull. But this 'Box' should be of great use]. I believe that this is a practical common-sense way to teach reading in English. It may be profitable for the little German child to work through all possibly dreary combinations of letters before he is permitted to have any joy in 'reading,' because wherever these combinations occur they will have the sounds the child has learned laboriously. The fact that English is anomalous as regards the connection between sign and sound, happily exonerates us from enforcing this dreary grind. [It is desirable that 'Tommy' should not begin to 'read' until his intelligence is equal to the effort required by these lessons. Even then, it may be well to break up one into two, or half a dozen, as he is able to take it].

VII.—Recitation

'The Children's Art' On this subject I cannot do better than refer the reader to Mr Arthur Burrell's Recitation. This book purports to be a handbook for teachers in elementary schools. I wish that it may be very largely used by such teachers, and may also become a family hand-book; though many of the lessons will not be called for in educated homes. There is hardly any 'subject' so educative and so elevating as that which Mr. Burrell has happily described as 'The Children's Art.' All children have it in them to recite; it is an imprisoned gift waiting to be delivered, like Ariel from the pine. In this most thoughtful and methodical volume we are possessed of the fit incantations. Use them duly, and out of the woodenness of even the most commonplace child steps forth the child-artist, a delicate sprite, who shall make you laugh and make you weep. Did not the great Sir Walter "sway to and fro, sobbing his fill," to his little 'Pet's' speaking of—

"For I am sick, and capable of fears,

Oppressed with wrong, and therefore full of fears;

A widow, husbandless, subject to fears;

A woman, naturally born to fears"?

Marjorie Fleming was, to be sure, a child-genius; but in this book we learn by what carefully graduated steps a child who is not a genius, is not even born of cultivated parents, may be taught the fine art of beautiful and perfect speaking; but that is only the first step in the acquisition of 'The Children's Art.' The child should speak beautiful thoughts so beautifully, with such delicate rendering of each nuance of meaning, that he becomes to the listener the interpreter of the author's thought. Now, consider what appreciation, sympathy, power of expression this implies, and you will grant that 'The Children's Art' is, as Steele said of the society of his wife, "a liberal education in itself." It is objected— 'Children are such parrots! They say a thing as they hear it said; as for troubling themselves to 'appreciate' and 'interpret,' not a bit of it!' Most true of the 'My name is Norval' style of recitation; but throughout this volume the child is led to find the just expression of thought for himself; never is the poor teacher allowed to set a pattern—'say this as I say it.' The ideas are kept well within the child's range, and the expression is his own. He is caught with guile, his very naughtiness is pressed into service, he finds a dozen ways of saying 'I shan't,' is led cunningly up to the point of expressing himself, and—he does it, to his own surprise and delight. The pieces given here for recitation are a treasure-trove of new joys. 'Winken, Blinken, and Nod,' "Miss Lilywhite's Party,' and 'The Two Kittens,' would compel any child to recite. Try a single piece over with the author's markings and suggestions, and you will find there is as much difference between the result and ordinary reading aloud as there is in a musical composition played with and without the composer's expression marks. I hope that my readers will train their children in the art of recitation; in the coming days, more even than in our own will it behove every educated man and woman to be able to speak effectively in public; and, in learning to recite you learn to speak.

Memorising.—Recitation and committing to memory are not necessarily the same thing, and it is well to store a child's memory with a good deal of poetry, learnt without labour. Some years ago I chanced to visit a house, the mistress of which had educational notions of her own, upon which she was bringing up a niece. She presented me with a large foolscap sheet written all over with the titles of poems, some of them long and difficult: Tintern Abbey, for example. She told me that her niece could repeat to me any of those poems that I liked to ask for, and that she had never learnt a single verse by heart in her life. The girl did repeat several of the poems on the list, quite beautifully and without hesitation; and then the lady unfolded her secret. She thought she had made a discovery, and I thought so too. She read a poem through to E.; then the next day, while the little girl was making a doll's frock, perhaps, she read it again; once again the next day, while E.'s hair was being brushed. She got in about six or more readings, according to the length of the poem, at odd and unexpected times, and in the end E. could say the poem which she had not learned.

I have tried the plan often since, and found it effectual. The child must not try to recollect or to say the verse over to himself, but, as far as may be, present an open mind to receive an impression of interest. Half a dozen repetitions should give children possession of such poems as 'Dolly and Dick,' 'Do you ask what the birds say?' Little lamb, who made thee?' and the like. The gains of such a method of learning are, that the edge of the child's enjoyment is not taken off by weariful verse by verse repetitions, and, also, that the habit of making mental images is unconsciously formed.

I remember once discussing this subject with the late Miss Anna Swanwick in some connection with Browning of which I do not recall, but in the course of talk an extremely curious incident transpired. A lady, a niece of Miss Swanwick's, said that after a long ill-ness, during which she had not been allowed to do anything, she read 'Lycidas' through, by way of a first treat to herself as a convalescent. She was surprised to find herself then next day repeating to herself long passages. Then she tried the whole poem and found she could say it off, the result of this single reading, for she had not learned the poem before her illness, nor read it with particular attention. She was much elated by the treasure-trove she had chanced upon, and to test her powers, she read the whole of 'Paradise Lost,' book by book, and with the same result,—she could repeat it book by book after a single reading! She enriched herself by acquiring other treasures dur-ing her convalescence; but as health returned, and her mind became preoccupied with many interests, she found she no longer had this astonishing power. It is possible that the disengaged mind of a child is as free to take and as strong to hold beautiful images clothed in beautiful words as was that of this lady during her convalescence. But, let me again say, every effort of the kind, however unconscious, means wear and tear of brain substance. Let the child lie fallow till he is six, and then, in this matter of memorizing, as in others, attempt only a little, and let the poems the child learns be simple and within the range of his own thought and imagination. At the same time, when there is so much noble poetry within a child's compass, the pity of it, that he should be allowed to learn twaddle!

VIII—Reading for Older Children

In teaching to read, as in other matters, c'est le premier pas qui coute. The child who has been taught to read with care and deliberation until he has mastered the words of a limited vocabulary, usually does the rest for himself. The attention of his teachers should be fixed on two points—that he acquires the habit of reading, and that he does not fall into slipshod habits of reading.

The Habit of Reading.—The most common and the monstrous defect in the education of the day is that children fail to acquire the habit of reading. Knowledge is conveyed to them by lessons and talk, but the studious habit of using books as a means of interest and delight is not acquired. This habit should be begun early; so soon as the child can read at all, he should read for himself, and to himself, history, legends, fairy tales, and other suitable matter. He should be trained from the first to think that one reading of any lesson is enough to enable him to narrate what he has read, and will thus get the habit of slow, careful reading, intelligent even when it is silent, because he reads with an eye to the full meaning of every clause.

Reading Aloud.— He should have practice, too, in reading aloud, for the most part, in the books he is using for his term's work. These should include a good deal of poetry, to accustom him to the delicate rendering of shades of meaning, and especially to make him aware that words are beautiful in themselves, that they are a source of pleasure, and are worthy of our honour; and that a beautiful word deserves to be beautifully said, with a certain roundness of tone and precision of utterance. Quite young children are open to this sort of teaching, conveyed, not in a lesson, but by a word now and then.

Limitation—In this connection the teacher should not trust to setting, as it were, a copy in reading for the children's imitation. They do imitate readily enough, catching tricks of emphasis and action in an amusing way; but these are mere tricks, an aping of intelligence. The child must express what he feels to be the author's meaning; and this sort of intelligent reading comes only of the habit of reading with understanding.

Reading to Children—It is a delight to older people to read aloud to children, but this should be only an occasional treat and indulgence, allowed before bedtime, for example. We must remember the natural inertness of a child's mind; give him the habit of being read to, and he will steadily shirk the labour of reading for himself; indeed, we all like to be spoon-fed with our intellectual meat, or we should read and think more for ourselves and be less eager to run after lectures.

Questions on the Subject-Matter—When a child is reading, he should not be teased with questions as to the meaning of what he has read, the signification of this word or that; what is annoying to older people is equally annoying to children. Besides, it is not of the least consequence that they should be able to give the meaning of every word they read. A knowledge of meanings, that is, an ample and correct vocabulary, is only arrived at in one way—by the habit of reading. A child unconsciously gets the meaning of a new word from the context, if not the first time he meets with it, then the second or the third: but he is on the look-out, and will find out for himself the sense of any expression he does not understand. Direct questions on the subject-matter of what a child has read are always a mistake. Let him narrate what he has read, or some part of it. He enjoys this sort of consecutive reproduction, but abominates every question in the nature of a riddle. If there must be riddles, let it be his to ask and the teacher's to direct him the answer. Questions that lead to a side issue or to a personal view are allowable because these interest children—'What would you have done in his place?'

Lesson-Books—A child has not begun his education until he has acquired the habit of reading to himself, with interest and pleasure, books fully on a level with his intelligence. I am speaking now of his lesson-books, which are all too apt to be written in a style of insufferable twaddle, probably because they are written by persons who have never chanced to meet a child. All who know children know that they do not talk twaddle and do not like it, and prefer that which appeals to their understanding. Their lesson-books should offer matter for their reading, whether aloud or to themselves; therefore they should be written with literary power. As for the matter of these books, let us remember that children can take in ideas and principles, whether the latter be moral or mechanical, as quickly and clearly as we do ourselves (perhaps more so); but detailed processes, lists and summaries, blunt the edge of a child's delicate mind. Therefore, the selection of their first lesson-books is a matter of grave importance, because it rests with these to give children the idea that knowledge is supremely attractive and that reading is delightful. Once the habit of reading his lesson-book with delight is set up in a child, his education is—not completed, but—ensured; he will go on for himself in spite of the obstructions which school too commonly throws in his way.

Slipshod Habits; Inattention—I have already spoken of the importance of a single reading. If a child is not able to narrate what he has read once, let him not get the notion that he may, or that he must, read it again. A look of slight regret because there is a gap in his knowledge will convict him. The power of reading with perfect attention will not be gained by the child who is allowed to moon over his lessons. For this reason, reading lessons must be short; ten minutes or a quarter of an hour of fixed attention is enough for children of the ages we have in view, and a lesson of this length will enable a child to cover two or three pages of his book. The same rule as to the length of a lesson applies to children whose lessons are read to them because they are not yet able to read for themselves.

Careless Enunciation—It is important that, when reading aloud, children should make due use of the vocal organs, and, for this reason, a reading lesson should be introduced by two or three simple breathing exercises, as, for a example, a long inspiration with closed lips and a slow expiration with open mouth. If a child read through his nose, it is well to consult a doctor; an operation for adenoids may be necessary, which is rarely distressing, and should be performed while children are young. Provincial pronunciation and slipshod enunciation must be guarded against. Practice in pure vowel sounds, and the respect for words which will not allow of their being hastily slurred over, should cure these defects. By the way, quite little children commonly enunciate beautifully, because a big word is a new acquirement which they delight in and make the most of; our efforts should be directed to make older children hold words in like esteem.

The habit of 'minding your stops' comes of intelligent reading. A child's understanding of the passage will lead him to correct pointing.

IX.—The Art of Narrating

Children Narrate by Nature.—Narrating is an art, like poetry-making or painting, because it is there, in every child's mind, waiting to be discovered, and is not the result of any process of disciplinary education. A creative fiat calls it forth. 'Let him narrate'; and the child narrates, fluently, copiously, in ordered sequence, with fit and graphic details, with a just choice of words, without verbosity or tautology, so soon as he can speak with ease. This amazing gift with which normal children are born is allowed to lie fallow in their education. Bobbie will come home with a heroic narrative of a fight he has seen between 'Duke' and a dog in the street. It is wonderful! He has seen everything, and he tells everything with splendid vigour in the true epic vein; but so ingrained is our contempt for children that we see nothing in this but Bobbie's foolish childish way! Whereas here, if we have eyes to see and grace to build, is the ground-plan of his education.

Until he is six, let Bobbie narrate only when and what he has a mind to. He must not be called upon to tell anything. Is this the secret of the strange long talks we watch with amusement between creatures of two, and four, and five? Is it possible that they narrate while they are still inarticulate, and that the other inarticulate person takes it all in? They try us, poor dear elders, and we reply 'Yes,' 'Really!' 'Do you think so?' to the babble of whose meaning we have no comprehension. Be this as it may; of what goes on in the dim region of 'under two' we have no assurance. But wait till the little fellow has words and he will 'tell' without end to whomsoever will listen to the tale, but, for choice, to his own compeers.

This Power should be used in their Education.— Let us take the goods the gods provide. When the child is six, not earlier, let him narrate the fairy-tale which has been read to him, episode by episode, upon one hearing of each; the Bible tale read to him in the words of the Bible; the well-written animal story; or all about other lands from some such volume as The World at Home [See Appendix]. The seven-years-old boy will have begun to read for himself, but must get most of his intellectual nutriment, by ear, certainly, but read to him out of books. Geography, sketches from ancient history, Robinson Crusoe, The Pilgrim's Progress, Tanglewood Tales, Heroes of Asgard, and much of the same calibre, will occupy him until he is eight. The points to be borne in mind are, that he should have no book which is not a child's classic; and that, given the right book, it must not be diluted with talk or broken up with questions, but given to the boy in fit proportions as wholesome meat for his mind, in the full trust that a child's mind is able to deal with its proper food.

The child of eight or nine is able to tackle the more serious material of knowledge; but our business for the moment is with what children under nine can narrate.

Method of Lesson.—In every case the reading should be consecutive from a well-chosen book. Before the reading for the day begins, the teacher should talk a little (and get the children to talk) about the last lesson, with a few words about what is to be read, in order that the children may be animated by expectation; but she should beware of explanation and, especially, of forestalling the narrative. Then, she may read two or three pages, enough to include an episode; after that, let her call upon the children to narrate,—in turns, if there be several of them. They not only narrate with spirit and accuracy, but succeed in catching the style of their author. It is not wise to tease them with corrections; they may begin with an endless chain of 'ands,' but they soon leave this off, and their narrations become good enough in style and composition to be put in a 'print book'!

This sort of narration lesson should not occupy more than a quarter of an hour.

The book should always be deeply interesting, and when the narration is over, there should be a little talk in which moral points are brought out, pictures shown to illustrate the lesson, or diagrams drawn on the blackboard. As soon as children are able to read with ease and fluency, they read their own lesson, either aloud or silently, with a view to narration; but where it is necessary to make omissions, as in the Old Testament narratives and Plutarch's Lives, for example, it is better that the teacher should always read the lesson which is to be narrated.

X.—Writing   Perfect

Accomplishment.—I can only offer a few hints on the teaching of writing, though much might be said. First, let the child accomplish something perfectly in every lesson—a stroke, a pothook, a letter. Let the writing lesson be short; it should not last more than five or ten minutes. Ease in writing comes by practice; but that must be secured later. In the meantime, the thing to be avoided is the habit of careless work—humpy 'm's, angular o's.

Printing.—But the child should have practice in printing before he begins to write. First, let him print the simplest of the capital letters with single curves and straight lines. When he can make the capitals and large letters, with some firmness and decision, he might go on to the smaller letters—'printed' as in the type we call 'italics,' only upright,—as simple as possible, and large.

Steps in Teaching.—Let the stroke be learned first; then the pothook; then the letters of which the pothook is an element—n, m, v, w, r, h, p, y; then o, and letters of which the curve is an element a, c, g, e, x, s, q; then looped and irregular letters—b, l, f, t, etc. One letter should be perfectly formed in a day, and the next day the same elemental forms repeated in another letter, until they become familiar. By-and-by copies, three or four of the letters they have learned grouped into a word—'man,' 'aunt'; the lesson to be the production of the written word once without a single fault in any letter. At this stage the chalk and blackboard are better than pen and paper, as it is well that the child should rub out and rub out until his own eye is satisfied with the word or letter he has written.

Of the further stages, little need be said. Secure that the child begins by making perfect letters and is never allowed to make faulty ones, and the rest he will do for himself; as for 'a good hand,' do not hurry him; his 'handwriting' will come by-and-by out of the character that is in him; but, as a child, he cannot be said, strictly speaking, to have character.

Set good copies before him, and see that he imitates his model dutifully: the writing lesson being not so many lines, or 'a copy'—that is, a page of writing—but a single line which is as exactly as possible a copy of the characters set. The child may have to write several lines before he succeeds in producing this.

Text-Hand—If he write in books with copperplate headlines (which are, on the whole, to be eschewed), discrimination should be exercised in the choice of these; in many of them the writing is atrocious, and the letters are adorned with flourishes which increase the pupil's labour but by no means improve his style. One word more; do not hurry the child into 'small hand'; it is unnecessary that he should labour much over what is called 'large hand,' but 'text-hand,' the medium size, should be continued until he makes the letters with ease. It is much easier for the child to get into an irregular scribble by way of 'small-hand,' than to get out of it again. In this, as in everything else, the care of the educator must be given, not only to the formation of good, but to the prevention of bad habits.

A 'New Handwriting.'—Some years ago I heard of a lady who was elaborating, by means of the study of old Italian and other manuscripts, a 'system of beautiful handwriting' which could be taught to children. I waited patiently, though not without some urgency, for the production of this new kind of 'copy-book.' The need for such an effort was very great, for the distinctly commonplace writing taught from existing copy-books, however painstaking and legible, cannot but have a rather vulgarizing effect both on the writer and the reader of such manuscript. At last the lady, Mrs Robert Bridges, has succeeded in her tedious and difficult undertaking, and this book for teachers will enable them to teach their pupils a style of writing which is pleasant to acquire because it is beautiful to behold. It is surprising how quickly young children, even those already confirmed in 'ugly' writing, take to this 'new handwriting.'

But Mrs. Bridges' purpose in A New Handwriting will be better understood by some passages quoted, with her permission, from her preface: "The accompanying ten plates are intended chiefly for those who teach writing: a few words, both of apology and explanation, are needed to introduce them. I was always interested in handwriting, and after making acquaintance with the Italianized Gothic of the sixteenth century, I consciously altered my hand towards some likeness with its forms and general character. The script happening to please, I was often asked to make alphabets and copies, and begged by professional teachers to have such a book as this printed, that they might use it in their schools. One can never quite satisfy oneself in the making of models for others to copy, but these plates are very much what I intended, though, owing to my inexperience, some of them have suffered in the reproduction...

A child must first learn to control his hand and constrain it to obey his eye; at this earliest stage, any simple forms will serve the purpose; and hence it might be further argued that the forms are always indifferent, and that full mastery of the hand can be as well attained by copying bad models as good; but this can hardly be: the ordinary copybook, the aim of which seems to be to economise the component parts of the letters, cannot train the hand as more varied shapes will; nor does this uniformity, exclusive of beauty, offer as good training to the eye. Moreover, I should say that variety and beauty of form are attractive, even to little children, and that the attempt to create something which interests them, cheers and crowns their stupendous efforts with a pleasure that cannot be looked for in the task of copying monotonous shapes. But whether such a hand as that here shown lends itself as easily as the more uniform model to the development of a quick, useful cursive, I cannot say; and it is possible that the degradations, inevitable in the habit of quick writing, might produce a mere untidiness, almost the worst reproach of penmanship. Some of the best English hands of to-day are as good a quick cursive as one can desire, and show points of real beauty; but such hands are rare, and are only those which have, as we say, character; which probably means that the writer would have done well for himself under any system: whereas the average hands, which are the natural outcome of the old copybook writing, degraded by haste, seem to owe their common ugliness to the mean type from which they sprang; and the writers, when they have occasion to write well, find they can do but little better, and only prove that haste was not the real cause of their bad writing."

How to Use.—The method of using Mrs Bridges' Handwriting [see Appendix], which we find most effectual, is to practise each form on the blackboard from the plate, and later to use pencil, and still later pen and ink. By-and-by the children will be promoted to transcribe little poems, and so on, in this very pleasing script.

Set headlines are to be avoided, as children fail to use the forms of the headline in their ordinary writing. It is sometimes objected that this rather elaborate and beautiful handwriting will interfere with a characteristic 'hand,' but it seems to me that to have a beautiful, instead of a commonplace, basis for handwriting is a great gain.

XI.—Transcription

Value of Transcription—The earliest practice in writing proper for children of seven or eight should be, not letter writing or dictation, but transcription, slow and beautiful work, for which the New Handwriting is to be preferred, though perhaps some of the more ornate characters may be omitted with advantage.

Transcription should be an introduction to spelling. Children should be encouraged to look at the word, see a picture of it with their eyes shut, and then write from memory.

Children should Transcribe favourite Passages.—A certain sense of possession and delight may be added to this exercise if children are allowed to choose for transcription their favourite verse in one poem and another. This is better than to write a favourite poem, an exercise which stales on the little people before it is finished. But a book of their own, made up of their own chosen verses, should give them pleasure.

Small Text-Hand—Double-ruled Lines—Double ruled lines, small text-hand, should be used at first, as children are eager to write very minute 'small hand,' and once they have fallen into this habit it is not easy to get good writing. A sense of beauty in their writing and in the lines they copy should carry them over this stage of their work with pleasure. Not more than ten minutes or a quarter of an hour should be given to the early writing-lessons. If they are longer the children get tired and slovenly.

Position in Writing.—For the writing position children should sit so that light reaches them from the left, and desk or table should be at a comfortable height.

It would be a great gain if children were taught from the first to hold the pen between the first and second fingers, steadying it with the thumb. This position avoids the un-comfortable strain on the muscles produced by the usual way of holding a pen—a strain which causes writer's cramp in later days when there is much writing to be done. The pen should be held in a comfortable position, rather near the point, fingers and thumb somewhat bent, and the hand resting on the paper. The writer should also be allowed to support himself with the left hand on the paper, and should write in an easy position, with bent head but not with stooping figure. It would be unnecessary to say that the flat of the nib should be used if children had not a happy gift for making spider marks with the nib held sideways. In all writing lessons, free use should be made of the black-board by both teacher and children by way of model and practice.

Desks.—The best desks I know are those recommended by Dr Roth, single desks which may be raised or lowered, moved backwards or forwards, with seat, back, and a back pad, and rests for the feet. There may be others as good, even better, in the market, but these seem to answer every purpose.

Children's Table.—For little children it is a good plan to have a table of the right height made by the house carpenter, to the top of the table consisting of two leaves with hinges. These leaves open in the middle, and disclose a sort of box in the space which is often used for a drawer, the table-top itself making the lids of the box. Such a receptacle for the children's books, writing materials, etc., is more easily kept neat by themselves than is an ordinary drawer or box.

XII.—Spelling And Dictation

Of all the mischievous exercises in which children spend their school hours, dictation, as commonly practised, is perhaps the most mischievous; and this, because people are slow to understand that there is no part of a child's work at school which some philosophic principle does not underlie.

A Fertile Cause of Bad Spelling.—The common practise is for the teacher to dictate a passage, clause by clause, repeating each clause, perhaps, three of our times under a fire of questions from the writers. Every line has errors in spelling, one, two, three, perhaps. The conscientious teacher draws her pencil under these errors, or solemnly underlines them with red ink. The children correct in various fashions; sometimes they change books, and each corrects the errors of another, copying the word from the book or from the blackboard. A few benighted teachers still cause children to copy their own error along with the correction, which last is written three or four times, learned, and spelt to the teacher. The latter is astonished at the pure perversity which causes the same errors to be repeated again and again, notwithstanding all these painstaking efforts.

The Rationale of Spelling.—But the fact is, the gift of spelling depends upon the power the eye possesses to 'take' (in a photographic sense) a detailed picture of a word; and this is a power and habit which must be cultivated in children from the first. When they have read 'cat,' they must be encouraged to see the word with their eyes shut, and the same habit will enable them to image 'Thermopylae.' This picturing of words upon the retina appears to be to be the only royal road to spelling; an error once made and corrected leads to fearful doubt for the rest of one's life, as to which was the wrong way and which is the right. Most of us are haunted by some doubt as to whether 'balance,' for instance, should have one 'l' or two; and the doubt is born of a correction. Once the eye sees a misspelt word, that image remains; and if there is also the image of the word rightly spelt, we are perplexed as to which is which. Now we see why there could not be a more ingenious way of making bad spellers than 'dictation' as it is commonly taught. Every misspelt word is in image in the child's brain not to be obliterated by the right spelling. It becomes, therefore, the teacher's business to prevent false spelling, and, if an error has been made, to hide it away, as it were, so that the impression may not become fixed.

Steps of a Dictation Lesson.—Dictation lessons, conducted in some such way as the following, usually result in good spelling. A child of eight or nine prepares a paragraph, older children a page, or two or three pages. The child prepares by himself, by looking at the word he is not sure of, and then seeing it with his eyes shut. Before he begins, the teacher asks what words he thinks will need his attention. He generally knows, but the teacher may point out any word likely to be a cause of stumbling. He lets his teacher know when he is ready. The teacher asks if there are any words he is not sure of. These she puts, one by one, on the blackboard, letting the child look till he has a picture, and then rubbing the word out. If anyone is still doubtful he should be called to put the word he is not sure of on the board, the teacher watching to rub out the word when a wrong letter begins to appear, and again helping the child to get a mental picture. Then the teacher gives out the dictation, clause by clause, each clause repeated once. She dictates with a view to the pointing, which the children are expected to put in as they write; but they must not be told 'comma,' 'semicolon,' etc. After the sort of preparation I have described, which takes ten minutes or less, there is rarely an error in spelling. If there be, it is well worth while for the teacher to be on the watch with slips of stamp-paper to put over the wrong word, that its image may be erased as far as possible. At the end of the lesson, the child should again study the wrong word in his book until he says he is sure of, and should write it correctly on the stamp-paper.

A lesson of this kind secures the hearty co-operation of children, who feel they take their due part in it; and it also prepares them for the second condition of good spelling, which is—much reading combined with the habit of imaging the words as they are read.

Illiterate spelling is usually a sign of sparse reading; but, sometimes, of hasty reading without the habit of seeing the words that are skimmed over.

Spelling must not be lost sight of in the children's other studies, though they should not be teased to spell. It is well to write a difficult proper name, for example, on the blackboard in the course of history or geography readings, rubbing the word out when the children say they can see it. The whole secret of spelling lies in the habit of visualizing words from memory, and children must be trained to visualize in the course of their reading. They enjoy this way of learning to spell.

XIII.—Composition

George Osborne's Essay—"What a prodigiously well-read and delightful person the Reverend Lawrence Veal was, George's Master! 'He knows everything,' Amelia said. 'He says there is no place in the bar or the senate that Georgy may not aspire to. Look here,' and she went to the piano-drawer and drew out a theme of George's composition. This great effort of genius, which is still in the possession of Georgy's mother, is as follows:

"'On Selfishness.—Of all the vices which degrade the human character, Selfishness is the most odious and contemptible. An undue love of Self leads to the most monstrous crimes and occasions of the greatest misfortunes both in States and Families. As a selfish man will impoverish his family and often bring them to ruin; so a selfish king brings ruin on his people and often plunges them into war. Example: The selfishness of Achilles, as remarked by the poet Homer, occasioned a thousand woes to the Greeks—[a sentence in Greek follows here, from Homer's Illiad, A. 2]. The selfishness of the late Napoleon Bonaparte occasioned innumerable wars in Europe, and caused him to perish, himself, in a miserable island—that of St. Helena in the Atlantic Ocean.

"'We see by these examples that we are not to consult our own interest and ambition, but that we are to consider the interests of others as well as our own.—George S. Osborne.

"'Athene House, 24 April 1827.'

"' Think of him' (George was 10) 'writing such a hand, and quoting Greek too, at his age,' the delighted mother said."

And well might Mrs. George Sedley be delighted. Would not many a mother to-day triumph in such a literary effort? What can Thackeray be laughing at? Or does he, in truth, give us this little 'theme' as a tour de force?

An Educational Futility.—I think this great moral teacher here throws down the gauntlet in challenge of an educational fallacy which is accepted, even in the twentieth century. That futility is the extraction of original composition from schoolboys and schoolgirls. The proper function of the mind of the young scholar is to collect material for the generalizations of after-life. If a child is asked to generalize, that is, to write an essay upon some abstract theme, a double wrong is done him. He is brought up before a stone wall by being asked to do what is impossible to him, and that is discouraging. But a worse moral injury happens to him in that, having no thought of his own to offer on the subject, he puts together such tags of commonplace thought as have come in his way and offers the whole as his 'composition,' an effort which puts a strain upon his conscience while it piques his vanity. In these days masters do not consciously put their hand to the work of their pupils as did that 'prodigiously well-read and delightful' master who had the educating of George Osborne. But, perhaps, without knowing it, they give the ideas which the cunning schoolboy seizes to 'stick' into the 'essay' he hates. Sometimes they do more. They deliberately teach children how to 'build a sentence' and how to 'bind sentences' together.

Lessons in Composition.—Here is a series of preliminary exercises (or rather a part of a series, which numbers 40) intended to help a child to write an essay on 'An Umbrella,' from a book of the hour proceeding from one of our best publishing houses: -

"Step I.

"1. What are you? "2. How did you get your name? "3. Who uses you? "4. What were you once? "5. What were like then? "6. Where were you obtained or found? "7. Of what stuff or materials are you made? "8. From what sources do you come? "9. What are your parts? "10. Are you made, grown, or fitted together?

"Step II.

"I am an umbrella, and am used by many people, young and old. "I get my name from a word which means a shade. "The stick came perhaps from America, and is quite smooth, even, and polished, so that the metal ring may slide easily up and down the stick. "My parts are a frame and a cover. My frame consists of a stick about a yard long, wires, and a sliding metal band. At the lower end of the stick is a steel ferrule or ring. This keeps the end from wearing away when I am used in walking.

"Step III.

"Now use it, is, and was, instead of I, have, my, and am.

"Exercise.

"Now write your own description of it."

Such Teaching a Public Danger.—And this is work intended for Standards VI. And VII.! That is to say, this kind of thing is the final literary effort to be exacted from children in our elementary schools!

The two volumes (I quote from near the end of the second and more advanced volume) are not to be gibbeted as exceptionally bad. A few years ago the appalling discovery was made that, both in secondary and elementary schools, 'composition' was dreadfully defective, and, therefore, badly taught. Since then many volumes have been produced, more or less on the lines indicated in the above citation, and distinguished publishers have not perceived that to offer to the public, with the sanction of their name, works of this sterilizing and injurious character, is an offence against society. The body of a child is sacred in the eye of the law, but his intellectual powers may be annihilated on such starvation diet as this, and nothing said! The worst of it is, both authors and publishers in every case act upon the fallacy that well intentioned effort is always excusable, if not praiseworthy. They do not perceive that no effort is permissible towards the education of children without an intelligent conception, both of children, and of what is meant by education.

'Composition' comes by Nature.—In fact, lessons on 'composition' should follow the model of that famous essay on "Snakes in Ireland"—"There are none." For children under nine, the question of composition resolves itself into that of narration, varied by some such simple exercise as to write a part and narrate a part, or write the whole account of a walk they have taken, a lesson they have studied, or of some simple matter that they know. Before they are ten, children who have been in the habit of using books will write good, vigorous English with ease and freedom; that is, if they have not been hampered by instructions. It is well for them not even to learn rules for the placing of full stops and capitals until they notice how these things occur in their books. Our business is to provide children with material in their lessons, and leave the handling of such material to themselves. If we would believe it, composition is as natural as jumping and running to children who have been allowed due use of books. They should narrate in the first place, and they will compose, later readily enough; but they should not be taught 'composition.'

XIV.—Bible Lessons

Children Enjoy the Bible.—We are apt to believe that children cannot be interested in the Bible unless its pages be watered down—turned into the slipshod English we prefer to offer them. Here is a suggestive anecdote of the childhood of Mrs Harrison, one of the pair of little Quaker maidens introduced to us in the Autobiography of Mary Howitt, the better known of the sisters. "One day she found her way into a lumber room. There she caught sight of an old Bible and turning over its yellow leaves she came upon words that she had not heard at the usual morning readings, the opening chapters of St. Luke—which her father objected to read aloud—and the closing chapter of Revelation. The exquisite picture of the Great Child's birth in the one chapter and the beauty of the description of the New Jerusalem in the other, were seized upon by the eager little girl of six years old with a rapture which, she used to say, no novel in after years ever produced."

And here is a mention of a child of five. "The little ones read every day the events of Holy Week with me. Z. is inexpressibly interesting in his deep, reverent interest, almost excitement."

We are probably quite incapable of measuring the religious receptivity of children. Nevertheless, their fitness to apprehend the deep things of God is a fact with which we are called to 'deal prudently,' and to deal reverently. And that, because, as none can appreciate more fully than the 'Darwinian,' the attitude of thought and feeling in which you place a child is the vital factor in his education.

Should know the Bible Text.—Children between the ages of six and nine should get a considerable knowledge of the Bible text. By nine they should have read the simple (and suitable) narrative portions of the Old Testament, and, say, two of the gospels.

The Old Testament should, for various reasons, be read to the children. The gospel stories they might be read for themselves as soon as they can read them beautifully. It is a mistake to use paraphrases of the text; the fine roll of Bible English appeals to children with a compelling music, and they will probably retain through life their first conception of the Bible scenes, and, also, the very words in which these scenes are portrayed. This is a great possession. Half the clever talk we hear to-day, and half the uneasiness which underlies this talk, are due to a thorough and perfect ignorance of the Bible text. The points of assault are presented to men's minds naked and jagged, without atmosphere, perspective, proportion; until the Bible comes to mean for many, the speaking of Balaam's ass or the standing still of the sun at Joshua's bidding.

But let the imaginations of children be stored with the pictures, their minds nourished upon the words, of the gradually unfolding story of the Scriptures, and they will come to look out upon a wide horizon within which persons and events take shape in their due place and due proportion. By degrees, they will see that the world is a stage whereon the goodness of God is continually striving with the wilfulness of man; that some heroic men take sides with God; and that others, foolish and headstrong, oppose themselves to Him. The fire of enthusiasm will kindle in their breast, and the children, too, will take their side, without much exhortation, or any thought or talk of spiritual experience.

Essential and Accidental Truth.—As for whether such and such a narrative be a myth, or a parable, or a circumstance that has actually occurred, such questions do not affect the sincere mind of a child, because they have nothing to do with the main issues. It is quite well to bring before children, in the course of their Bible readings, whatever new light modern research puts in our way; the more we can help them in this way, the more vivid and real will Bible teaching become to them. But this grace, at any rate, the children may claim at our hands, that they shall not be disturbed by questions of authenticity in their Bible reading any more than in their reading of English history. Let them hear the story of the Garden of Eden, for example, as it stands; just so, we might even let them have the story of the man who went fishing and found a goodly pearl; and this, because the thing that matters in both stories is the essential truths they embody, and not the mere accidents of time and place. It is conceivable that the 'pearl of great price' was matter of current talk at the time; a so-called 'fact' seized upon by upon our Lord to make of it the vehicle for essential truth. If we will believe it, the minds of children are, perhaps, more fit than our own to appropriate and deal with truth. By-and-by they will perceive and discard, if necessary, the accidental circumstances with which the truth is clothed upon; but let us be very chary of our own action. Let us remember that neither we nor the children can bear the white light of naked truth; that if, for example, we succeed in destroying the clothing that covers the story of the first fall—the tree and its fruit, the tempting serpent, the yielding woman—we have no other clothing at hand for the fundamental truths of responsibility, temptation, sin; and, once uncovered, with no vesture which we can lay hold upon, the truths themselves will assuredly slip from our grasp.

We need not be at the pains to discriminate, in teaching children Bible narratives, between essential and accidental truth—the truth which interprets our own lives, and that which concerns only the time, place, and circumstances proper to the narrative. The children themselves will discern and keep fast hold of the essential, while the merely accidental slips from their memory as from ours. Therefore, let the minds of young children be well stored with the beautiful narratives of the Old Testament and of the gospels; but, in order that these stories may be always fresh and delightful to them, care must be taken lest Bible teaching stale upon their minds. Children are more capable of being bored than even we ourselves and many a revolt has been brought about by the undue rubbing-in of the Bible, in season and out of season, even in nursery days. But we are considering, not the religious life of children, but their education by lessons; and their Bible lessons should help them to realize in early days that the knowledge of God is the principal knowledge, and, therefore, that their Bible lessons are their chief lessons.

Method of Bible Lessons.—The method of such lessons is very simple. Read aloud to the children a few verses covering if possible, an episode. Read reverently, carefully, and with just expression. Then require the children to narrate what they have listened to as nearly as possible in the words of the Bible. It is curious how readily they catch the rhythm of the majestic and simple Bible English. Then, talk the narrative over with them in the light of research and criticism. Let the teaching, moral and spiritual, reach them without much personal application. I know of no better help in the teaching of young children than we get in Canon Paterson Smyth's Bible for the Young. Mr. Smyth brings both modern criticism and research to bear, so that children taught from his little manuals will not be startled to be told that the world was not made in six days; and, at the same time, they will be very sure that the world was made by God. The moral and spiritual teaching in these manuals is on broad and convincing lines. It is rather a good plan occasionally to read aloud Mr. Smyth's lesson on the subject after the Bible passage has been narrated. Children are more ready to appropriate lessons that are not directly levelled at themselves; while the teacher makes the teaching her own by the interest with which she reads, the pictures and other illustrations she shows, and her conversational remarks. Click here for a Sample of one of Paterson Smyth's books

Picture Illustrations.—The pictures in the Illustrated New Testament are, at the same time, reverent and actual, an unusual combination, and children enjoy them greatly. It would be well for them to have only the penny gospel they are reading, but it should perhaps be protected (and honoured) by an embroidered cover. A tattered Bible is not a wholesome sight for children. The Holy Gospels with Illustrations from the Old Masters, published by the S.P.C.K., is admirable. The study of such pictures as are here repro-duced should be a valuable part of a child's education; it is no slight thing to realize how the Nativity and the visit of the Wise Men filled the imagination of the early Mas-ters, and with what exceeding reverence and delight they dwelt upon every detail of the sacred story. This sort of impression is not to be had from any up-to-date treatment, or up-to-date illustrations; and the child who gets it in early days, will have a substratum of reverent feeling upon which should rest his faith. But it is well to let the pictures tell their own tale. The children should study a subject quietly for a few minutes; and then, the picture being removed, say what they have seen in it. It will be found that they miss no little reverent or suggestive detail which the artist has thought well to include.

The various R.T.S. publications issued in the series of Bypaths of Bible Knowledge will be found very helpful by the teacher as illustrating modern research; notably, Professor Sayce's Fresh Light from Ancient Monuments, and Budge's Dwellers on the Nile.

Bible Recitations.—The learning by heart of Bible passages should begin while the children are quite young, six or seven. It is a delightful thing to have the memory stored with beautiful, comforting, and inspiring passages, and we cannot tell when and how this manner of seed may spring up, grow, and bear fruit; but the learning of the parable of the Prodigal son, for example, should not be laid on the children as a burden. The whole parable should be read to them in a way to bring out its beauty and tenderness; and then, day by day, the teacher should recite a short passage, perhaps two or three verses, saying it over some three or four times until the children think they know it. Then, but not before, let them recite the passage. Next day the children will recite what they have already learned, and so on, until they are able to say the whole parable.

XV.—Arithmetic

Educative Value of Arithmetic.—Of all his early studies, perhaps none is more important to the child as a means of education than that of arithmetic. That he should do sums is of comparatively small importance; but the use of those functions which 'summing' calls into play is a great part of education so much so, that the advocates of mathematics and of language as instruments of education have, until recently, divided the field pretty equally between them.

The practical value of arithmetic to persons in every class of life goes without remark. But the use of the study in practical life is the least of its uses. The chief value of arithmetic, like that of the higher mathematics, lies in the training it affords the reasoning powers, and in the habits of insight, readiness, accuracy, intellectual truthfulness it engenders. There is no one subject in which good teaching effects more, as there is none in which slovenly teaching has more mischievous results. Multiplication does not produce the 'right answer,' so the boy tries division; that again fails, but subtraction may get him out of the bog. There is no must be to him he does not see that one process, and one process only, can give the required result. Now, a child who does not know what rule to apply to a simple problem within his grasp, has been ill taught from the first, although he may produce slatefuls of quite right sums in multiplication or long division.

Problems within the Child's Grasp.—How is this insight, this exercise of the reasoning powers, to be secured? Engage the child upon little problems within his comprehension from the first, rather than upon set sums. The young governess delights to set a noble 'long division sum,'—, 953,783,465/873—which shall fill the child's slate, and keep him occupied for a good half-hour; and when it is finished, and the child is finished too, done up with the unprofitable labour, the sum is not right after all: the last two figures in the quotient are wrong, and the remainder is false. But he cannot do it again—he must not be discouraged by being told it is wrong; so, 'nearly right' is the verdict, a judgment inadmissible in arithmetic. Instead of this laborious task, which gives no scope for mental effort, and in which he goes to sea at last from sheer want of attention, say to him—

"Mr. Jones sent six hundred and seven, and Mr. Stevens eight hundred and nineteen, apples to be divided amongst the twenty-seven boys at school on Monday. How many apples apiece did they get?"

Here he must ask himself certain questions. 'How many apples altogether? How shall I find out? Then I must divide the apples into twenty-seven heaps to find out each boy's share.' That is to say, the child perceives what rules he must apply to get the required information. He is interested; the work goes on briskly; the sum is done in no time, and is probably right, because the attention of the child is concentrated on his work. Care must be taken to give the child such problems as he can work, but yet which are difficult enough to cause him some little mental effort.

Demonstrate.—The next point is to demonstrate everything demonstrable. The child may learn the multiplication-table and do a subtraction sum without any insight into the rationale of either. He may even become a good arithmetician, applying rules aptly, without seeing the reason of them; but arithmetic becomes an elementary mathematical training only in so far as the reason why of every process is clear to the child. 2+2=4, is a self-evident fact, admitting of little demonstration; but 4x7=28 may be proved.

He has a bag of beans; places four rows with seven beans in a row; adds the rows thus: 7 and 7 are 14, and 7 are 21, and 7 are 28; how many sevens in 28? 4. Therefore it is right to say 4x7=28; and the child sees that multiplication is only a short way of doing addition.

A bag of beans, counters, or buttons should be used in all the early arithmetic lessons, and the child should be able to work with these freely, and even to add, subtract, multiply, and divide mentally, without the aid of buttons or beans, before he is set to 'do sums' on his slate.

He may arrange an addition table with his beans, thus—

    0 0   0   = 3 beans

    0 0   0 0   = 4 beans

    0 0   0 0 0 = 5 beans

and be exercised upon it until he can tell, first without counting, and then without looking at the beans, that 2+7=9, etc.

Thus with 3, 4, 5,—each of the digits: as he learns each line of his addition table he is exercised upon imaginary objects, '4 apples and 9 apples,' '4 nuts and 6 nuts' etc.; and lastly, with abstract numbers—6+5, 6+8.

A subtraction table is worked out simultaneously with the addition table. As he works out each line of additions, he goes over the same ground, only taking away one bean, or two beans, instead of adding, until he is able to answer quite readily, 2 from 7? 2 from 5? After working out each line of addition or subtraction, he may put it on his slate with the proper signs, that is, if he have learned to make figures. It will be found that it requires a much greater mental effort on the child's part to grasp the idea of subtraction than that of addition, and the teacher must be content to go slowly—one finger from four fingers, one nut from three nuts, and so forth, until he knows what he is about.

When the child can add and subtract numbers pretty freely up to twenty, the multiplication and division tables may be worked out with beans, as far as 6x12; that is, 'twice six are 12' will be ascertained by means of two rows of beans, six beans in a row.

When the child can say readily, without even a glance at his beans, 2x8=16, 2x7=14, etc., he will take 4, 6, 8, 10, 12 beans, and divide them into groups of two: then, how many twos in 10, in 12, in 20? And so on, with each line of the multiplication table that he works out.

Problems—Now he is ready for more ambitious problems: thus, 'A boy had twice ten apples; how many heaps of 4 could he make?' He will be able to work with promiscuous numbers, as 7+5-3. If he must use beans to get his answer, let him; but encourage him to work with imaginary beans, as a step towards working with abstract numbers. Carefully graduated teaching and daily mental effort on the child's part at this early stage may be the means of developing real mathematical power, and will certainly promote the habits of concentration and effort of mind.

Notation—When the child is able to work pretty freely with small numbers, a serious difficulty must be faced, upon his thorough mastery of which will depend his appreciation of arithmetic as a science; in other words, will depend the educational value of all the sums he may henceforth do. He must be made to understand our system of notation. Here, as before, it is best to begin with the concrete: let the child get the idea of ten units in one ten after he has mastered the more easily demonstrable idea of twelve pence in one shilling.

Let him have a heap of pennies, say fifty: point out the inconvenience of carrying such weighty money to shops. Lighter money is used—shillings. How many pennies is a shilling worth? How many shillings, then, might he have for his fifty pennies? He divides them into heaps of twelve, and finds that he has four such heaps, and two pennies over; that is to say, fifty pence are (or are worth) four shillings and two pence. I buy ten pounds of biscuits at fivepence a pound; they cost fifty pence, but the shopman gives me a bill for 4s. 2d.; show the child how to put down: the pennies, which are worth least, to the right; the shillings, which are worth more, to the left.

When the child is able to work freely with shillings and pence, and to understand that 2 in the right-hand column of figures is pence, 2 in the left-hand column, shillings, introduce him to the notion of tens and units, being content to work very gradually. Tell him of uncivilized peoples who can only count so far as five—who say 'five-five beasts in the forest,' 'five-five fish in the river,' when they wish to express an immense number. We can count so far that we might count all day long for years without coming to the end of the numbers we might name; but after all, we have very few numbers to count with, and very few figures to express them by. We have but nine figures and a nought: we take the first figure and the nought to express another number, ten; but after that we must begin again until we get two tens, then, again, till we reach three tens, and so on. We call two tens, twenty, three tens, thirty, because 'ty' (tig) means ten. But if I see figure 4, how am I to know whether it means four tens or four ones? By a very simple plan. The tens have a place of their own; if you see figure 6 in the ten-place, you know it means sixty. The tens are always put behind the units: when you see two figures standing side by side, thus, '55,' the left-hand figure stands for so many tens; that is, the second 5 stands for ten times as many as the first.

Let the child work with tens and units only until he has mastered the idea of the ten-fold value of the second figure to the left, and would laugh at the folly of writing 7 in the second column of figures, knowing that thereby it becomes seventy. Then he is ready for the same sort of drill in hundreds, and picks up the new idea readily if the principle have been made clear to him, that each remove to the left means a tenfold increase in the value of a number. Meantime, 'set' him no sums. Let him never work with figures the notation of which is beyond him, and when he comes to 'carry' in an addition or multiplication sum, let him not say he carries 'two,' or 'three,' but 'two tens,' or 'three hundreds,' as the case may be.

Weighing and Measuring.—If the child do not get the ground under his feet at this stage, he works arithmetic ever after by rule of thumb. On the same principle, let him learn 'weights and measures' by measuring and weighing; let him have scales and weights, sand or rice, paper and twine, and weigh, and do up, in perfectly made parcels, ounces, pounds, etc. The parcels, though they are not arithmetic, are educative, and afford considerable exercise of judgment as well as of neatness, deftness, and quickness. In like manner, let him work with foot-rule and yard measure, and draw up his tables for himself. Let him not only measure and weigh everything about him that admits of such treatment, but let him use his judgment on questions of measure and weight. How many yards long is the tablecloth? How many feet long and broad a map, or picture? What does he suppose a book weighs that is to go by parcel post? The sort of readiness to be gained thus is valuable in the affairs of life, and, if only for that reason, should be cultivated in the child. While engaged in measuring and weighing concrete quantities, the scholar is prepared to take in his first idea of a 'fraction,' half a pound, a quarter of a yard, etc.

Arithmetic a Means of Training.—Arithmetic is valuable as a means of training children in habits of strict accuracy, but the ingenuity which makes this exact science tend to foster slipshod habits of mind, a disregard of truth and common honesty, is worthy of admiration! The copying, prompting, telling, helping over difficulties, working with an eye to the answer which he knows, that are allowed in the arithmetic lesson, under an inferior teacher, are enough to vitiate any child; and quite as bad as these is the habit of allowing that a sum is nearly right, two figures wrong, and so on, and letting the child work it over again. Pronounce a sum wrong, or right—it cannot be something between the two. That which is wrong must remain wrong: the child must not be let run away with the notion that wrong can be mended into right. The future is before him: he may get the next sum right, and the wise teacher will make it her business to see that he does, and that he starts with new hope. But the wrong sum must just be let alone. Therefore his progress must be carefully graduated; but there is no subject in which the teacher has a more delightful consciousness of drawing out from day to day new power in the child. Do not offer him a crutch: it is in his own power he must go. Give him short sums, in words rather than in figures, and excite him in the enthusiasm which produces concentrated attention and rapid work. Let his arithmetic lesson be to the child a daily exercise in clear thinking and rapid, careful execution, and his mental growth will be as obvious as the sprouting of seedlings in the spring.

The A B C Arithmetic—Instead of entering further into the subject of teaching elementary arithmetic, I should like to refer the reader to the A B C Arithmetic by Messrs Sonnenschein & Nesbit. The authors found their method upon the following passage from Mill's Logic:

"The fundamental truths of the science of Number all rest on the evidence of sense; they are proved by showing to our eyes and our fingers that any given number of objects, ten balls for example, may by separation and re-arrangement exhibit to our sense all the different sets of numbers the sum of which is equal to ten. All the improved methods of teaching arithmetic to children proceed on a knowledge of this fact. All who wish to carry the child's mind along with them in learning arithmetic, all who wish to teach numbers and not mere ciphers, now teach it through the evidence of the senses in the manner we have described."

Here we may, I think, trace the solitary source of weakness in a surpassingly excellent manual. It is quite true that the fundamental truths of the science of number all rest on the evidence of sense but, having used eyes and fingers upon ten balls or twenty balls, upon ten nuts, or leaves, or sheep, or what not, the child has formed the association of a given number with objects, and is able to conceive of the association of various other numbers with objects. In fact, he begins to think in numbers and not in objects, that is, he begins mathematics. Therefore I incline to think that an elaborate system of staves, cubes, etc., instead of tens, hundreds, thousands, errs by embarrassing the child's mind with too much teaching, and by making the illustration occupy a more prominent place than the thing illustrated.

Dominoes, beans, graphic figures drawn on the blackboard, and the like, are, on the other hand, aids to the child when it is necessary of him to conceive of a great number with the material of a small one; but to see a symbol of the great numbers and to work with such a symbol are quite different matters.

With the above trifling exception, which does not interfere at all with the use of the books, nothing can be more delightful than the careful analysis of numbers and the beautiful graduation of the work, "only one difficulty at a time being presented to the mind." The examples and the little problems could only have been invented by writers in sympathy with children. I advise the reader who is interested in the teaching of arithmetic to turn to Mr. Sonnenschein's paper on 'The Teaching of Arithmetic in Elementary Schools,' in one of the volumes published by the Board of Education.

Preparation for Mathematics.—In the 'forties' and 'fifties' it was currently held that the continual sight of the outward and visible signs (geometrical forms and figures) should beget the inward and spiritual grace of mathematical genius, or, at any rate, of an inclination to mathematics. But the educationalists of those days forgot, when they gave children boxes of 'form' and stuck up cubes, hexagons, pentagons, and what not, in every available schoolroom space, the immense capacity for being bored which is common to us all, and is far more strongly developed in children than in grown-up people. The objects which bore us, or the persons who bore us, appear to wear a bland place in the mind, and thought turns from them with sick aversion. Dickens showed us the pathos of it in the schoolroom of the little Gradgrinds, which was bountifully supplied with objects of uncompromising outline. Ruskin, more genially, exposes the fallacy. No doubt geometric forms abound,—the skeletons of which living beauty, in contour and gesture, in hill and plant, is the covering; and the skeleton is beautiful and wonderful to the mind which has already entered within the portals of geometry. But children should not be presented with the skeleton, but with the living forms which clothe it. Besides, is it not an inverse method to familiarise the child's eye with patterns made by his compasses, or stitched upon his card, in the hope that the form will beget the idea? For the novice, it is probably the rule that the idea must beget the form, and any suggestion of an idea from a form comes only to the initiated. I do not think that any direct preparation for mathematics is desirable. The child, who has been allowed to think and not compelled to cram, hails the new study with delight when the due time for it arrives. The reason why mathematics are a great study is because there exists in the normal mind an affinity and capacity for this study; and too great an elaboration, whether of teaching or of preparation, has, I think, a tendency to take the edge off this manner of intellectual interest.

XVI.—Natural Philosophy

A Basis of Facts.—Of the teaching of Natural Philosophy, I will only remind the reader of what was said in an earlier chapter—that there is no part of a child's education more important than that he should lay, by his own observation, a wide basis of facts towards scientific knowledge in the future. He must live hours daily in the open air, and, as far as possible, in the country; must look and touch and listen; must be quick to note, consciously, every peculiarity of habit or structure, in beast, bird, or insect; the manner of growth and fructification of every plant. He must be accustomed to ask why—Why does the wind blow? Why does the river flow? Why is a leaf-bud sticky? And do not hurry to answer his questions for him; let him think his difficulties out so far as his small experience will carry him. Above all, when you come to the rescue, let it not be in the 'cut and dried' formula of some miserable little text-book; let him have all the insight available and you will find that on many scientific questions the child may be brought at once to the level of modern thought. Do not embarrass him with too much scientific nomenclature. If he discover for himself (helped, perhaps, by a leading question or two), by comparing an oyster and his cat, that some animals have backbones and some have not, it is less important that he should learn the terms vertebrate and invertebrate than that he should class the animals he meets with according to this difference.

Eyes and No-eyes.—The method of this sort of instruction is shown in Evenings at Home, where 'Eyes and No-eyes' go for a walk. No-eyes come home bored; he has seen nothing, been interested in nothing: while Eyes is all agog to discuss a hundred things that have interested him. As I have already tried to point out, to get this sort of instruction for himself is simply the nature of a child: the business of the parent is to afford him abundant and varied opportunities, and to direct his observations, so that, knowing little of the principles of scientific classification, he is, unconsciously, furnishing himself with the materials for such classification. It is needless to repeat what has already been said on this subject; but, indeed, the future of the man or woman depends very largely on the store of real knowledge gathered, and the habits of intelligent observation acquired, by the child. "Think you," says Mr. Herbert Spencer, "that the rounded rock marked with parallel scratches calls up as much poetry in an ignorant mind as in the mind of the geologist, who knows that over this rock a glacier slid a million of years ago? The truth is, that those who have never entered on scientific pursuits are blind to most of the poetry by which they are surrounded. Whoever has not in youth collected plants and insects, knows not half the halo of interest which lanes and hedgerows can assume."

Principles.—In this connection I should like to recommend The Sciences, by Mr. Holden. America comes to the fore with a schoolbook after my own heart. The Sciences is a forbidding title, but since the era of Joyce's Scientific Dialogues I have met with nothing on the same lines which makes so fit an approach to the sensible and intelligent mind of a child. This is what we may call a 'first-hand' book. The knowledge has of course all been acquired; but then it has been assimilated, and Mr. Holden writes freely out of his own knowledge both of his subject-matter and of his readers. The book has been thrown into the form of conversations between children—simple conversations without padding. About three hundred topics are treated of: Sand-dunes, Back-ice, Herculaneum, Dredging, Hurricanes, Echoes, the Prism, the Diving-bell, the Milky Way, and, shall I say, everything else? But the amazing skill of the author is shown in the fact that there is nothing scrappy and nothing hurried in the treatment of any topic, but each falls naturally and easily under the head of some principle which it elucidates. Many simple experiments are included, which the author insists shall be performed by the children themselves. I venture to quote from the singularly wise preface, a vade mecum for teachers:—

"The object of the present volume is to present chapters to be read in school or at home that shall materially widen the outlook of American schoolchildren in the domain of science, and of the applications of science to the arts and to daily life. It is in no sense a text-book, although the fundamental principles underlying the sciences treated are here laid down. Its main object is to help the child to understand the material world about him.

To be Comprehended by Children.—"All natural phenomena are orderly; they are governed by law; they are not magical. They are comprehended by someone; why not by the child himself? It is not possible to explain every detail of a locomotive to a young pupil, but it is perfectly practicable to explain its principles so that this machine, like others, becomes a mere special case of certain well-understood general laws. The general plan of the book is to awaken the imagination; to convey useful knowledge; to open the doors towards wisdom. Its special aim is to stimulate observation and to excite a living and lasting interest in the world that lies about us.

"The sciences of astronomy, physics, chemistry, meteorology, and physiography are treated as fully and as deeply as the conditions permit; and the lessons that they teach are enforced by examples taken from familiar and important things. In astronomy, for example, emphasis is laid upon phenomena that the child himself can observe, and he is instructed how to go about it. The rising and setting of the stars, the phases of the moon, the uses of the telescope, are explained in simple words. The mystery of these and other matters is not magical, as the child at first supposes. It is to deeper mysteries that his attention is here directed. Mere phenomena are treated as special cases of very general laws. The same process is followed in the exposition of the other sciences.

"Familiar phenomena, like those of steam, of shadows, of reflected light, of musical instruments, of echoes, etc., are referred to their fundamental causes. Whenever it is desirable, simple experiments are described and fully illustrated, and all such experiments can very well be repeated in the schoolroom. . . . The volume is the result of a sincere belief that much can be done to aid young children to comprehend the material world in which they live, and of a desire to have a part in a work so very well worth doing."

I cannot help quoting also in this connection from an article (Parents' Review, April 1904) by the Rev. H. H. Moore dealing with a forgotten pioneer of a rational education and his experiment. This pioneer was the Rev. Richard Dawes, at one time Rector of Kings Somborne parish, Hampshire, who, in 1841, worked out the problem of rational education in an agricultural village, in which he found the population unusually ignorant and debased. The whole story is of great interest, but our concern is with the question of Natural Philosophy, the staple of the teaching given in this school.

As taught in a Village School.—Mr. Dawes thus explained his object:—"I aimed at teaching what would be profitable and interesting to persons in the position in life which the children were likely to occupy. I aimed at their being taught what may be called the philosophy of common things of everyday life. They were shown how much there is that is interesting, and which it is advantageous for them to know, in connection with the natural objects with which they are familiar; they had explained to them, and were made acquainted with, the principles of a variety of natural phenomena, as well as the principles and construction of various instruments of a useful kind. A practical turn was given to everything the uses and fruits of the knowledge they were acquiring were never lost sight of." A list of some of the subjects included in this kind of teaching will be the best commentary on Mr. Dawes' scheme:—

"Some of the properties of air, explaining how its pressure enables them to pump up water, to amuse themselves with squirts and popguns, to suck up water through a straw; explaining also the principles and construction of a barometer, the common pump, the diving-bell, a pair of bellows. That air expands by heat, shown by placing a half-blown bladder near the fire, when the wrinkles disappear. Why the chimney-smoke sometimes rises easily in the air, sometimes not; why there is a draught up the chimney, and under the door, and towards the fire. Air as a vehicle of sound, and why the flash of a distant gun fired is seen before the report is heard; how to calculate the distance of a thunderstorm; the difference in the speeds at which different materials conduct sound. Water and its properties, its solid, fluid, and vaporous state; why water-pipes are burst by frost; why ice forms and floats on the surface of ponds, and not at the bottom; why the kettle-lid jumps up when the water is boiling on the fire; the uses to which the power of steam is applied; the gradual evolution of the steam-engine, shown by models and diagrams; how their clothes are dried, and why they feel cold sitting in damp clothes; why a damp bed is so dangerous; why one body floats in water, and another sinks; the different densities of sea and fresh water; why, on going into the school on a cold morning, they sometimes see a quantity of water on the glass, and why on the inside and not on the outside; why, on a frosty day, their breath is visible as vapour; the substances water holds in solution, and how their drinking water is affected by the kind of soil through which it has passed. Dew, its value, and the conditions necessary for its formation; placing equal portions of dry wool on gravel, glass, and the grass, and weighing them the next morning. Heat and its properties; how it is that the blacksmith can fit iron hoops so firmly on the wheels of carts and barrows; what precautions have to be taken in laying the iron rails of railways and in building iron bridges, etc.; what materials are good, and what bad, conductors of heat; why at the same temperature some feel colder to our touch than others; why a glass sometimes breaks when hot water is poured into it, and whether thick or thin glass would be more liable to crack; why water can be made to boil in a paper kettle or an eggshell without its being burned. The metals, their sources, properties, and uses; mode of separating from the ores. Light and its properties, illustrated by prisms, etc; adaptation of the eye; causes of long and short-sightedness. The mechanical principles of the tools more commonly used, the spade, the plough, the axe, the lever, etc."

"It may surprise some who read carefully the above list that such subjects should have been taught to the children of a rural elementary school. But it is an undeniable fact that they were taught in Kings Somborne School, and so successfully that the children were both interested and benefited by the teaching. Mr. Dawes, in answer to the objection that such subjects are above the comprehension of the young, said:—'The distinguishing mark of Nature's laws is their extreme simplicity. It may doubtless require intellect of a high order to make the discovery of these laws; yet, once evolved, they are within the capacity of a child,—in short, the principles of natural philosophy are the principles of common sense, and if taught in a simple and common-sense way, they will be speedily understood and eagerly attended to by children; and it will be found that with pupils of even from ten to twelve years of age much may be done towards forming habits of observation and inquiry.' Such a fact, I think, suggests some valuable practical lessons for those who have the responsibility of deciding what subjects to include in an educational system for children."

In reading of this remarkable experiment, we feel that we must at once secure a man, all-informed like the late Dean Dawes, to teach our own Jack and Elsie; but it is something to realize what these young persons should know, and Mr. Holden has done a great deal for us. Some of the chapters in The Sciences may be beyond children under nine, but they will be able to master a good deal. One thing is to be borne in mind: nothing should be done without its due experiment. By the way, our old friend, Joyce's Scientific Dialogues, if it is still to be had, describes a vast number of easy and interesting experiments which children can work for themselves.

XVII.—Geography

Geography is, to my mind, a subject of high educational value; though not because it affords the means of scientific training. Geography does present its problems, and these of the most interesting, and does afford materials for classification; but it is physical geography only which falls within the definition of a science, and even that is rather a compendium of the results of several sciences than a science itself. But the peculiar value of geography lies in its fitness to nourish the mind with ideas, and to furnish the imagination with pictures. Herein lies the educational value of geography.

As commonly Taught.—Now, how is the subject commonly taught? The child learns the names of the capital cities of Europe, or of the rivers of England, or of the mountain-summits of Scotland, from some miserable text-book, with length in miles, and height in feet, and population, finding the names on his map or not, according as his teacher is more or less up to her work. Poor little fellow! the lesson is hard work to him; but as far as education goes—that is, the developing of power, the furnishing of the mind—he would be better employed in watching the progress of a fly across the window-pane. But, you will say, geography has a further use than this strictly educative one; everybody wants the sort of information which the geography lesson should afford. That is true, and is to be borne in mind in the schoolroom; the child's geography lesson should furnish just the sort of information which grown-up people care to possess. Now, do think how unreasonable we are in this matter; nothing will persuade us to read a book of travel unless it be interesting, graphic, with a spice of personal adventure. Even when we are going about with Murray in hand, we skip the dry facts and figures, and read the suggestive pictorial scraps; these are the sorts of things we like to know, and remember with ease. But none of this pleasant padding for the poor child, if you please; do not let him have little pictorial sentences that he may dream over; facts and names and figures—these are the pabulum for him!

Geography should be Interesting.—But, you say, this sort of knowledge, though it may be a labour to the child to acquire it, is useful in after life. Not a bit of it; and for this reason—it has never been really received by the brain at all; has never got further than the floating nebulae of mere verbal memory of which I have already had occasion to speak. Most of us have gone through a good deal of drudgery in the way of 'geography' lessons, but how much do we remember? Just the pleasant bits we heard from travelled friends, about the Rhine, or Paris, or Venice, or bits from The Voyages of Captain Cook, or other pleasant tales of travel and adventure. We begin to see the lines we must go upon in teaching geography: for educative purposes, the child must learn such geography, and in such a way, that his mind shall thereby be stored with ideas, his imagination with images; for practical purposes he must learn such geography only as, the nature of his mind considered, he will be able to remember; in other words, he must learn what interests him. The educative and the practical run in one groove, and the geography lesson becomes the most charming occupation of the child's day.

How to begin.—But, how to begin? In the first place, the child gets his rudimentary notions of geography as he gets his first notions of natural science, in those long hours out of doors of which we have already seen the importance. A pool fed by a mere cutting in the fields will explain the nature of a lake, will carry the child to the lovely lakes of the Alps, to Livingstone's great African lake, in which he delighted to see his children 'paidling'—"his own children 'paidling' in his own lake." In this connection will come in a great deal of pleasant talk about places, 'pictorial geography,' until the child knows by name and nature the great rivers and mountains, deserts and plains, the cities and countries of the world. At the same time, he gets his first notions of a map from a rude sketch, a mere few lines and dots, done with pencil and paper, or, better still, with a stick in the sand or gravel. 'This crooked line is the Rhine; but you must imagine the rafts, and the island with the Mouse Tower, and the Nuns' Island, and the rest. Here are the hills, with their ruined castles—now on this side, now on that. This dot is Cologne,' etc. Especially, let these talks cover all the home scenery and interests you are acquainted with, so that, by-and-by, when he looks at the map of England, he finds a score of familiar names which suggest landscapes to him—places where 'mother has been,'—the woody, flowery islets of the Thames; the smooth Sussex downs, delightful to run and roll upon, with soft carpet of turf and nodding harebells; the York or Devon moors, with bilberries and heather:—and always give him a rough sketch-map of the route you took in a given journey.

What next?—Give him next intimate knowledge, with the fullest details, of any country or region of the world, any county or district of his own country. It is not necessary that he should learn at this stage what is called the 'geography' of the countries of Europe, the continents of the world—mere strings of names for the most part: he may learn these, but it is tolerably certain that he will not remember them. But let him be at home in any single region; let him see, with the mind's eye, the people at their work and at their play, the flowers and fruits in their seasons, the beasts, each in its habitat; and let him see all sympathetically, that is, let him follow the adventures of a traveller; and he knows more, is better furnished with ideas, than if he had learnt all the names on all the maps. The 'way' of this kind of teaching is very simple and obvious; read to him, or read for him, that is, read bit by bit, and tell as you read, Hartwig's Tropical World, the same author's Polar World, Livingstone's missionary travels, Mrs. Bishop's Unbeaten Tracks in Japan—in fact, any interesting, well-written book of travel. It may be necessary to leave out a good deal, but every illustrative anecdote, every bit of description, is so much towards the child's education. Here, as elsewhere, the question is, not how many things does he know, but how much does he know about each thing.

Maps.—Maps must be carefully used in this type of work,—a sketch-map following the traveller's progress, to be compared finally with a complete map of the region; and the teacher will exact a description of such and such a town, and such and such a district, marked on the map, by way of testing and confirming the child's exact knowledge. In this way, too, he gets intelligent notions of physical geography; in the course of his readings he falls in with a description of a volcano, a glacier, a cañon, a hurricane; he hears all about, and asks and learns the how and the why, of such phenomena at the moment when his interest is excited. In other words, he learns as his elders elect to learn for themselves, though they rarely allow the children to tread in paths so pleasant.

What General Knowledge a Child of Nine should have.—Supposing that between the child's sixth and his ninth year half a dozen well-chosen standard books of travel have been read with him in this way, he has gained distinct ideas of the contours, the productions, and the manners of the people, of every great region of the world; has laid up a store of reliable, valuable knowledge, that will last his lifetime; and besides, has done something to acquire a taste for books and the habit of reading. Such books as Lady Brassey's Voyage in the 'Sunbeam' should be avoided, as covering too much ground, and likely to breed some confusion of ideas.

Particular Knowledge.—But we are considering lessons as 'Instruments of Education;' and the sort of knowledge of the world I have indicated will be conveyed rather by readings in the 'Children's Hour' and at other times than by way of lessons. I know of nothing so good as the old-fashioned World at Home by Mary and Elizabeth Kirby (for lessons) for children between six and seven. As they hear, they wonder, admire, imagine, and can even 'play at' a hundred situations. The first ideas of geography, the lessons on place, which should make a child observant of local geography, of the features of his own neighbourhood, its heights and hollows, and level lands, its streams and ponds, should be gained, as we have seen, out of doors, and should prepare him for a certain amount of generalization—that is, he should be able to discover definitions of river, island, lake, and so on, and should make these for himself in a tray of sand, or draw them on the blackboard.

Definitions.—But definitions should come in the way of recording his experiences. Before he is taught what a river is, he must have watched a stream and observed that it flows; and so on with the rest.

Children easily simulate knowledge, and at this point the teacher will have to be careful that nothing which the child receives is mere verbiage, but that every generalisation is worked out somewhat in this way:—The child observes a fact, as, for example, a wide stretch of flat ground; the teacher amplifies. He reads in his book about Pampas, the flat countries of the north-west of Europe, the Holland of our own eastern coast, and, by degrees, he is prepared to receive the idea of a plain, and to show it on his tray of sand.

Fundamental Ideas.—By the time he is seven, or before, he finds himself in need of further knowledge. He has read of hot countries and cold countries, has observed the seasons and the rising and setting of the sun, has said to himself—

"Twinkle, twinkle, little star,

How I wonder what you are!"—

Knows something of ocean and sea, has watched the tide come in and go out, has seen many rough sketch-maps made and has made some for himself, and has, no doubt, noticed the criss-cross lines on a 'proper' map; that is to say, his mind is prepared for knowledge in various directions; there are a number of things concerned with geography which he really wants to know.

The shape and motions of the earth are fundamental ideas, however difficult to grasp, but the difficulty is of a kind which increases with years.

The principle in each case is simple enough, and a child does not concern himself, as do his elders, with the enormous magnitude of the scale upon which operations in space are carried on. It is probable that a child's vivid imagination puts him on a level with the mathematician in dealing with the planetary system, with the behaviour and character of Earth, with the causes of the seasons, and much besides.

Meaning of a Map.—Then, again, geography should be learned chiefly from maps. Pictorial readings and talks introduce him to the subject, but so soon as his geography lessons become definite they are to be learned, in the first place, from the map. This is an important principle to bear in mind. The child who gets no ideas from considering the map, say of Italy or of Russia, has no knowledge of geography, however many facts about places he may be able to produce. Therefore he should begin this study by learning the meaning of a map and how to use it. He must learn to draw a plan of his schoolroom, etc., according to scale, go on to the plan of a field, consider how to make the plan of his town, and be carried gradually from the idea of a plan to that of a map; always beginning with the notion of an explorer who finds the land and measures it, and by means of sun and stars, is able to record just where it is on the earth's surface, east or west, north or south.

Now he will arrive at the meaning of the lines of latitude and longitude. He will learn how sea and land are shown on a map, how rivers and mountains are represented; and having learned his points of direction and the use of his compass, and knowing that maps are always made as if the beholder were looking to the north, he will be able to tell a good deal about situation, direction, and the like, in very early days. The fundamental ideas of geography and the meaning of a map are subjects well fitted to form an attractive introduction to the study. Some of them should awaken the delightful interest which attaches in a child's mind to that which is wonderful, incomprehensible, while the map lessons should lead to mechanical efforts equally delightful. It is only when presented to the child for the first time in the form of stale knowledge and foregone conclusions that the facts taught in such lessons appear dry and repulsive to him. An effort should be made to treat the subject with the sort of sympathetic interest and freshness which attracts children to a new study.

XVIII.—History

A Storehouse of Ideas.—Much that has been said about the teaching of geography applies equally to that of history. Here, too, is a subject which should be to the child an inexhaustible storehouse of ideas, should enrich the chambers of his House Beautiful with a thousand tableaux, pathetic and heroic, and should form in him, insensibly, principles whereby he will hereafter judge of the behaviour of nations, and will rule his own conduct as one of a nation. This is what the study of history should do for the child; but what is he to get out of the miserable little chronicle of feuds, battles, and death which is presented to him by way of 'a reign'—all the more repellent because it bristles with dates? As for the dates, they never come right; the tens and units he can get, but the centuries will go astray; and how is he to put the right events in the right reign, when, to him, one king differs from another only in number, one period from another only in date? But he blunders through with it; reads in his pleasant, chatty little history book all the reigns of all the kings, from William the Conqueror to William IV., and back to the dim days of British rule. And with what result? This: that, possibly, no way of warping the judgment of the child, of filling him with crude notions, narrow prejudices, is more successful than that of carrying him through some such course of English history; and all the more so if his little text-book be moral or religious in tone, and undertake to point the moral as well as to record the fact. Moral teaching falls, no doubt, within the province of history; but the one small volume which the child uses affords no scope for the fair and reasonable discussion upon which moral decisions should be based, nor is the child old enough to be put into the judicial attitude which such a decision supposes.

'Outlines' Mischievous—The fatal mistake is in the notion that he must learn 'outlines,' or a baby edition of the whole history of England, or of Rome, just as he must cover the geography of all the world. Let him, on the contrary, linger pleasantly over the history of a single man, a short period, until he thinks the thoughts of that man, is at home in the ways of that period. Though he is reading and thinking of the lifetime of a single man, he is really getting intimately acquainted with the history of a whole nation for a whole age. Let him spend a year of happy intimacy with Alfred, 'the truth-teller,' with the Conqueror, with Richard and Saladin, or with Henry V.—Shakespeare's Henry V.—and his victorious army. Let him know the great people and the common people, the ways of the court and of the crowd. Let him know what other nations were doing while we at home were doing thus and thus. If he come to think that the people of another age were truer, larger-hearted, simpler-minded than ourselves, that the people of some other land were, at one time, at any rate, better than we, why, so much the better for him.

So are most History Books written for Children—For the matter for this intelligent teaching of history, eschew, in the first place, nearly all history books written expressly for children; and in the next place, all compendiums, outlines, abstracts whatsoever. For the abstracts, considering what part the study of history is fitted to play in the education of the child, there is not a word to be said in their favour; and as for what are called children's books, the children of educated parents are able to understand history written with literary power, and are not attracted by the twaddle of reading-made-easy little history books. Given judicious skipping, and a good deal of the free paraphrasing mothers are so ready at, and the children may be taken through the first few volumes of a well-written, illustrated, popular history of England, say as far as the Tudors. In the course of such reading a good deal of questioning into them, and questioning out of them, will be necessary, both to secure their attention and to fix the facts. This is the least that should be done; but better than this would be fuller information, more graphic details about two or three early epochs.

Early History of a Nation best fitted for Children.—The early history of a nation is far better fitted than its later records for the study of children, because the story moves on a few broad, simple lines; while statesmanship, so far as it exists, is no more than the efforts of a resourceful mind to cope with circumstances. Mr. Freeman has provided interesting early English history for children; but is it not on the whole better to take them straight to the fountainhead, where possible? In these early years, while there are no examinations ahead, and the children may yet go leisurely, let them get the spirit of history into them by reading, at least, one old Chronicle written by a man who saw and knew something of what he wrote about, and did not get it at second-hand. These old books are easier and pleasanter reading than most modern works on history, because the writers know little of the 'dignity of history'; they purl along pleasantly as a forest brook, tell you 'all about it,' stir your heart with the story of a great event, amuse you with pageants and shows, make you intimate with the great people, and friendly with the lowly. They are just the right thing for the children whose eager souls want to get at the living people behind the words of the history book, caring nothing at all about progress, or statutes, or about anything but the persons, for whose action history is, to the child's mind, no more than a convenient stage. A child who has been carried through a single old chronicler in this way has a better foundation for all historical training than if he knew all the dates and names and facts that ever were crammed for examination.

Some old Chronicles.—First in order of time, and full of the most captivating reading, is the Ecclesiastical History of England (see Appendix) of the Venerable Bede, who, writing of himself so early as the seventh century, says, "It was always sweet to me to learn, to teach, and to write." "He has left us," says Professor Morley, "a history of the early years of England, succinct, yet often warm with life; business-like, and yet childlike in its tone; at once practical and spiritual, simply just, and the work of a true scholar, breathing love to God and man. We owe to Bede alone the knowledge of much that is most interesting in our early history." William of Malmesbury (twelfth century) says of Bede, "That almost all knowledge of past events was buried in the same grave with him"; and he is no bad judge, for in his Chronicles of the Kings of England he himself is considered to have carried to perfection the art of chronicle-making. He is especially vivid and graphic about contemporary events—the story of the dreary civil war of Stephen and Matilda. Meantime, there is Asser, who writes the life of Alfred, whose friend and fellow-worker he is. "It seems to me right," he says, "to explain a little more fully what I have heard from my lord Alfred." He tells us how, "When I had come into his presence at the royal vill, called Leonaford, I was honourably received by him, and remained that time with him at his court about eight months, during which I read to him whatever books he liked, and such as he had at hand; for this is his most usual custom, both night and day, amid his many other occupations of mind and body, either himself to read books or to listen whilst others read them." When he was not present to see for himself, as at the battle of Ashdown, Asser takes pains to get the testimony of eyewitnesses. "But Alfred, as we have been told by those who were present and would not tell an untruth, marched up promptly, with his men to give them battle; for King Ethelred remained a long time in his tent in prayer." Then there are Chronicles of the Crusades, contemporary narratives of the crusades of Richard Coeur de Lion, by Richard of Devizes, and Geoffrey de Vinsany, and of the crusade of St. Louis, by Lord John de Joinville.

It is needless to extend the list; one such old chronicle in a year, or the suitable bits of one such chronicle, and the child's imagination is aglow, his mind is teeming with ideas; he has had speech of those who have themselves seen and heard; and the matter-of-fact way in which the old monks tell their tales is exactly what children prefer. Afterwards, you may put any dull outlines into their hands, and they will make history for themselves.

Age of Myths.—But every nation has its heroic age before authentic history begins: these were giants in the land in those days, and the child wants to know about them. He has every right to revel in such classic myths as we possess as a nation; and to land him in a company of painted savages, by way of giving him his first introduction to his people, is a little hard; it is to make his vision of the past harsh and bald as a Chinese painting. But what is to be done? If we ever had an Homeric age, have we not, being a practical people, lost all record thereof? Here is another debt that we owe to those old monkish chroniclers: the echoes of some dim, rich past had come down to, at any rate, the twelfth century: they fell upon the ear of a Welsh priest, one Geoffrey of Monmouth; and while William of Malmesbury was writing his admirable History of the Kings of England, what does Geoffrey do but weave the traditions of the people into an orderly History of the British Kings, reaching back all the way to King Brut, the grandson of Aeneas. How he came to know about kings, that no other historian had heard of, is a matter that he is a little roguish about; he got it all, he says, out of "that book in the British language which Walter, Archdeacon of Oxford, brought out of Britainy." Be that as it may, here we read of Gorboduc, King Lear, Merlin, Uther Pendragon, and, best of all, of King Arthur, the writer making 'the little finger of his Arthur stouter than the back of Alexander the Great.' Here is, indeed, a treasure-trove which the children should be made free of ten years before they come to read the Idylls of the King. Some caution must, however, be exercised in reading Geoffrey of Monmouth. His tales of marvel are delightful; but when he quits the marvellous and romances freely about historical facts and personages, he becomes a bewildering guide. Many of these 'chronicles,' written in Latin by the monks, are to be had in readable English; the only caution to be observed is, that the mother should run her eye over the pages before she reads them aloud. (Bohn's Antiquarian Library [5s. a volume] includes Bede, William of Malmesbury, Dr. Giles's Six Old English Chronicles—Asser and Geoffrey of Monmouth being two of them—Chronicles of the Crusaders, etc.)

Froissart, again, most delightful of chroniclers, himself 'tame' about the court of Queen Phillippa, when he chose to be in England—from whom else should the child get the story of the French wars? And so of as much else as there is time for; the principle being, that, whenever practicable, the child should get his first notions of a given period, not from the modern historian, the commentator and reviewer, but from the original sources of history, the writings of contemporaries. The mother must, however, exercise discrimination in her choice of early 'Chronicles,' as all are not equally reliable.

Plutarch's 'Lives.'—In the same way, readings from Plutarch's Lives will afford the best preparation for the study of Grecian or of Roman history. Alexander the Great is something more than a name to the child who reads this sort of thing:—

"When the horse Bucephalus was offered in sale to Philip, at the price of thirteen talents (= £2518, 15s.), the king, with the prince and many others, went into the field to see some trial made of him. The horse appeared very vicious and unmanageable, and was so far from suffering himself to be mounted, that he would not bear to be spoken to, but turned fiercely upon all the grooms. Philip was displeased at their bringing him so wild and ungovernable a horse, and bade them take him away. But Alexander, who had observed him well, said, 'What a horse they are losing for want of skill and spirit to manage him!'

"Philip at first took no notice of this; but upon the prince's often repeating the same expression, and showing great uneasiness, he said, 'Young man, you find fault with your elders as if you knew more than they, or could manage the horse better.'

"'And I certainly could,' answered the prince.

"'If you should not be able to ride him, what forfeiture will you submit for your rashness?'

"'I will pay the price of the horse.'"

"Upon this all the company laughed; but the king and prince agreeing as to the forfeiture, Alexander ran to the horse, and laying hold on the bridle, turned him to the sun, for he had observed, it seems, that the shadow which fell before the horse, and continually moved as he moved, greatly disturbed him. While his fierceness and fury lasted, he kept speaking to him softly and stroking him; after which he gently let fall his mantle, leaped lightly upon his back, and got his seat very safe. Then, without pulling the reins too hard, or using either whip or spur, he set him agoing. As soon as he perceived his uneasiness abated, and that he wanted only to run, he put him in a full gallop, and pushed him on both with the voice and spur.

"Philip and all his court were in great distress for him at first, and a profound silence took place; but when the prince had turned him and brought him safe back, they all received him with loud exclamations, except his father, who wept for joy, and kissing him, said 'Seek another kingdom, my son, that may be worthy of thy abilities, for Macedonia is too small for thee.'"

Here, again, in North's inimitable translation, we get the sort of vivid graphic presentation which makes 'History' as real to the child as are the adventures of Robinson Crusoe.

To sum up, to know as much as they may about even one short period, is far better for the children than to know the 'outlines' of all history. And in the second place, children are quite able to take in intelligent ideas in intelligent language, and should by no means be excluded from the best that is written on the period they are about.

History Books—It is not at all easy to choose the right history books for children. Mere summaries of facts must, as we have seen, be eschewed; and we must be equally careful to avoid generalisations.

The natural function of the mind, in the early years of life, is to gather the material of knowledge with a view to that very labour of generalisation which is proper to the adult mind; a labour which we should all carry on to some extent for ourselves.

As it is, our minds are so poorly furnished that we accept the conclusions presented to us without demur; but we can, at any rate, avoid giving children cut-and-dried opinions upon the course of history while they are yet young. What they want is graphic details concerning events and persons upon which imagination goes to work; and opinions tend to form themselves by slow degrees as knowledge grows.

Mr. York Powell has, perhaps more than others, hit upon the right teaching for the young children I have in view. In the preface to his Old Stories from British History, he says:—"The writer has chosen such stories as he thought would amuse and please his readers, and give them at the same time some knowledge of the lives and thoughts of their forefathers. To this end he has not written solely of great folk—kings and queens and generals—but also of plain people and children, ay, and birds and beasts too"; and we get the tale of King Lear and of Cuculain, and of King Canute and the poet Otter, of Havelock and Ubba, and many more, all brave and glorious stories; indeed, Mr. York Powell gives us a perfect treasure-trove in his two little volumes of Old Stories and Sketches from British History, which are the better for our purpose, because children can read them for themselves so soon as they are able to read at all. These tales, written in good and simple English, and with a certain charm of style, lend themselves admirably to narration.

Indeed, it is most interesting to hear children of seven or eight go through a long story without missing a detail, putting every event in its right order. These narrations are never a slavish reproduction of the original. A child's individuality plays about what he enjoys, and the story comes from his lips, not precisely as the author tells it, but with a certain spirit and colouring which express the narrator. By the way, it is very important that children should be allowed to narrate in their own way, and should not be pulled up or helped with words and expressions from the text.

A narration should be original as it comes from the child—that is, his own mind should have acted upon the matter it has received.

Narrations which are mere feats of memory are quite valueless.

I have already spoken of the sorts of old chronicles upon which children should be nourished; but these are often too diffuse to offer good matter for narration, and it is well to have quite fitting short tales for this purpose.

I should like to mention two other little volumes in which children delight, which feed patriotic sentiment and lay a broad basis for historical knowledge. I mean Mrs Frewen Lord's Tales from St. Paul's and Tales from Westminister Abbey. It is a beautiful and delightful thing to take children informed by these tales to the Abbey or St Paul's, and let them identify for themselves the spots consecrated to their heroes. They know so much and are so full of vivid interest that their elders stand by instructed and inspired. There are, no doubt, multitudes of historical tales and sketches for children, and some of them, like Miss Brooke Hunt's Prisoners of the Tower, are very good; but let the mother beware: there is nothing which calls for more delicate tact and understanding sympathy with the children than this apparently simple matter of choosing their lesson-books, and especially, perhaps, their lesson-books in history.

Many children of eight or nine will be quite ready to read with pleasure A History of England, by H.O. Arnold Forster, who has long since won his spurs in the field of educational literature. In this, as in matters of more immediate statecraft, Mr Arnold Forster has the gift to see a defect and a remedy, an omission and the means of supplying it. He saw that English children grew up without any knowledge of the conditions under which they live, and of the laws which govern them; but since the appearance of The Citizen Reader and The Laws of Every-day Life, we have changed all that.

The History of England, or, as the children call it, History, ignoring the fact that there is any other history than that of England, has hitherto been presented to young people as "outlines of dates and facts, or as collections of romantic stories, with little coherence and less result on the fortunes of the country." Mr Arnold Forster says in his preface that he "is reluctant to introduce his book by any such repellent title as 'A Summary,' or 'An Outline of English History.'

Such titles seem on the face of them to imply that the element of interest and the romance inseparable from the life and doings of individuals are excluded, and that an amplified chronological table has been made to do duty for history. But to read English history and fail to realize that it is replete with interest, sparkling with episode, and full of dramatic incident, is to miss all the pleasure and most of the instruction which its study, if properly pursued, can give." The author fulfills his implied promise, and his work is, I venture to say, as "replete with interest, sparkling with episode, and full of dramatic incident" as is possible, considering the limitations imposed upon him by the facts that he writes for uneducated readers, and gives us a survey of the whole of English History in a pleasant, copiously and wisely illustrated volume of some eight hundred pages. How telling and lucid this is, for example, and how we all wish we had come across such a paragraph in our early studies of architecture:—"On page 23 we have pictures of two windows. One of them is what is called a Pointed window. All the arches in it go up to a point. It was built a long time before the Tudor period. The other was built in the time of Queen Elizabeth. In it the upright shaft, or mullion, of the window goes straight up to the top without forming an arch. This style of building a window is called the Perpendicular Style, because the mullions of the window are 'perpendicular.' Some of the most famous buildings in England built in Tudor times, and in the perpendicular style, are the Chapel of King's College, Cambridge, and Hatfield House, the residence of the Marquis of Salisbury, in Hertfordshire." Mr. Arnold Forster has done in this volume for children and the illiterate, what Professor Green did in his Shorter History of England for somewhat more advanced students, awakening many to the fact that history is an entrancing subject of study. This is a real introduction to real history. The portraits are an especially valuable feature of the work.

Dates.—In order to give definiteness to what may soon become a pretty wide knowledge of history—mount a sheet of cartridge-paper and divide it into twenty columns, letting the first century of the Christian era come in the middle, and let each remaining column represent a century B.C. or A.D., as the case may be.

Then let the child himself write, or print, as he is able, the names of the people he comes upon in due order, in their proper century.

We need not trouble ourselves at present with more exact dates, but this simple table of the centuries will suggest a graphic panorama to the child's mind, and he will see events in their time-order.

Illustrations by the Children—History readings afford admirable material for narration, and children enjoy narrating what they have read or heard. They love, too, to make illustrations. Children who had been reading Julius Caesar (and also, Plutarch's Life), were asked to make a picture of their favourite scene, and the results showed the extraordinary power of visualizing which the little people possess. Of course that which they visualize, or imagine clearly, they know; it is a life possession.

The drawings of the children in question are psychologically interesting as showing what various and sometimes obscure points appeal to the mind of a child; and also, that children have the same intellectual pleasure as persons of cultivated mind in working out new hints and suggestions. The drawings, be it said, leave much to be desired, but they have this in common with the art of primitive peoples: they tell the tale directly and vividly. A girl of nine and a half pictures Julius Caesar conquering Britain. He rides in a chariot mounted on scythes, he is robed in blue, and bits of blue sky here and there give the complementary colour. In the distance, a soldier plants the ensign bearing the Roman eagle, black on a pink ground.

In the foreground, is a hand-to-hand combat between Roman and Briton, each having a sword of enormous length. Other figures are variously employed.

Another, gives us Antony 'making his speech after the death of Caesar.' This girl, who is older, gives us architecture; you look through an arch, which leads into a side street, and, in the foreground, Antony stands on a platform at the head of a flight of marble steps. Antony's attitude expresses indignation and scorn. Below, is a crowd of Romans wearing the toga, whose attitudes show various shades of consternation and dismay. Behind, is Antony's servant in uniform, holding his master's horse; and on the platform, in the rear of Antony, lies Caesar, with the royal purple thrown over him. The chief value of the drawing, as a drawing, is that it tells the tale.

Another girl draws Calpurnia begging Caesar not to go to the Senate. Caesar stands armed and perturbed, while Carpurnia holds his outstretched hand with both of hers as she kneels before him, her face raised in entreaty; her loose blue night-robe and long golden hair give colour to the picture. This artist is fourteen, and the drawing is better done.

Another artist presents Brutus and Portia in the orchard with a 'south-wall' of red brick, espaliers, and two dignified figures which hardly tell their tale.

Another child gives us the scene in the forum, Caesar seated in royal purple, Brutus kneeling before him, and Casca standing behind his chair with out-stretched hand holding a dagger, saying "Speak, hands, for me," while Caesar says, "Doth not Brutus bootless kneel?"

Again, we get Lucius playing to Brutus in the tent. Brutus, armed cap-a-pie, seated on a stool, is vainly trying to read, while Lucius, a pretty figure, seated before him, plays the harp. The two sentries, also fully armed, are stretched on the floor sound asleep.

Another, gives us Claudius dressed as a woman at the women's festival—the ladies with remarkable eyes, and each carrying a flaming torch.

Another pictures, with great spirit, Caesar reading his history to the conquered Gauls, who stand in rows on the hillside listening to the great man with exemplary patience.

In these original illustrations (several of them by older children than those we have in view here), we get an example of the various images that present themselves to the minds of children during the reading of a great work; and a single such glimpse into a child's mind convinces us of the importance of sustaining that mind upon strong meat. Imagination does not stir at the suggestion of the feeble, much-diluted stuff that is too often put into children's hands.

'Playing at' History—Children have other ways of expressing the conceptions that fill them when they are duly fed. They play at history lessons, dress up, make tableaux, act scenes; or they have a stage, and their dolls act, while they paint the scenery and speak the speeches. There is no end to the modes of expression children find when there is anything in them to express.

The mistake we make is to suppose that imagination is fed by nature, or that it works on the insipid diet of children's storybooks.

Let a child have the meat he requires in his history readings, and in the literature which naturally gathers round this history, and imagination will bestir itself without any help of ours; the child will live out in detail a thousand scenes of which he only gets the merest hint.

XIX.—Grammar

Grammar a Difficult Study.—Of grammar, Latin and English, I shall say very little here. In the first place, grammar, being a study of words and not of things, is by no means attractive to the child, nor should he be hurried into it. English grammar, again, depending as it does on the position and logical connection of words, is peculiarly hard for him to grasp. In this respect the Latin grammar is easier; a change in the form, the shape of the word, to denote case, is what a child can see with his bodily eye, and therefore is plainer to him than the abstract ideas of nominative and objective case as we have them in English. Therefore, if he learns no more at this early stage than the declensions and a verb or two, it is well he should learn thus much, if only to help him to see what English grammar would be at when it speaks of a change in case or mood, yet shows no change in the form of a word.

Latin Grammar.—Of the teaching of Latin grammar, I think I cannot do better than mention a book for beginners that really answers. Children of eight and nine take to this First Latin Course (Scott and Jones) very kindly, and it is a great thing to begin a study with pleasure. It is an open question, however, whether it is desirable to begin Latin at so early an age.

English Grammar a Logical Study.—Because English grammar is a logical study, and deals with sentences and the positions that words occupy in them, rather than with words, and what they are in their own right, it is better that the child should begin with the sentence, and not with the parts of speech; that is, that he should learn a little of what is called analysis of sentences before he learns to parse; should learn to divide simple sentences into the thing we speak of, and what we say about it—'The cat-sits on the hearth'—before he is lost in the fog of person, mood, and part of speech.

"So then I took up the next book. It was about grammar. It said extraordinary things about nouns and verbs and particles and pronouns, and past participles and objective cases and subjunctive moods. 'What are all these things?' asked the King. 'I don't know, your Majesty,' and the Queen did not know, but she said it would be very suitable for children to learn. 'It would keep them quiet.'"(2)

It is so important that children should not be puzzled as were this bewildered King and Queen, that I add a couple of introductory grammar lessons; as a single example is often more useful than many precepts.

Lesson I

Words put together so as to make sense form what is called a sentence.

'Barley oats chair really good and cherry' is not a sentence, because it makes no(n) sense.

'Tom has said his lesson' is a sentence.

It is a sentence because it tells us something about Tom.

Every sentence speaks of someone or of something, and tells us something about that of which it speaks.

So a sentence has two parts: (1) The thing we speak of; (2) What we say about it.

In our sentence we speak of 'Tom.'

We say about him that he 'has learned his lesson.'

The thing we speak of is often called the subject, which just means that which we talk about.

People sometimes say 'the subject of conversation was so and so,' which is another way of saying 'the thing we were speaking about was so and so.'

To be learnt—

Words put together so as to make sense form a sentence. A sentence has two parts: that which we speak of, and what we say about it. That which we speak of is the subject.

Exercises on Lesson I

1. Put the first part to—

    —has a long mane.

    —is broken.

    —cannot do his sums.

    —played for an hour;

    etc., etc.

2. Put the second part to—

    That poor boy—.

    My brother Tom—.

    The broken flowerpot—.

    Bread and jam—.

    Brown's tool-basket—;

    etc., etc.

3. Put six different subjects to each half sentence in 1.

4. Make six different sentences with each subject in 2.

5. Say which part of the sentence is wanting, and supply it in—

Has been mended

Tom's knife

That little dog

Cut his finger

Ate too much fruit

My new book

The snowdrops in our garden, etc., etc.

N.B.—Be careful to call the first part of each sentence the subject.

Draw a line under the subject of each sentence in all the exercises.

Lesson II

We may make a sentence with only two words—the name of the thing we speak of, and what we say about it:—

John writes.

Birds sing.

Mary sews.

We speak about 'John.' We say about him that he 'writes.' We speak about 'birds.' We say about them that they 'sing.'

These words, writes, sing, sews, all come out of the same group of words, and the words in that group are the chief words of all, for this reason—we cannot make sense, and therefore cannot make a sentence, without using at least one of them.

They are called verbs, which means words, because they are the chief words of all.

A verb always tells one of two things about the subject. Either it tells what the subject is, as—

I am hungry.

The chair is broken.

The birds are merry;

or it tells what the subject does, as—

Alice writes.

The cat mews.

He calls.

To be learnt—

We cannot make a sentence without a verb. Verb means word. Verbs are the chief words. Verbs show that the subject is something—

He is sleepy;

or does something—

He runs.

Exercises on Lesson II

1. Put in a verb of being:—

Mary—sleepy.

Boys—rough.

Girls—quiet.

He—first yesterday.

I—a little boy.

Tom and George—swinging before dinner.

We—busy to-morrow.

He—punished;

etc., etc.

2. Make three sentences with each of the following verbs:—

Is, are, should be, was, am, were, shall be, will be.

3. Make six sentences with verbs of being in each.

4. Put a verb of doing to—

Tigers—.

The boy with the pony—.

My cousins—;

etc., etc.

5. Make twenty sentences about—

That boy in kilts,

with verbs showing what he does.

6. Find the verbs, and say whether of being or doing, in—

The bright sun rises over the hill.

We went away.

You are my cousin.

George goes to school.

He took his slate.

We are seven.

7. Count how many verbs you use in your talk for the next ten minutes.

8. Write every verb you can find in these exercises, and draw a line under it.

XX.—French

French should be acquired as English is, not as a grammar, but as a living speech. To train the ear to distinguish and the lips to produce the French vocables is a valuable part of the education of the senses, and one which can hardly be undertaken too soon. Again, all educated persons should be able to speak French. Sir Lyon Playfair, once speaking a conference of French masters, lamented feelingly our degeneracy in this respect, and instanced the grammar school of Perth to show that in a Scotch school in the sixteenth century the boys were required to speak Latin during school hours, and French at all other times. There is hardly another civilised nation so dull in acquiring foreign tongues as we English of the present time; but, probably, the fault lies rather in the way we set about the study than in any natural incapacity for languages.

As regards French, for instance, our difficulties are twofold—the want of a vocabulary, and a certain awkwardness in producing unfamiliar sounds. It is evident that both these hindrances should be removed in early childhood. The child should never see French words in print until he has learned to say them with as much ease and readiness as if they were English. The desire to give printed combinations of letters the sounds they would bear in English words is the real cause of our national difficulty in pronouncing French. Again, the child's vocabulary should increase steadily, say, at the rate of half a dozen words a day. Think of fifteen hundred words in a year! The child who has that number of words, and knows how to apply them, can speak French. Of course, his teacher, will take care that, in giving words, she gives idioms also, and that as he learns new words, they are put into sentences and kept in use from day to day. A note-book in which she enters the child's new words and sentences will easily enable the teacher to do this. The young child has no foolish shame about saying French words—he pronounces them as simply as if they were English.

But it is very important that he should acquire a pure accent from the first. It is not often advisable that young English children should be put into the hands of a French governess or nurse; but would it not be possible for half a dozen families, say, to engage a French lady, who would give half an hour daily to each family?

M. Gouin's Method—A serious effort is being made to approach the study of foreign languages rationally and scientifically. I have no hesitation in saying that M. [Monsieur Francois] Gouin's work (The Art of Teaching and Studying Languages) is the most important attempt that has yet been made to bring the study of languages within the sphere of practical education. Indeed, the great reform in our methods of teaching modern languages owe their origin to this remarkable work. The initial idea, that we must acquire a new language as a child acquires his mother tongue, is absolutely right, whether the attempt to follow this idea out by analyzing a language into a certain number, say fifteen, exhaustive 'series,' be right or not. Again, it is incontestable that the ear, and not the eye, is the physical organ for apprehending a language, just as truly as it is by the mouth, and not the ear, we appropriate food. If M. Gouin's book establish these two points only, it will be a valuable contribution to educational thought. Equally important is his third position, that the verb is the key to the sentence, and more, is the living bridge between thought and act. He maintains, too, that the child thinks in sentences, not in words; that his sentences have a logical sequence; that this sequence is one of time —the order of the operations in, for example, the growth of a plant, or the grinding of corn in a mill; that, as the child perceives the operations, he has an absolute need to express them; that his ear solicits, his memory cherishes, his tongue reproduces, the words which say the thing he thinks.

No doubt M. Gouin's method should be more successful than any other in steeping the student (child or man) in German or French thought. If you are all day long trying to work out a 'series' in French, say, you come to think in French, to dream in French, to speak French. Moreover, one has a delightful sense that at last the way is made clear to us to conduct all teaching in the language under study. You have the 'Art Series' and the 'Bee Series' and the 'River' and the 'Character Series' and the 'Poet Series,' and any series you like. You think the thing out in the order of time and natural sequence; you get the right verbs, nouns, and such epithets as are necessary, follow suit, and in amazingly few sentences, very short sentences too, connected by 'and,' you have said all that is essential to the subject. The whole thing is a constant surprise, like the children's game which unearths the most extraordinary and out-of-the-way thing you can think of by means of a dozen or so questions.

The 'Series.'—Thus, a language learned by M. Gouin's method is 'a liberal education in itself.' One learns how few and simple are, after all, the conceptions of which the human mind is cognisant, and how few and simple, putting mere verbiage aside, are the words necessary to express these.

You really learn to think in the new language, because you have no more than vague impressions about these acts or facts in your mother tongue.

You order your thoughts in the new language, and, having done so, the words which express these are an inalienable possession.

Here is an example of an elementary 'Series,' showing how 'the servant lights the fire':

"The servant takes a box of matches, (takes.)

She opens the match-box, (opens.)

She takes out a match, (takes out.)

She shuts up the match-box, (shuts up.)

She strikes the match on the cover, (strikes.)

The match takes fire, (takes fire.)

The match smokes, (smokes.)

The match flames, (flames.)

The match burns, (burns.)

And spreads a smell of burning over the kitchen, (spreads.)

The servant bends down to the hearth, (bends down.)

Puts out her hand, (puts out.)

Puts the match under the shavings, (puts.)

Holds the match under the shavings, (holds.)

The shavings take fire, (take fire.)

The servant leaves go of the match, (leave go.)

Stands up again, (stands up.)

Looks at her fire burning, (looks.)

And puts back the box of matches in its place, (puts back.)

But any attempt to quote gives an uncertain and unsatisfactory idea of this important work.

How does the Child learn?—Whatever may be said of M. Gouin's methods, the steps by which he arrives at them are undoubtedly scientific. He learns from a child:

"Unhappily the child has remained up to the present a hackneyed riddle, which we have never taken sufficient trouble to decipher or examine...."

The little child, which at the age of two years utters nothing but meaningless exclamations, at the age of three finds itself in possession of a complete language. How does it accomplish this? Does this miracle admit of explanation or not? Is it a problem of which there is a possibility of finding the unknown quantity? . . . The organ of language—ask the little child—is not the eye: it is the ear. The eye is made for colours, and not for sounds and words . . . This tension, continuous and contrary to nature, of the organ of sight, the forced precipitancy of the visual act, produced what it was bound to produce, a disease of the eyesight."

This refers to M. Gouin's herculean labours in the attempt to learn German. He knew everybody's 'Method,' learned the whole dictionary through, and found at the end that he did not know one word of German 'as she is spoke.'

He returned to France, after a ten months' absence, and found that his little nephew—whom he had left a child of two and a half, not yet able to talk—had in the interval done what his uncle had signally failed to do. "'What!' I thought; 'this child and I have been working for the same time, each at a language. He, playing round his mother, running after flowers, butterflies and birds, without weariness, without apparent effort, without even being conscious of his work, is able to say all he thinks, express all he sees, understand all he hears; and when he began his work, his intelligence was yet a futurity, a glimmer, a hope. And I, versed in the sciences, versed in philosophy, armed with a powerful will, gifted with a powerful memory . . . have arrived at nothing, or at practically nothing!'"

"The linguistic science of the college has deceived me, has misguided me. The classical method, with its grammar, its dictionary, and its translations, is a delusion." "To surprise Nature's secret, I must watch this child."

M. Gouin watches the child—the work in question is the result of his observations.

The method of teaching may be varied, partly because that recommended by M. Gouin requires a perfect command of the French tongue, and teachers who are diffident find a conversational method founded on book and picture easier to work and perhaps as effectual—more so, some people think; but, be this as it may, it is to M. Gouin we owe the fundamental idea.

It is satisfactory to find principles, which we have urged continually, enunciated in this most thoughtful work. For example: "If one learns French without being able to read it—as the child does—there will be no longer much greater difficulty in pronouncing it than in pronouncing words in English. 'How about the spelling?' you will ask. The spelling? You would learn it as the young French children learn it, as you yourself have learnt the English spelling, ten times more difficult than the French; and this without letting the study of the spelling spoil your already acquired pronunciation. Besides, the spelling is a thing that can be reformed—the pronunciation hardly at all. We must choose between the two evils." M. Gouin speaks of the possibility of a child's picking up another tongue—even Chinese from a Chinese nurse; and his words remind me of an extraordinary instance of a child's facility in picking up languages, which once came before me. Having occasion to speak in public of three little children, all aged three, belonging to different families, where one parent was English, the other German, I said that these three children of my acquaintance could each say everything they had to say, express the whole range of their ideas, with equal ease and fluency in the two languages. At the close of the meeting, a gentleman present came forward and endorsed my remarks. He said he had a son whose wife was a German lady, and who was now a missionary in Bagdad. They have a child of three, and their child speaks three languages with perfect fluency—English, German, and Arabic! No doubt the child will forget two of the three, and this is no argument for teaching foreign tongues to babies, but surely it does prove that the acquisition of a foreign tongue need not present insuperable difficulties to any of us.

XXI.—Pictorial Art

Study of Pictures.—The art training of children should proceed on two lines. The six-year-old child should begin both to express himself and to appreciate, and his appreciation should be well in advance of his power to express what he sees or imagines. Therefore it is a lamentable thing when the appreciation of children is exercised only upon the coloured lithographs of their picture-books or of the 'Christmas number.' But the reader will say, 'A young child cannot appreciate art; it is only the colour and sentiment of a picture that reach him. A vividly coloured presentation of Bobbie's Birthday, or of Barbara's Broken Doll, will find its way straight to his "business and bosom."' 'Therefore,' says the reader, 'Nature indicates the sort of art proper for the children!' But, as a matter of fact, the minds of children and of their elders alike accommodate themselves to what is put in their way; and if children appreciate the vulgar and sentimental in art, it is because that is the manner of art to which they become habituated. A little boy of about nine was (with many others) given reproductions of some half dozen of the pictures of Jean Francois Millet to study during a school term. At the end, the children were asked to describe the one of these pictures which they liked best. Of course they did it, and did it well. This is what a little boy I mentioned makes of it:—"I liked the Sower best. The sower is sowing seeds; the picture is all dark except high up on the right-hand side where there is a man ploughing the field. While he is ploughing the field the sower sows. The sower has got a bag in his left hand and is sowing with this right hand. He has wooden clogs on. He is sowing at about six o'clock in the morning. You can see his head better than his legs and body, because it is against the light."

A little girl of seven prefers the 'Angelus', and says:—"The picture is about people in the fields, man and a woman. By the woman is a basket with something in it; behind her is a wheelbarrow. They are praying; the man has his hat off in his hand. You can tell that it is evening, because the wheelbarrow and the basket are loaded."

Should be Regular.—When children have begun regular lessons (that is, as soon as they are six), this sort of study of pictures should not be left to chance, but they should take one artist after another, term by term, and study quietly some half-dozen reproductions of his work in the course of the term.

The little memory outlines I have quoted show his studies; but this is the least of the gains. We cannot measure the influence that one or another artist has upon the child's sense of beauty, upon his power of seeing, as in a picture, the common sights of life; he is enriched more than we know in having really looked at even a single picture. It is a mistake to think that colour is quite necessary to children in their art studies. They find colour in many places, and are content, for the time, with form and feeling in their pictures. By the way, for schoolroom decorations, I know of nothing better than the Fitzroy Pictures [see Appendix.], especially those of the Four Seasons, where you get beauty, both of line and colour, and poetic feeling. I should like, too, to quote Ruskin's counsel that English children should be brought up on Jean Richter's picture-books for children, the Unser Vater, Sontag [see Appendix], and the rest.

I subjoin notes of a lesson on a Picture-talk [by a student of the House of Education] given to children of eight and nine, to show how this sort of lesson may be given.

Picture-Talk   "Objects

"1. To continue the series of Landseer's pictures the children are taking in school. "2. To increase their interest in Landseer's works. "3. To show the importance of his acquaintance with animals. "4. To help them to read a picture truly. "5. To increase their powers of attention and observation.

"Step I.—Ask the children if they remember what their last picture-talk was about, and what artist was famous for animal-painting. Tell them Landseer was acquainted with animals when he was quite young: he had dogs for pets, and because he loved them he studied them and their habits—so was able to paint them.

"Step II.—Give them the picture 'Alexander and the Diogenes' to look at, and ask them to find out all they can about it themselves, and to think what idea the artist had in his mind, and what idea or ideas he meant his picture to convey to us.

"Step III.—After three or four minutes, take the picture away and see what the children have noticed. Then ask them what the different dogs suggest to them; the strength of the mastiff representing Alexander; the dignity and stateliness of the bloodhounds in his rear; the look of the wise counselor on the face of the setter; the rather contemptuous look of the rough-haired terrier in the tub. Ask the children if they have noticed anything in the picture which shows the time of day: for example, the tools thrown down by the side of the workman's basket suggesting the mid-day meal; and the bright sunshine on the dogs who cast a shadow on the tub shows it must be somewhere about noon.

"Step IV.—Let them read the title, and tell any facts they know about Alexander and Diogenes; then tell them Alexander was a great conqueror who lived B.C. 356-323, famous for the battles he won against Persia, India, and along the coast of the Mediterranean He was very proud, strong, and boastful. Diogenes was a cynic philosopher. Explain cynic, illustrating by the legend of Alexander and Diogenes; and from it find out which dog represents Alexander and which Diogenes.

"Step V.—Let the children draw the chief lines of the picture, in five minutes, with a pencil and paper."

Original Illustrations.—I have spoken, from time to time, of original illustrations drawn by the children. It may be of use to subjoin notes of a lesson [By a student of the House of Education] showing the sort of occasional help a teacher may give in this kind of work; but in a general way it is best to leave children to themselves.

"Objects

"1. To help the children to make clear mental pictures from description, and to reproduce the same in painting. "2. To increase their power of imagination. "3. To help them in their ideas of form and colour. "4. To increase their interest in the story of Beowulf by letting them illustrate a scene from the book they are reading. "5. To bring out their idea of an unknown creature (Grendel).

Steps

"Step I.—To draw from the children what they know of the poem 'Beowulf', and of the hero himself. "Step II.—To tell them any points they may miss in the story, as far as they have read (i.e. to the death of Grendel).

"Step III.—To read the description of the dress at that time, and the account of Grendel's death (including three possible pictures).

"Step IV.—To draw from the children what mental pictures they have made—and to re-read the passage.

"Step V.—To let them produce their mental picture with brush and paint.

"Step VI.—To show them George Harrow's 'original illustration' of Beowulf in "Heroes of Chivalry and Romance."

Drawing Lessons.—But 'for their actual drawing lessons,' says the reader, 'I suppose you use "blobs"?'—'i.e. splashes of paint made with the flat of the brush, which take an oval form. I think blobs have one use—they give certain freedom in using colour. Otherwise 'blobs' seem to me a sort of apparatus of art which a child acquires with a good deal of labour, and which, by proper combinations into flowers, and so on he can produce effects beyond his legitimate power as an artist, while all the time he can do this without a particle of the feeling for the natural object which is the very soul of the art. The power of effective creation by a sort of clever trick maims those delicate feelers of a child's nature by which he apprehends art.

"Let the eye (says Ruskin) "but rest on rough piece of branch for curious form during a conversation with a friend, rest, however unconsciously, and though the conversation be forgotten, though every circumstance connected with it be as utterly lost to the memory as though it had not been, yet the eye will, through the whole life after, take a certain pleasure in such boughs which it had not before, a pleasure so slight, a trace of feeling so delicate, as to leave us utterly unconscious of its peculiar power, but undestroyable by any reasoning, a part thence-forward of our constitution."

This is what we wish to do for children in teaching them to draw—to cause the eye to rest, not unconsciously, but consciously, on some object of beauty which will leave in their minds an image of delight for all their lives to come. Children of six and seven draw budding twigs of oak and ash, beech and larch, with such tender fidelity to colour, tone, and gesture, that the crude little drawings are in themselves things of beauty.

Children have 'Art' in them.—With art, as with so many other things in a child, we must believe that it is there, or we shall never find it. Once again, here is a delicate Ariel whom it is our part to deliver from his bonds. Therefore we set twig or growing flower before a child and let him deal with it as he chooses. He will find his own way to form and colour, and our help may very well be limited at first to such technical matters as the mixing of colours and the like. In order that we may not impede the child's freedom or hinder the deliverance of the art that is in him, we must be careful not to offer any aids in the way of guiding lines, points, and such other crutches; and, also, he should work in the easiest medium, that is, with paint brush or with charcoal, and not with a black-lead pencil. Boxes of cheap colours are to be avoided. Children are worthy of the best, and some half-dozen tubes of really good colours will last a long time, and will satisfy the eye of the little artists.

Clay-modelling.—While speaking of the art training of children, it may be as well to give a word to clay-modelling. Neat little birds-nests, baskets of eggs, etc., are of no use in the way of art development, and soon cease to be amusing. The chief thing the teacher has to do is to show the child how to prepare his clay so as to expel air-bubbles, and to give him the idea of making a little platform for his work, so that it may from the first have an artistic effect. Then put before him an apple, a banana, a Brazil nut, or the like; let him, not take a lump of clay and squeeze it into shape, but build up the shape he desires morsel by morsel. His own artistic perception seizes on the dint in the apple, the crease in the child's shoe, the little notes of expression in the objects which break uniformity and make for art.

The Piano and Singing.—I must close, with the disappointing sense that subjects of importance in the child's education have been left out of count, and that no one matter has been adequately treated.

Certain subjects of peculiar educational value, music, for instance, I have said nothing about, partly for want of space, and partly because if the mother have not Sir Joshua Reynold's 'that!' in her, hints from an outsider will not produce the art-feeling which is the condition of success in this sort of teaching. If possible, let the children learn from the first under artists, lovers of their work: it is a serious mistake to let the child lay the foundation of whatever he may do in the future under ill-qualified mechanical teachers, who kindle in him none of the enthusiasm which is the life of art. I should like, in connection with singing, to mention the admirable educational effects of the Tonic Sol-fa method. [See Appendix] Children learn by it in a magical way to produce sign for sound and sound for sign, that is, they can not only read music, but can write the notes for, or make the proper hand signs for, the notes of a passage sung to them. Ear and Voice are simultaneously and equally cultivated.

Mrs. Curwen's Child Pianist [See Appendix] method is worked out, with minute care, upon the same lines; that is, the child's knowledge of the theory of music and his ear training keep pace with his power of execution, and seem to do away with the deadly dreariness of 'practising.'

Handicrafts and Drills.—It is not possible to do more than mention two more important subjects—the Handicrafts and Drills—which should form a regular part of a child's daily life. For physical training nothing is so good as Ling's Swedish Drill, and a few of the early exercises are the reach of children under nine. Dancing, and the various musical drills, lend themselves to grace of movement, and give more pleasure, if less scientific training, to the little people.

The Handicrafts best fitted for children under nine seem to me to be chair-caning, carton-work, basket-work, Smyrna rugs, Japanese curtains, carving in cork, samplers on coarse canvas showing a variety of stitches, easy needlework, knitting (big needles and wool), etc. The points to be borne in mind in children's handicrafts are: (a) that they should not be employed in making futilities such as pea and stick work, paper mats, and the like; (b) that they should be taught slowly and carefully what they are to do; (c) that slipshod work should not allowed; (d) and that, therefore, the children's work should be kept well within their compass.

May I hope, in concluding this short review of the subjects proper for a child's intellectual education, that enough has been said to show the necessity of grave consideration on the mother's part before she allows promiscuous little lesson-books to be put into the hands of her children, or trust ill-qualified persons to strike out methods of teaching for themselves?

Part VI

The Will—The Conscience—The Divine Life in the Child

I.—The Will

Government of Mansoul.—We have now to consider a subject of unspeakable importance to every being called upon to sustain a reasonable life here, with the hope of the fuller life hereafter; I mean, the government of the kingdom of Mansoul. Every child who lives long enough in the world is invested, by degrees, with this high function, and it is the part of his parents to instruct him in his duties, and to practise him in his tasks. Now, the government of this kingdom of Mansoul is, like that of some well-ordered states, carried on in three chambers, each chamber with its own functions, exercised, not by a multitude of counsellors, but by a single minister.

Executive Power vested in the Will.—In the outer of the three chambers sits the Will. Like that Roman centurion, he has soldiers under him: he says to this man, Go, and he Goeth; to another, Come, and he cometh; to a third, Do this, and he doeth it. In other words, the executive power is vested in the will. If the will have the habit of authority, if it deliver its mandates in the tone that constrains obedience, the kingdom is, at any rate, at unity with itself. If the will be feeble, of uncertain counsels, poor Mansoul is torn with disorder and rebellion.

What is the Will?—I do not know what the will is; it would appear to be an ultimate fact, not admitting of definition: but there are few subjects on which those who have the education of children in their hands make more injurious mistakes; and therefore it is worth while to consider, as we may, what are the functions of the will, and what are its limitation.

Persons may go through life without deliberate act of Will.—In the first place, the will does not necessarily come into play in any of the aspects in which we have hitherto considered the child. He may reflect and imagine; be stirred by the desire of knowledge, of power, of distinction; may love and esteem; may form habits of attention, obedience, diligence, sloth, involuntarily—that is, without ever intending, purposing, willing these things for himself. So far is this true, that there are people who live through their lives without an act of deliberate will: amiable, easy-going people, on the one hand, hedged in by favouring circumstances; and poor souls, on the other, whom circumstances have not saved, who have drifted from their moorings, and are hardly to be named by those to whom they belong. Great intellectual powers by no means imply a controlling will. We read how Coleridge had to be taken care of, because he had so little power of willing. His thoughts were as little under his own volition as his actions, and the fine talk people went to hear was no more than an endless pouring forth of ideas connected by no other link than that of association; though so fine was his mind, that his ideas flowed methodically—of their own accord, so to speak.

Character the Result of Conduct regulated by Will.—It is not necessary to say a word about the dignity and force of character which a confirmed will gives to its possessors. In fact, character is the result of conduct regulated by will. We say, So-and-so has a great deal of character, such another is without character; and we might express the fact equally by saying, So-and-so has a vigorous will, such another has no force of will. We all know of lives, rich in gifts and graces, which have been wrecked for the lack of a determining will.

Three Functions of the Will.—The will is the controller of the passions and emotions, the director of the desires, the ruler of the appetites. But observe, the passions, the desires, the appetites, are there already, and the will gathers force and vigour only as it is exercised in the repression and direction of these; for though the will appears to be of purely spiritual nature, yet it behaves like any member of the body in this—that it becomes vigorous and capable in proportion as it is duly nourished and fitly employed.

A Limitation of the Will disregarded by some Novelists.—The villain of a novel, it is true, is, or rather used to be, an interesting person, because he was always endowed with a powerful will, which acted, not in controlling his violent passions, but in aiding and abetting them: the result was a diabolical being out of the common way of nature. And no wonder, for, according to natural law, the member which does not fulfil its own functions is punished by loss of power; if it does not cease to be, it becomes as though it were not; and the will, being placed in the seat of authority, is not able to carry its forces over to the mob—the disorder would be too fearful; just as when the executive powers of a state are seized upon by a riotous mob, and there are shootings in the highways and hangings from the lanterns, infinite confusion everywhere.

Parents fall into this Metaphysical Blunder.—I am anxious to bring before you this limitation of the will to its own proper functions, because parents often enough fall into the very metaphysical blunder we have seen in the novel-writer. They admire a vigorous will, and rightly. They know that if their child is to make his mark in the world, it must be by force of will. What follows? The baby screams himself into fits for a forbidden plaything, and the mother says, 'He has such a strong will.' The little fellow of three stands roaring in the street, and will neither go hither or thither with his nurse, because 'he has such a strong will.' He will rule the sports of the nursery, will monopolise his sisters' playthings, all because of this 'strong will.' Now we come to a divergence of opinion: on the one hand, the parents decide that, whatever the consequence, the child's will is not to be broken, so all his vagaries must go unchecked; on the other, the decision is, that the child's will must be broken at all hazards, and the poor little being is subjected to a dreary round of punishment and repression.

Wilfulness indicates want of Will Power.—But, all the time, nobody perceives that it is the mere want of will that is the matter with the child. He is in a state of absolute 'wilfulness,'—the rather unfortunate word we use to describe the state in which the will has no controlling power; willessness, if there were such a word, would describe this state more truly. Now, this confusion, in the minds of many persons, between the state of wilfulness and that of being dominated by will, leads to mischievous results even where wilfulness is not fostered nor the child unduly repressed: it leads to the neglect of the due cultivation and training of the will, that almost divine possession, upon the employment of which every other gift, be it beauty or genius, strength or skill, depends for its value.

What is Wilfulness?—What, then, is wilfulness, if it be not an exercise of will? Simply this: remove bit and bridle—that is, the control of the will—from the appetites, the desires, the emotions, and the child who has mounted his hobby, be it resentment, jealousy, desire of power, desire of property, is another Mazeppa, borne along with the speed of the swift and the strength of the strong, and with no power at all to help himself. Appetite, passion, there is no limit to their power and their persistence if the appointed check be removed; and it is this impetus of appetite or of passion, this apparent determination to go in one way and no other, which is called wilfulness and mistaken for an exercise of will. Whereas the determination is only apparent; the child is, in fact, hurried along without resistance, because that opposing force which should give balance to his character is undeveloped and untrained.

The Will has Superior and Inferior Functions.—The will has its superior and its inferior, what may be called its moral and its mechanical, functions; and that will which, for want of practice, has grown flaccid and feeble in the exercise of it higher functions, may yet be able for the ordering of such matters as going or coming, sitting or standing, speaking or refraining from speech.

The Will not a Moral Faculty.—Again, though it is impossible to attain moral excellence of character without the agency of a vigorous will, the will itself is not a moral faculty, and a man may attain great strength of will in consequence of continued efforts in the repression or direction of his appetites or desires, and yet be an unworthy man; that is, he may be keeping himself in order from unworthy motives, for the sake of appearances, for his own interest, even for the injury of another.

A Disciplined Will necessary to Heroic Christian Character.—Once again, though a disciplined will is not a necessary condition of the Christian life, it is necessary to the development of the heroic Christian character. A Gordon, a Havelock, a Florence Nightingale, a St. Paul, could not be other than a person of vigorous will. In this respect, as in all others, Christianity reaches the feeblest souls. There is a wonderful Guido 'Magdalen' in the Louvre, with a mouth which has plainly never been set to any resolve for good or ill—a lower face moulded by the helpless following of the inclination of the moment; but you look up to the eyes, which are raised to meet the gaze of eyes not shown in the picture, and the countenance is transfigured, the whole face is aglow with a passion of service, love, and self-surrender. All this the divine grace may accomplish in weak unwilling souls, and then they will do what they can; but their power of service is limited by their past. Not so the child of the Christian mother, whose highest desire is to train him for the Christian life. When he wakes to the consciousness of whose he is and whom he serves, she would have him ready for that high service, with every faculty in training—a man of war from his youth; above all, with an effective will, to will and to do of His good pleasure.

The sole Practical Faculty of Man.—Before we consider how to train this 'sole practical faculty of man,' we must know how the will operates—how it manages the ordering of all that is done and thought in the kingdom of Mansoul. "Can't you make yourself do what you wish to do?" says Guy, in the Heir of Redclyffe [by Mary Charlotte Yonge], to poor Charlie Edmonston, who has never been in the habit of making himself do anything. There are those, no doubt, who have not even arrived at wishing, but most of us desire to do well; what we want to know is, how to make ourselves do what we desire. And here is the line which divides the effective from the non-effective people, the great from the small, the good from the well-intentioned and respectable; it is in proportion as a man has self-controlling, self-compelling power that he his able to do, even of his own pleasure; that he can depend upon himself, and be sure of his own action in emergencies.

How the Will operates.—Now, how does this autocrat of the bosom behave? Is it with a stern 'Thou shalt,' 'Thou shalt not,' that the subject man is coerced into obedience? By no means. Is it by a plausible show of reasons, mustering of motives? Not this either. Since Mr. John Stuart Mill taught us that "all that man does, or can do, with matter" is to "move one thing to or from another," we need not be surprised if great moral results are brought about by what seem inadequate means; and a little bit of nursery experience will show better than much talking what is possible to the will. A baby falls, gets a bad bump, and cries piteously. The experienced nurse does not "kiss the place to make it well," or show any pity for the child's trouble—that would make matters worse; the more she pities, the more he sobs. She hastens to 'change his thoughts,' so she says; she carries him to the window to see the horses, gives him his pet picture-book, his dearest toy, and the child pulls himself up in the middle of a sob, though he is really badly hurt. Now this, of the knowing nurse, is precisely the part the will plays towards the man. It is by force of will that a man can 'change his thoughts,' transfer his attention from one subject of thought to another, and that, with a shock of mental force of which he is indistinctly conscious. And this is enough to save a man and to make a man, this power of making himself think only of those things which he has beforehand decided that it is good to think upon.

The Way of the Will—Incentives.—His thoughts are wandering on forbidden pleasure, to the hindrance of his work; he pulls himself up, and deliberately fixes his attention on those incentives which have most power to make him work, the leisure and pleasure which follow honest labour, the duty which binds him to the fulfilling of his task. His thoughts run in the groove he wills them to run in, and work is no longer an effort.

Diversion.—Again, some slight affront has called up a flood of resentful feeling: So-and-so should not have done it, he had no right, it was mean, and so on, through all the hard things we are ready enough to say in our hearts of an offender against our amour propre. But the man under the control of his own will does not allow this to go on: he does not fight it out with himself, and say, 'This is very wrong in me. So-and-so is not so much to blame, after all.' He is not ready for that yet; but he just compels himself to think of something else—the last book he has read, the next letter he must write, anything interesting enough to divert his thoughts. When he allows himself to go back to the cause of offence, behold, all rancour is gone, and he is able to look at the matter with the coolness of a third person. And this is true, not only of the risings of resentment, but of every temptation that besets the flesh and spirit.

Change of Thought.—Again, the sameness of his duties, the weariness of doing the same thing over and over, fills him with disgust and despondency, and he relaxes his efforts;—but not if he be a man under the power of his own will, because he simply does not allow himself in idle discontent; it is always within his power to give himself something pleasant, something outside of himself, to think of, and he does so; and, given what we call a 'happy frame of mind,' no work is laborious.

The Way of the Will should be taught to Children.—It is something to know what to do with ourselves when we are beset, and the knowledge of this way of the will is so far the secret of a happy life, that it is well worth imparting to the children. Are you cross? Change your thoughts. Are you tired of trying? Change your thoughts. Are you craving for things you are not to have? Change your thoughts; there is a power within you, your own will, which will enable you to turn your attention from thoughts that make you unhappy and wrong, to thoughts that make you happy and right. And this is the exceedingly simple way in which the will acts; this is the sole secret of the power over himself which the strong man wields—he can compel himself to think of what he chooses, and will not allow himself in thoughts that breed mischief.

Power of Will implies Power of Attention.—But you perceive that, though the will is all-powerful within certain limits, these are but narrow limits after all. Much must go before and along with a vigorous will if it is to be a power in the ruling of conduct. For instance, the man must have acquired the habit of attention, the great importance of which we have already considered. There are bird-witted people, who have no power of thinking connectedly for five minutes under any pressure, from within or from without. If they have never been trained to apply the whole of their mental faculties to a given subject, why, no energy of will, supposing they had it, which is impossible, could make them think steadily thoughts of their own choosing or of anyone else's. Here is how the parts of the intellectual fabric dovetail: power of will implies power of attention; and before the parent can begin to train the will of the child, he must have begun to form in him the habit of attention.

Habit may Frustrate the Will.—Again, we have already considered the fatal facility in evil, the impulse towards good, which habit gives. Habit is either the ally or the opponent, too often the frustrator, of the will. The unhappy drunkard does will with what strength there is in him; he turns away the eyes of his mind from beholding his snare; he plies himself assiduously with other thoughts; but alas, his thoughts will only run in the accustomed groove of desire, and habit is too strong for his feeble will. We all know something of this struggle between habit and will in less vital matters. Who is without some dilatory, procrastinating, in some way tiresome, habit, which is in almost daily struggle with the rectified will? But I have already said so much about the duty of parents to ease the way of their children by laying down for them the lines of helpful habits, that it is unnecessary to say a word more here of habit as an ally or a hinderer of will.

Reasonable Use of so effective an Instrument.—And, once more, only the man of cultivated reason is capable of being ruled by a well-directed will. If his understanding does not show good cause why he should do some solid reading every day, why he should cling to the faith of his fathers, why he should take up his duties as a citizen,—the movement of his will will be feeble and fluctuating, and very barren of results. And, indeed, worse may happen: he may take up some wrong-headed, or even vicious, notion and work a great deal of mischief by what he feels to be a virtuous effort of will. The parent may venture to place the power of will in the hands of his child only in so far as he trains him to make a reasonable use of so effective an instrument.

How to Strengthen the Will.—One other limitation of the will we shall consider presently; but supposing the parent take pains that the child shall be in a fit state to use his will, how is he to strengthen that will, so that by and by the child may employ it to control his own life by? We have spoken already of the importance of training the child in the habit of obedience. Now, obedience is valuable only in so far as it helps the child towards making himself do that which he knows he ought to do. Every effort of obedience which does not give him a sense of conquest over his own inclinations, helps to enslave him, he will resent the loss of his liberty by running into license when he can. That is the secret of the miscarrying of many strictly brought-up children. But invite his co-operation, let him heartily intend and purpose to do the thing he is bidden, and then it is his own will that is compelling him, and not yours; he has begun the greatest effort, the highest accomplishment of human life—the making, the compelling of himself. Let him know what he is about, let him enjoy a sense of triumph, and of your congratulation, whenever he fetches his thoughts back to his tiresome sum, whenever he makes his hands finish what they have begun, whenever he throws the black dog off his back, and produces a smile from a clouded face.

Habit of Self-management.—Then, as was said before, let him know the secret of willing; let him know that, by an effort of will, he can turn his thoughts to the thing he wants to think of—his lessons, his prayers, his work, and away from the things he should not think of;—that, in fact, he can be such a brave strong little fellow, he can make himself think of what he likes; and let him try little experiments—that if he once get his thoughts right, the rest will take care of itself, he will be sure to do right then; that if he feels cross, naughty thoughts coming upon him, the plan is, to think hard about something else, something nice—his next birthday, what he means to do when he is a man. Not all this at once, of course; but line upon line, precept upon precept, here a little and there a little, as opportunity offers. Let him get into the habit of managing himself, controlling himself, and it is astonishing how much self-compelling power quite a young child will exhibit. "Restrain yourself, Tommy," I once heard a wise aunt say to a boy of four, and Tommy restrained himself, though he was making a terrible hullabaloo about some small trouble.

Education of the Will more important than that of the Intellect.—All this time, the will of the child is being both trained and strengthened; he is learning how and when to use his will, and it is becoming every day more vigorous and capable. Let me add one or two wise thoughts from Dr. Morell's Introduction to Mental Philosophy: "The education of the will is really of far greater importance, as shaping the destiny of the individual, than that of the intellect. . . . Theory and doctrine, and inculcation of laws and propositions, will never of themselves lead to the uniform habit of right action. It is by doing, that we learn to do; by overcoming, that we learn to overcome; and every right act which we cause to spring out of pure principles, whether by authority, precept, or example, will have a greater weight in the formation of character than all the theory in the world."

II.—The Conscience

Conscience is Judge and Lawgiver.—But the will by no means carries on the government of the kingdom of Mansoul single-handed. True, the will wields the executive power; it is only by willing we are enabled to do; but there is a higher power behind, whose mandate the will does no more than express. Conscience sits supreme in the inner chamber. Conscience is the lawgiver, and utters the 'Thou shalt' and the 'Thou shalt not' whereon the will takes action; the judge, too, before whom the offending soul is summoned; and from the 'Thou art the man' of conscience, there is no appeal.

'I am, I ought, I can, I will.'—'I am, I ought, I can, I will'—these are the steps of that ladder of St. Augustine, whereby we

> "rise on stepping stones
> Of our dead selves to higher things."

'I am'—we have the power of knowing ourselves. "I ought'—we have within us a moral judge, to whom we feel ourselves subject, and who points out and requires of us our duty. 'I can'—we are conscious of power to do that which we perceive we ought to do. 'I will'—we determine to exercise that power with a volition which is in itself a step in the execution of that which we will. Here is a beautiful and perfect chain, and the wonder is that, so exquisitely constituted as he is for right-doing, error should be even possible to man. But of the sorrowful mysteries of sin and temptation it is not my place to speak here; you will see that it is because of the possibilities of ruin and loss which lie about every human life that I am pressing upon parents the duty of saving their children by the means put into their hands. Perhaps it is not too much to say, that ninety-nine out of a hundred lost lives lie at the door of parents who took no pains to deliver them from sloth, from sensual appetites, from willfulness, no pains to fortify them with the habits of a good life.

Inertness of Parents not supplemented by Divine Grace.—We live in a redeemed world, and infinite grace and help from above attend every rightly directed effort in the training of the children; but I do not see much ground for hoping that divine grace will step in as a substitute for any and every power we choose to leave unused or misdirected. In the physical world, we do not expect miracles to make up for our neglect of the use of means; the rickety body, the misshapen limb, for which the child has to thank his parents, remain with him through life, however much else he may have to thank God for; and a feeble will, bad habits, an uninstructed conscience, stick by many a Christian man through his life, because his parents failed in their duty to him, and he has not had force enough in himself to supply their omission.

Conscience not an Infallible Guide.—In this matter of conscience, for instance, the laissez-faire habit of his parents is the cause of real wrong and injury to many a child. The parents are thankful to believe that their child is born with a conscience; they hope his conduct may be ruled thereby: and the rest they leave; the child and his conscience may settle it between them. Now this is to suppose, either that a fully-informed conscience is born into an infant body, or that it grows, like the hair and the limbs, with the growth of the body, and is not subject to conditions of spiritual progress proper to itself. In other words, it is to suppose that conscience is an infallible guide, a delusion people cling to in spite of common sense and of everyday experience of the wrong-headed things men do from conscientious motives. The vagaries of the uninstructed conscience are so familiar as to have given rise to popular proverbs: 'Honour among thieves,' 'To strain out the gnat and swallow the camel,' point to cases of misguided conscience; while 'The wish is father to the thought,' 'None is so blind as he who won't see,' point to the still more common cases, in which a man knowingly tricks his conscience into acquiescence.

But a real Power.—Then, if conscience be not an infallible guide—if it pass blindfold by heinous offences, and come down heavily upon some mere quibble, tithing mint, rue, and all manner of herbs, and neglecting the weightier matters of the law—if conscience be liable to be bamboozled, persuaded into calling evil good and good evil, when Desire is the special pleader before the bar, where is its use, this broken reed? Is this stern law-giver of the breast no more, after all, than a fiction of the brain? Is your conscience no more than what you happen to think about your own actions and those of other people? On the contrary, these aberrations of conscience are perhaps the strongest proof that it exists as a real power. As Adam Smith has well said, "The supreme authority of conscience is felt and tacitly acknowledged by the worst, no less than by the best, of men; for even they who have thrown off all hypocrisy with the world, are at pains to conceal their real character from their own eyes."

That Spiritual Sense whereby we know Good and Evil.—What conscience is, how far it lies in the feelings, how far in the reason, how far it is independent of both, are obscure questions which it is not necessary for practical purposes to settle; but this much is evident—that conscience is as essential a part of human nature as are the affections and the reason, and that conscience is that spiritual sense whereby we have knowledge of good and evil. The six-months-old child who cannot yet speak exhibits the workings of conscience; a reproving look will make him drop his eyes and hide his face. But, observe, the mother may thus cover him with confusion by way of an experiment when the child is all sweetness, and the poor little untutored conscience rises all the same, and condemns him on the word of another.

Facts like this afford a glimpse of the appalling responsibility that lies upon parents. The child comes into the world with a moral faculty, a delicate organ whereby he discerns the flavour of good and evil, and at the same time has a perception of delight in the good—in himself or others,—of loathing and abhorrence of the evil. But, poor little child, he is like a navigator who does not know how to box his compass. He is born to love the good, and to hate the evil, but he has no real knowledge of what is good and what is evil; what intuitions he has, he puts no faith in, but yields himself in simplicity to the steering of others. The wonder that Almighty God can endure so far to leave the very making of an immortal being in the hands of human parents is only matched by the wonder that human parents can accept this divine trust with hardly a thought of its significance.

A Child's Conscience Undeveloped Capability rather than a Supreme Authority.— Looking, then, upon conscience in the child rather as an undeveloped capability than as a supreme authority, the question is, how is this nascent lord of the life to be educated up to its high functions of informing the will and decreeing the conduct? For though the ill-taught conscience may make fatal blunders, and a man may carry slaughter amongst the faithful because his conscience bids; yet, on the other hand, no man ever attained a godly, righteous, and sober life except as he was ruled by a good conscience—a conscience with not only the capacity to discern good and evil, but trained to perceive the qualities of the two. Many man may have the great delicacy of taste which should qualify him for a tea-taster, but it is only as he has trained experience in the qualities of teas that his nice taste is valuable to his employers, and a source of income to himself.

The Uninstructed Conscience.—As with that of the will, so with the education of the conscience; it depends upon much that has gone before. Refinement of conscience cannot coexist with ignorance. The untutored savage has his scruples that we cannot enter into; we cannot understand to this day how it was that the horrors of the Indian Mutiny arose from the mere suspicion that mixture of hog's lard and beef fat had been used to grease the cartridges dealt out to the Sepoys. Those scruples which are beyond the range of our ideas we call superstitions and prejudices, and are unwilling to look upon conduct as conscientious, even when prompted by the uninstructed conscience, unless in so far as it is reasonable and right in itself.

The Processes implied in a 'Conscientious' Decision.—Therefore, it is plain that before conscience is in a position to pronounce its verdict on the facts of a given case, the cultivated reason must review the pros and cons; the practiced judgment must balance these, deciding which have the greater weight. Attention must bring all the powers of the mind to bear on the question; habits of right action must carry the feelings, must make right-doing seem the easier and the pleasanter. In the meantime, desire is clamorous; but conscience, the unbiased judge, duly informed in full court of the merits of the case, decides for the right. The will carries out the verdict of conscience; upon the verdicts of conscience is the conscientious man, of whose actions and opinions you may be sure beforehand, and then what becomes of these elaborate proceedings? That is just the advantage of an instructed conscience backed by a trained intelligence; the judge is always sitting, the counsel always on the spot.

The Instructed Conscience nearly always right.—Here is, indeed, a high motive for the all-round training of the child's intelligence; he wants the highest culture you can give him, backed by carefully formed habits, in order that he may have a conscience always alert, supported by every power of the mind; and such a conscience is the very flower of a noble life. The instructed conscience may claim to be, if not infallible, at any rate nearly always right. It is not generally mature until the man is mature; young people, however right-minded and earnest, are apt to err, chiefly because they fix their attention too much upon some one duty, some one theory of life, at the expense of much besides.

The Good Conscience of a Child.—But even the child, with the growing conscience and the growing powers, is able to say, 'No, I can't; it would not be right'; 'Yes, I will; for it is right.' And once able to give either of these answers to the solicitations that assail him, the child is able to live; for the rest, the development, and what may be called the adjustment, of conscience will keep pace with his intellectual growth. But allowing that a great deal of various discipline must go to secure that final efflorescence of a good conscience, what is to be done by way of training the conscience itself, quickening the spiritual taste so that the least soupçon [suspicion] of evil is detected and rejected?

Children play with Moral Questions.—There is no part of education more nice and delicate than this, nor any in which grown-up people are more apt to blunder. Everyone knows how tiresome it is to discuss any nice moral question with children; how they quibble, suggest a hundred ingenious explanations or evasions, fail to be shocked or to admire in the right place—in fact, play with the whole question; or, what is more tiresome still, are severe and righteous overmuch, and 'deal damnation round' with much heartiness and goodwill. Sensible parents are often distressed at this want of conscience in the children; but they are not greatly in fault; the mature conscience demands to be backed up by the mature intellect, and the children have neither the one nor the other. Discussions of the kind should be put down; the children should not be encouraged to give their opinions on questions of right and wrong, and little books should not be put into their hands which pronounce authoritatively upon conduct.

The Bible the Chief Source of Moral Ideas.—It would be well if the reticence of the Bible in this respect were observed by the writers of children's books, whether of story or history. The child hears the history of Joseph (with reservations) read from the Bible, which rarely offers comment or explanation. He does not need to be told what was 'naughty' and what was 'good'; there is no need to press home the teaching, or the Bible were written in vain, and good and bad actions carry no witness with them. Let all the circumstances of the daily Bible reading—the consecutive reading, from the first chapter of Genesis onwards, with necessary omissions—be delightful to the child; let him be in his mother's room, in his mother's arms; let that quarter of an hour be one of sweet leisure and sober gladness, the child's whole interest being allowed to go to the story without distracting moral considerations; and then, the less talk the better; the story will sink in, and bring its own teaching, a little now, and more every year as he is able to bear it.

Once such story will be in him a constantly growing, fructifying moral idea.

Tales fix attention upon Conduct.—The Bible (the fitting parts of it, that is) first and supreme; but any true picture of life, whether a tale of golden deeds or of faulty and struggling human life, brings aliment to the growing conscience. The child gets into the habit of fixing his attention on conduct; actions are weighed by him, at first, by their consequences, but by degrees his conscience acquires discriminating power, and such and such behavior is bad or good to him whatever its consequences. And this silent growth of the moral faculty takes place all the more surely if the distraction of chatter on the subject is avoided; for a thousand small movements of vanity and curiosity and mere love of talk are easily called into play, and these take off the attention from the moral idea which should be conveyed to the conscience. It is very important, again, that the child should not be allowed to condemn the conduct of the people about him. Whether he is right or wrong in him verdict, is not the question; the habit of bestowing blame will certainly blunt his conscience, deaden his sensibility to the injunction, "Judge not, that ye be not judged."

Ignorance of a Child's Conscience.—But the child's own conduct: surely he may be called upon to look into that? His conduct, including his words, yes; but his motives, no; nothing must be done to induce the evil habit of introspection. Also, in setting the child to consider his ways, regard must be had to the extreme ignorance of the childish conscience, a degree of ignorance puzzling to grown-up people when they chance to discover it, which is not often, for the children, notwithstanding their endless chatter and their friendly, loving ways, live very much to themselves. They commit serious offences against truth, modesty, love, and do not know that they have done wrong, while some absurd featherweight of transgression oppresses their souls. Children will bite and hurt one another viciously, commit petty thefts, do such shocking things that their parents fear they must have very bad natures: it is not necessarily so; it is simply that the untaught conscience sees no clear boundary line between right and wrong, and is as apt to err on the one side as the other. I once saw a dying child of twelve who was wearing herself out with her great distress because she feared she had committed 'the unpardonable sin,' so she said (how she picked up the phrase nobody knew); and that was—that she had been saying her prayers without even kneeling up in bed! The ignorance of children about the commonest matters of right and wrong is really pathetic; and yet they are too often treated as if they knew all about it, because 'they have consciences,' as if conscience were any more than a spiritual organ waiting for direction!

Instructing the Conscience—Kindness.—That the children do wrong knowingly is another matter, and requires, alas, no proving; all I am pressing for is the real need there exists to instruct them in their duty; and this, not at all haphazard, but regularly and progressively. Kindness, for instance, is, let us say, the subject of instruction this week. There is one of the talks with their mother that the children love—a short talk is best—about kindness. Kindness is love, showing itself in act and word, look and manner. A well of love, shut up and hidden in a little boy's heart, does not do anybody much good; the love must bubble up as a spring, flow out in a stream, and then it is kindness. Then will follow short daily talks about kind ways, to brothers and sisters, to playmates, to parents, to grown-up friends, to servants, to people in pain and trouble, to dumb creatures, to people we do not see but yet can think about—all in distress, the heathen. Give the children one thought at a time, and every time some lovely example of loving-kindness that will fire their hearts with the desire to do likewise.

Take our Lord's parable of the 'Good Samaritan' for a model of instruction in morals. Let tale and talk make the children emulous of virtue, and then give them the "Go and do likewise," the law. Having presented to them the idea of kindness in many aspects, end with the law: Be kind, or, "Be kindly affectioned one to another." Let them know that this is the law of God for children and for grown-up people. Now, conscience is instructed, the feelings are enlisted on the side of duty, and if the child is brought up, it is for breaking the law of kindness, a law that he knows of, that his conscience convicts him in the breaking. Do not give children deterrent examples of error, because of the sad proclivities of human nature, but always tell them of beautiful 'Golden Deeds,' small and great, that shall stir them as trumpet-calls to the battle of life.

The Conscience made effective by Discipline.—Be courteous, be candid, be grateful, be considerate, be true; there are aspects of duty enough to occupy the attention of mother and child for every day of the child-life; and all the time, the idea of duty is being formed, and conscience is being educated and developed. At the same time, the mother exercises the friendly vigilance of a guardian angel, being watchful, not to catch the child tripping, but to guide him into the acting out of the duty she has already made lovely in his eyes; for it is only as we do that we learn to do, and become strong in the doing. As she instructs her child in duty, she teaches him to listen to the voice of conscience as to the voice of God, a 'Do this,' or 'Do it not,' within the breast, to be obeyed with full assurance. It is objected that we are making infallible, not the divinely implanted conscience, but that same conscience made effective by discipline. It is even so; in every department of life, physical or spiritual, human effort appears to be the condition of the Divine energizing; there must be a stretching forth of the withered arm before it receives strength; and we have every reason to believe that the instructedconscience, being faithfully followed, is divinely illuminated.

III. The Divine Life In The Child

"The very Pulse of the Machine."—It is evident we have not yet reached

"The very pulse of the machine."

Habits, feeling, reason, conscience—we have followed these into the inmost recesses of the child's life; each acts upon the other, but what acts upon the last: what acts upon them all? "It is," says a writer who has searched into the deep things of God—"it is a King that our spirits cry for, to guide them, discipline them, unite them to each other; to give them a victory over themselves, a victory over the world. It is a Priest that our spirits cry out for, to lift them above themselves to their God and Father,—to make them partakers of his nature, fellow-workers in one authentic testimony that He is both the Priest and King of Men." [Maurice, Sermons on Sacrifice.] [Possibly The Doctrine of Sacrifice by John Frederick Denison Maurice, (1805–1872), whom Charles Kingsley called 'the most beautiful human soul whom God has ever allowed me to meet with.']

Parents have some Power to Enthrone the King.—Conscience, we have seen, is effective only as it is moved from within, from that innermost chamber of Mansoul, that Holy of Holies, the secrets of which are only known to the High-Priest, who "needed not that any man should tell Him, for He knew what was in man." It is necessary, however, that we should gather up crumbs of fact and inference and set in order such knowledge as we have; for the keys even of this innermost chamber are placed in the hands of parents, and it is a great deal in their power to enthrone the King, to induct the Priest, that every human cries for.

The Functions and Life of the Soul.—We take it for granted in common speech that every soul is a 'living soul,' a fully developed, full-grown soul; but the language of the Bible and that of general experience seem to point to startling conclusions. It has been said of a great poet—with how much justice is not the question here—that if we could suppose any human being to be made without a soul, he was such an abortive attempt; for while he had reason, imagination, passions, all the appetites and desires of an intelligent being, he appeared to exercise not one of the functions of the soul. Now, what are these functions, the suspension of which calls the very existence of a man's soul in question? We must go back to the axiom of Augustine—"The soul of man is for God, as God is for the soul." The soul has one appetite, for the things of God; breathes one air, the breath, the Spirit of God; has one desire, for the knowledge of God; one only joy, in the face of God. "I want to live in the Light of a Countenance which never ceases to smile upon me," [Christmas Day, and other Sermons] is the language of the soul. The direct action of the soul is all Godward, with a reflex action towards men. The speech of the soul is prayer and praise, the right hand of the soul is faith, the light of the soul is love, the love of God shed abroad upon it. Observe, these are the functions, this, the life of the soul, the only functions, the only life it can have: if it have not these, it has no power to turn aside and find the "life of its hand" elsewhere. As the conscience, the will, the reason, is ineffective till it be nourished with its proper food, exercised in its proper functions, so of the soul; and its chamber is dull, with cobwebbed doors and clouded windows, until it awake to its proper life; not quite empty, though, for there is the nascent soul; and the awakening into life takes place, sometimes with the sudden shock, the gracious miracle, which we call conversion; sometimes, when the parents so will, the soul of the child expands with a gentle, sweet growth and gradual unfolding as of a flower. There are torpid souls, which are yet alive; there are feeble, sickly souls, which are yet alive; and there are souls which no movement Godward ever quickens.

What is the Life of the Soul?—This life of the soul, what is it? Communicated life, as when one lights a torch at the fire? Perhaps; but it is something more intimate, more unspeakable: "I am the Life"; "In Him was life, and the life was the light of men"; "Abide in Me and I in you." The truth is too ineffable to be uttered in any words but those given to us. But it means this, at least, that the living soul does not abide alone in its place; that place becomes the temple of the living God. "Surely the Lord is in this place, and I knew it not. How dreadful is this place!"

The Parent must present the idea of God to the Soul of the Child.—But this holy mystery, this union and communion of God and the soul, how may human parents presume to meddle with it? What can they do? How can they promote it? and is there not every risk that they may lay rude hands upon the ark? In the first place, it does not rest with the parent to choose whether he will or will not attempt to quicken and nourish this divine life in his child. To do so this is his bounden duty and service. If he neglect or fail in this, I am not sure how much it matters that he has fulfilled his duties in the physical, moral and mental culture of his child, except in so far as the child is the fitter for the divine service should the divine life be awakened in him. But what can the parent do? Just this, and no more: he can present the idea of God to the soul of the child. Here, as throughout his universe, Almighty God works by apparently inadequate means. Who would say that a bee can produce apple trees? Yet a bee flies from an apple tree laden with the pollen of its flowers: this it unwittingly deposits on the stigmas of the flowers of the next tree it comes to. The bee goes, but the pollen remains, but with all the length of the style between it and the immature ovule below. That does not matter; the ovule has no power to reach the pollen grain, but the latter sends forth a slender tube, within the tube of the style; the ovule is reached; behold, then, the fruit, with its seed, and, if you like, future apple trees! Accept the parable: the parent is little better in this matter than the witless bee; it is his part to deposit, so to speak, within reach of the soul of the child some fruitful idea of God; the immature soul makes no effort towards that idea, but the living Word reaches down, touches the soul,—and there is life; growth and beauty, flower and fruit.

Must not make Blundering Efforts.—I venture to ask you to look, for once, at these divine mysteries from the same philosophical standpoint we have taken up in regarding all the capabilities and functions of the child, partly, because it is instructive to see how the mysteries of the religious life appear when it is looked at from without its own sphere; partly, because I wish to rise by unbroken steps to the supreme function of the parent in the education of his child. For here the similitude of the bee and the apple tree fails. The parent must not make blundering, witless efforts: as this is the highest duty imposed upon him, it is also the most delicate; and he will have infinite need of faith and prayer, tact and discretion, humility, gentleness, love, and sound judgement, if he would present his child to God, and the thought of God to the soul of his child.

God presented to Children as an Exactor and a Punisher.—"If we think of God as an exactor and not a giver," it has been well said, "exactors and not givers shall we become." Yet is not this the light in which God is most commonly set before the children— a Pharoah demanding his tale of bricks, bricks of good behaviour and right-doing? Do not parents deliberately present God as an exactor, to back up the feebleness of their own government; and do they not freely utter, on the part of God, threats they would be unwilling to utter on their own part? Again, what child has not heard from his nurse this, delivered with much energy, 'God does not love you, you naughty boy! He will send you to the bad place!' And these two thoughts of God, as an exactor and a punisher, make up, often enough, all the idea the poor child gets of his Father in heaven. What fruit can come of this but aversion, the turning away of the child from the face of his Father? What if, instead, were given to him the thought well expressed in the words, "The all-forgiving gentleness of God"?

Parents must select Inspiring Ideas.—These are but two of many deterrent thoughts of God commonly presented to the tender soul; and the mother, who realizes that the heart of her child may be irrevocably turned against God by the ideas of Him imbibed in the nursery, will feel the necessity for grave and careful thought, and definite resolve, as to what teaching her child shall receive on this momentous subject. She will most likely forbid any mention of the Divine Name to the children, except by their parents, explaining at the same time that she does so because she cares so much that her children should get none but right thoughts on this great matter. It is better that children should receive a few vital ideas that their souls may grow than a great deal of indefinite teaching.

We must Teach only what we Know.—How to select these few quickening thoughts of the infinite God? The selection is not so difficult to make as would appear at first sight. In the first place, we must teach that which we know, know by the life of the soul, not with any mere knowledge of the mind. Now, of the vast mass of the doctrines and the precepts of religion, we shall find that there are only a few vital truths that we have so taken into our being that we live upon them—this person, these; that person, those; some of us, not more than a single one. One or more, these are the truths we must teach the children, because these will come straight out of our hearts with the enthusiasm of conviction which rarely fails to carry its own idea into the spiritual life of another. There is no more fruitful source of what it is hardly too much to call infant infidelity than the unreal dead words which are poured upon children about the best things, with an artificial solemnity of tone and manner intended to make up for the want of living meaning in the words. Let the parent who only knows one thing from above teach his child that one; more will come to him by the time the child is ready for more.

Fitting and Vital Ideas.—Again, there are some ideas of the spiritual life more proper than others to the life and needs of the child. Thus, Christ the Joy-giver is more to him than Christ the Consoler.

And there are some few ideas which are as the daily bread of the soul, without which life and growth are impossible. All other teaching may be deferred until the child's needs bring him to it; but whoever sends his child out into life without these vital ideas of the spiritual life, sends him forth with a dormant soul, however well-instructed he may be in theology.

The Knowledge of God distinct from Morality.—Again, the knowledge of God is distinct from morality, or what the children call 'being good', though 'being good' follows from that knowledge. But let these come in their right order. Do not bepreach the child to weariness about 'being good' as what he owes to God, without letting in upon him first a little of that knowledge which shall make him good.

We are no longer suffering from an embarrassment of riches; these limitations shut out so much of the ordinary teaching about divine things that the question becomes rather, What shall we teach? than, How shall we choose?

The Times and the Manner of Religious Instruction.—The next considerations that will press upon the mother are of the times, and the manner, of this teaching in the things of God. It is better that these teachings be rare and precious, than too frequent and slighty valued; better not at all, than that the child should be surfeited with the mere sight of spiritual food, rudely served. At the same time, he must be built up in the faith, and his lessons must be regular and progressive; and here everything depends upon the tact of the mother. Spiritual teaching, like the wafted odour of flowers, should depend on which way the wind blows. Every now and then there occurs a holy moment, felt to be holy by mother and child, when the two are together—that is the moment for some deeply felt and softly spoken word about God, such as the occasion gives rise to. Few words need be said, no exhortation at all; just the flash of conviction from the soul of the mother to the soul of the child. Is 'Our Father' the thought thus laid upon the child's soul? there will be, perhaps, no more than a sympathetic meeting of eyes hereafter, between mother and child, over thousand showings forth of 'Our Father's' love; but the idea is growing, becoming part of the child's spiritual life. This is all: no routine of spiritual teaching; a dread of many words, which are apt to smother the fire of the sacred life; much self-restraint shown in the allowing of seeming opportunities to pass; and all the time, earnest purpose of heart, and a definite scheme for the building up of the child in the faith. It need not be added that, to make another use of our Lord's words, "this kind cometh forth only by prayer." It is as the mother gets wisdom liberally from above, that she will be enabled for this divine task.

The Reading of the Bible.—A word about the reading of the Bible. I think we make a mistake in burying the text under our endless comments and applications. Also, I doubt if the picking out of individual verses, and grinding these into the child until they cease to have any meaning for him, is anything but a hindrance to the spiritual life. The Word is full of vital force, capable of applying itself. A seed, light as thistledown, wafted into the child's soul will take root downwards and bear fruit upwards. What is required of us is, that we should implant a love of the Word; that the most delightful moments of the child's day should be those in which his mother reads for him, with sweet sympathy and holy gladness in voice and eyes, the beautiful stories of the Bible; and now and then in the reading will occur one of those convictions, passing from the soul of the mother to the soul of the child, in which is the life of the Spirit. Let the child grow, so that,

"New thoughts of God, new hopes of heaven,"

are a joy to him, too; things to be counted first amongst the blessings of a day. Above all, do not read the Bible at the child: do not let any words of the Scriptures be occasions for gibbeting his faults. It is the office of the Holy Ghost to convince of sin; and He is able to use the Word for this purpose, without risk of that hardening of the heart in which our clumsy dealings too often result.

The matter for this teaching of divine things will come out of every mother's own convictions. I will attempt to speak of only one or two of those vital truths on which the spiritual life must sustain itself.

Father and Giver.—"Our Father, who is in heaven," is perhaps the first idea of God which the mother will present to her child—Father and Giver, straight from whom comes all the gladness of every day. 'What a happy birthday our Father has given to my little boy!' 'The flowers are coming again; our Father has taken care of the life of the plants all through the winter cold!' 'Listen to the skylark! It is a wonder how our Father can put so much joy into the heart of one little bird.' 'Thank God for making my little girl so happy and merry!' Out of this thought comes prayer, the free utterance of the child's heart, more often in thanks for the little joys of the day counted up than in desire, just yet. The words do not matter; any simple form the child can understand will do; the rising Godward of the child-heart is the true prayer. Out of this thought , too, comes duty—the glad acknowledgement of the debt of service and obedience to a Parent so gracious and benign—not One who exacts service at the sword's point, as it were, but One whom His children run to obey.

The Essence of Christianity is Loyalty to a Person.—Christ, our King. Here is a thought to unseal the fountains of love and loyalty, the treasures of faith and imagination, bound up in the child. The very essence of Christianity is personal loyalty, passionate loyalty to our adorable Chief. We have laid other foundations—regeneration, sacraments, justification, works, faith, the Bible—any one of which, however necessary to salvation in its due place and proportion may become a religion about Christ and without Christ. And now a time of sifting has come upon us, and thoughtful people decline to know anything about our religious systems; they write down all our orthodox beliefs as things not knowable. Perhaps this may be because, in thinking much of our salvation, we have put out of sight our King, the divine fact which no soul of man to whom it is presented can ignore. In the idea of Christ is life; let the thought of Him once get touch of the soul, and it rises up, a living power, independent of all formularies of the brain. Let us save Christianity for our children by bringing them into allegiance to Christ, the King. How? How did the old Cavaliers bring up sons and daughters, in passionate loyalty and reverence for not too worthy princes? Their own hearts were full of it; their lips spake it; their acts proclaimed it; the style of their clothes, the ring of their voices, the carriage of their heads—all was one proclamation of boundless devotion to their king and his cause. That civil war, whatever else it did, or missed doing, left a parable for Christian people. If a Stuart prince could command such measure of loyalty, what shall we say of "the Chief amongst ten thousand, the altogether lovely"?

Jesus, our Saviour. Here is a thought to be brought tenderly before the child in the moments of misery that follow wrong-doing. 'My poor little boy, you have been very naughty to-day! Could you not help it?' 'No, mother,' with sobs. 'No, I suppose not; but there is a way of help.' And then the mother tells her child how the Lord Jesus is our Saviour, because He saves us from our sins. It is a matter of question when the child should first learn the 'Story of the Cross.' One thinks it would be very delightful to begin with Moses and the prophets: to go through the Old Testament history, tracing the gradual unfolding of the work and character of the Messiah; and then, when their minds are full of the expectation of the Jews, to bring before them the mystery of the Birth in Bethlehem, the humiliation of the Cross. But perhaps no gain in freshness of presentation would make up to the children for not having grown up with the associations of Calvary and Bethlehem always present to their minds. One thing in this connection: it is not well to allow the children in a careless familiarity with the Name of Jesus, or in the use of hymns whose tone is not reverent. "Ye call Me Master and Lord; and ye say well, for so I am."

The Indwelling of Christ is a thought particularly fit for the children, because their large faith does not stumble at the mystery, their imagination leaps readily to the marvel, that the King Himself should inhabit a little child's heart. 'How am I to know He is come, mother?' 'When you are quite gentle, sweet, and happy, it is because Christ is within,—

> "And when He comes, He makes your face so fair,
>
> Your friends are glad, and say, 'The King is there.'"

I will not attempt to indicate any more of the vital truths which the Christian mother will present to her child; having patience until they blossom and bear, and his soul is as a very fruitful garden which the Lord hath blessed. But, once more, "This kind cometh forth only by prayer."

Appendix
Questions for the Use of Students

Part I: Some Preliminary Considerations

1. Show that children are a public trust. What follows? 2. What questions does Pestalozzi put to mothers? 3. What is Mr Herbert Spencer's argument for the study of education? 4. How do parents usually proceed? 5. What is the strenuous part of a parent's work?

I. A Method of Education

1. Contrast four or five older theories with later and perhaps sounder notions. 2. Point out the opposite characters of a system and a method. 3. Why is a system tempting to parents?

II. The Child's Estate

1. What do the Gospel sayings about children indicate? 2. What are the three commandments of the Gospel code of education?

III. Offending the Children

1. Distinguish between 'offending' and 'despising' children. 2. What is to be said of parents whose children have 'no sense of ought'? 3. Trace the steps by which a mother's 'no' comes to be disregarded. 4. Why must parents themselves be law-compelled? 5. Show that parents may offend their children by disregarding the laws of health. 6. By disregarding the laws of the intellectual life. 7. Of the moral life.

IV. Despising the Children

1. Show that children may be despised in the choice of a nurse. 2. By taking their faults too lightly.

V. Hindering the Children

1. In what ways may parents hinder their children's access to God?

VI. Conditions of Healthy Brain Activity

1. What is the first condition of successful education? 2. Show that daily efforts, intellectual, moral, and physical, are necessary for children. 3. On what principle is the blood-supply regulated? 4. Show the importance of rest after meals. 5. What is the best time for lessons? Why? 6. On what principle should a time-table be arranged? 7. Show that brain activity is affected by nourishment. 8. Under what conditions does food increase the vital quality of the blood? 9. Why must food be varied? 10. Show that children are spendthrifts of vitality. 11. Give a few useful hints concerning meals. 12. Why should there be talk at meals? 13. Give some rules to secure variety. 14. Show fully that air is as important as food. 15. What have you to say of the children's daily walk ? 16. What is meant by the oxygenation of the blood? 17. Show that oxygen has its limitations. 18. What are the dangers of unchanged air in spacious rooms? 19. 'I feed Alice on beef-tea.' Why? 20. What of Alice's mind? 21. What are the joys of Wordsworth's 'Lucy'? 22. Show the danger of stuffy rooms. 23. What principle must regulate ventilation? 24. Why is night air wholesome? 25. Upon what physical facts does the need of sunshine depend? 26. Show that the skin does much scavenger's work. 27. Why do persons die of external scalds or burns? 28. Why is a daily bath necessary? 29. Give some instructions for clothing children.

VII. 'The Reign of Law' in Education

1. What should be the method of all education? 2. Why are common sense and good intentions not sufficient? 3. How may we meet the danger to religion arising from the blameless lives of some non-religious persons? 4. Account for the superior morality of such nonbelievers. 5. Show that all observance of law brings its reward. 6. Show that parents should not lay up crucial difficulties for their children. 7. Why should parents study mental and moral science?

Part II Out-of-door Life for the Children

I. A Growing Time

1. Why is out-of-door life for young children especially important in these days? 2. What are the gains of meals out of doors? 3. What might be accomplished by dwellers in towns and suburbs? 4. What five or six points should be remembered in a day in the open? 5. What of story-books or tale-telling on such occasions? 6. What of 'the baby'?

II. 'Sight-seeing'

1. Give an example of 'sight-seeing.' 2. What five or six educational uses may be made of 'sight-seeing'? 3. Show the value of discriminating observation.

III. 'Picture Painting'

1. What is meant by 'picture painting'? 2. Give an example. 3. Show the value of this exercise. 4. What caution must be borne in mind? 5. What invaluable habit should this play tend to form? 6. What is the mother's part in the play? 7. What is the after-reward for taking pains in the act of seeing?

IV. Flowers and Trees

1. With what field crops may children become acquainted in your neighbourhood? 2. What should a child know about any wild flower of his neighbourhood? 3. How should children take up the study of trees? 4. Show how the seasons should be followed in this study. 5. What does Leigh Hunt say about flowers? 6. What use should be made of calendars and notebooks? 7. What of the child who says, 'I can't stop thinking'?

V. 'Living Creatures'

1. What part of the pleasure in living creatures may be secured for town dwellers? 2. Of what 'creatures' may children observe the habits? 3. What points about an insect should children observe? 4. How did White of Selborne and Audubon get their bent towards nature? 5. What can town children do in getting a knowledge of 'living creatures'? 6. Show that nature-knowledge is the most important knowledge for young children. 7. What intellectual powers are trained in the child naturalist? 8. Show that nature-work is especially valuable for girls.

VI. Field Lore and Naturalists' Books

1. Should young children be taught the elements of natural science? 2. Show the value of rough classifications. 3. Contrast with classifications learnt from books. 4. What are the uses of Naturalists' books? 5. Name a few. 6. Why should mothers and teachers have some knowledge of nature?

VII. The Child Gets Knowledge by Means of His Senses

1. Show, from the behaviour of a baby, that a child gets knowledge by means of his senses. 2. Characterise Nature's teaching. 3. Wherein lies the danger of over-pressure? 4. Why are object lessons inefficient? 5. Why does a child learn most from things? 6. Give some examples showing that a sense of beauty comes from early contact with nature. 7. What does Dickens say on the subject of a child's observing powers ?

VIII. The Child Should Be Made Familiar with Natural Objects

1. Compare town and country as to things worth observing. 2. How does the fact that every natural object is a member of a series affect education? 3. 'Power win pass more and more into the hands of scientific men'—how should this influence parents and teachers? 4. In what ways does intimacy with nature make for personal well-being?

IX. Out-of-Door Geography

1. Show that small things may suggest great in pictorial geography. 2. What should children be taught to observe about the position of the sun? 3. What, of clouds, rain, snow, and hail? 4. Show how, by pacing, a child should get the idea of distance. 5. What is the first step towards a knowledge of direction? 6. What practice should a child have in finding direction? 7. What compass-drill would you give him? 8. How should a child get the notion of boundaries? 9. When should he begin to make 'plans'? 10. What geographical ideas should he get from his own neighbourhood?

X. The Child and Mother Nature

1. Why must the mother refrain from much talk? 2. How is a new acquaintance begun? 3. What are the two things permissible to the mother?

XI. Out-of-door Games, Etc.

1. Why should not the French lesson be omitted? 2. Why should children indulge in cries and shouts out of doors? 3. Why should rondes be preserved? 4. What are the best ways of using skipping-rope and shuttlecock? 5. What is to be said for climbing? 6. What, for woollen garments?

XII. Walks in Bad Weather

1. Why are winter walks as necessary as summer walks? 2. What pleasures are connected with frost and snow? 3. How may children be kept alert on dull days? 4. How does winter lend itself to observation? 5. Why are wet weather tramps wholesome and necessary? 6. What sort of garments are necessary? Why? 7. What precautions should be borne in mind?

XIII. 'Red Indian' Life

1. What do you understand by 'scouting'? Show the value of scouting. 2. Describe a 'bird-stalking' expedition. 3. In what ways should these things afford training?

XIV. The Children Require Country Air

1. How may the essential proportion of oxygen be diminished? 2. How is excess of carbonic acid gas produced? 3. Why do children, especially, need unvitiated, unimpoverished air? 4. Show that children require solar light. 5. Describe a physical ideal for a child, and show the use of having such an ideal.

Part III 'Habit Is Ten Natures'

I. Education Based upon Natural Law

1. Show that a healthy brain and outdoor life are conditions of education. 2. Show that habit is the instrument by which parents work.

II. The Children Have No Self-compelling Power

1. Show that education is commonly a cul-de-sac. 2. Name three great educational forces. 3. Why are not these forces sufficient? 4. Why are children incapable of steady effort? 5. Why should young children be, to some extent, saved the effort of decision?

III. What Is 'Nature'?

1. What may we state of the child as a human being? 2. Show that all persons are born with the same primary desires. 3. And affections. 4. Name affections common to us all. 5. What does the most elemental notion of human nature include? 6. What have you to say of the strength of nature plus heredity? 7. What manner of differences may physical conditions bring about? 8. Of what is human nature the sum? 9. Why must not the child be left to his human nature? 10. What is the problem before the educator? 11. Show that divine grace works on the lines of human effort. 12.. Why must not the trust of parents be supine?

IV. Habit May Supplant 'Nature'

1. Show that habit runs on the lines of nature. 2. How must habit work to be a lever? 3. Show that a mother forms her children's habits involuntarily. 4. Illustrate the fact that habit may force nature into new channels. 5. To what end must parents and teachers lay down the lines of habit?

V. the Laying down of Lines of Habit

1. Show that parents initiate their children's habits of thought and feeling by their

own behaviour. 2. Does education in habit interfere with free-will? 3. Show how good it is that habit should rule our thoughts. 4. Show that habit is powerful even when the will decides.

VI. The Physiology of Habit

1. Illustrate the fact that growing tissues form themselves to the modes of action required of them. 2. Show fully and exactly why children should learn dancing, swimming, etc., at an early age. 3. To what fact is the strength of moral habits probably due? 4. Show the danger of persistent trains of thought. 5. What does the incessant regeneration of brain tissue imply to the educator? 6. Show that to acquire artificial reflex action in certain directions is a great part of education. 7. What are the aims of intellectual and moral education? 8. Show that character is affected by the acquired modification of brain tissue. 9. Show the need for care with regard to outside influences.

VII. The Forming of a Habit—'Shut the Door after You'

1. What remains to be tried when neither time, reward, nor punishment is effective in curing a bad habit? 2. Show that habit is a delight in itself. 3. Show that misguided sympathy is a hindrance in the formation of habits. 4. What are the qualities necessary in the mother who would form habits in her children? 5. What are the stages in the formation of a habit? 6. Which is the dangerous stage?

VIII. Infant Habits

1. Show the necessity for cleanliness in the nursery. 2. How do cleanliness, order, etc., educate a child? 3. Why is the training of a sensitive nose an important part of education? 4. Why should nurses know that the baby is ubiquitous? 5. Show that personal cleanliness should be made an early habit. 6. How may parents approach the subjects of modesty and purity? 7. Show how the habit of obedience and the sense of honour are safeguards. 8. What manner of life is the best safeguard? 9. Give some suggestions with regard to 'order' in the nursery. 10. Show how and why the child of two should put away his playthings. 11. Distinguish between neatness and order. 12. What occasions are there for regularity with an incant? 13. Show that irregularity leads to self-indulgence.

IX. Physical Exercises

1. Show the importance of daily physical exercises. 2. What moral qualities appear in alert movements? 3. Suggest a drill of good manners. 4. How would you train the ear and voice? 5. How may the habit of music be cultivated? 6. Show that the mother who trains habits can let her children alone.

Part IV Some Habits of Mind—Some Moral Habits

1. What can a knowledge of the science of education effect? 2. Show that education in habit favours an easy life. 3. Show how the mother's labours are eased by the fact that training in habits becomes a habit. 4. Instance some habits inspired with the home atmosphere.

I. The Habit of Attention

1. Why is the habit of attention of supreme importance? 2. Instance minds at the mercy of associations. 3. Give instances from literature of the habit of wandering attention. 4. Where is the harm of wandering attention? 5. How may the habit of attention be cultivated in the infant? 6. How would you cultivate attention to lessons? 7. What principles should help the teacher to. make lessons attractive? 8. Show the value of definite work in a given time. 9. On what principle must a time-table be drawn up? 10. What is the natural reward of attention at lessons? 11. What is to be said for and against emulation? 12. What is the risk in employing affection as a motive? 13. Show that the attractiveness of knowledge is a sufficient motive to the learner. 14. What is attention? 15. How would you induce self-compelled attention? 16. What is the secret of over-pressure? 17. How may parents be of use in the home-work of the day-schoolboy? 18. Describe a wholesome home-treatment for 'mooning.' 19. What have you to say of the discipline of consequences? 20. Show that rewards and punishments should be relative, rather than natural, consequences of conduct. 21. Distinguish between natural and educative consequences.

II. The Habits of Application, Etc.

1. How may rapid mental effort be secured? 2. How may zeal be stimulated?

III. The Habit of Thinking

1. Give the example of thinking cited. 2. What operations are included in 'thinking'?

IV. The Habit of Imagining

1. What is the double danger of many books ministering to the sense of the incongruous? 2. Show that commonplace tales leave nothing to the imagination. 3. In what way do tales of the imagination afford children a second life? 4. Show that we can have great conceptions only as we have imagination. 5. Upon what does imagination grow? 6. What lessons should feed imagination? 7. Why? 8. Show the educative value of the right story-books. 9. How would you promote the habit of thinking?

V. The Habit of Remembering

1. Distinguish between remembering and recollecting. 2. Describe what is here called a 'spurious' memory. 3. What results from the fact that memory is a record on the brain substance? 4. Made under what conditions? 5. Show that recollection depends upon the law or association of ideas. 6. What is the condition for recollecting a course of lessons? 7. Given what conditions may we say there is no limit to the recording power of the brain? 8. Show that links of association are a condition of recollection. Where are these to be discovered?

VI. The Habit of Perfect Execution

1. What national error hinders us from the effort to throw perfection into all we do? 2. Show the danger of the habit of turning out imperfect work. 3. How may a child be taught to execute perfectly?

VII. Some Moral Habits—Obedience

1. What is the whole duty of a child? 2. What is the state opposed to obedience? 3. Show that a parent has no right to forego obedience. 4. What is the true motive for obedience? 5. Account for the fact that strictly brought up children are often failures. 6. Why may parents and teachers expect obedience? 7. How may children be brought up to 'do as they choose'? 8. What manner of obedience is of lasting value to the child? 9. How may children be trained towards liberty?

VIII. Truthfulness, Etc.

1. What are the causes of lying? 2. Show that all kinds of lying are vicious. 3. How is it that only one kind is visited on children? 4. How would you train a child in accuracy of statement? 5. How would you deal with exaggeration? 6. With ludicrous embellishments? 7. Show that reverence, consideration, etc., claim special attention in these days. 8. Is temper born in a child? 9. Show that, not temper, but tendency is 'born.' 10. How must parents correct such tendency? 11. Show fully the efficacy of changing the child's thoughts. 12. Distinguish between changing a child's thoughts and conveying to him the thought you intend him to think.

Part V Lessons as Instruments of Education

I. The Matter and Method of Lessons 1. Discuss the statement, This is 'an age of pedagogy.' 2. Why must parents reflect on the subject-matter of instruction? 3. Show that home is the best growing ground for young children. 4. Why must a mother have definite views? 5. What are the three questions for the mother? 6. Show that children learn, to grow. 7. Show that any doctoring of the material of knowledge is unnecessary for a healthy child. 8. What is an idea? 9. Show that an idea feeds, grows, and produces. 10. What did Sir Walter Scott and George Stephenson each do with an idea? 11. Show the value of dominant ideas. 12. Why must lessons furnish ideas? 13. What quality of knowledge should children get? 14. What is the evil of 'diluted knowledge'? 15. Illustrate a child's power of getting knowledge (Dr Arnold). 16. What is the harm of lesson-books with pretty pictures and easy talk? 17. What are the four tests which should be applied to children's lessons? 18. Give a resume of six points already considered.

II. The Kindergarten as a Place of Education

1. Show that the mother is the best Kindergartnerin, 2. How may the child get education out of his daily nursery life? 3. Show that the children's pursuit of real knowledge may be hindered by the kindergarten. 4. Show that a just eye and a faithful hand may be trained at home. 5. In what respects does the kindergarten give a hint of the discipline proper for the nursery. 6. What temper should be cultivated in the nursery? 7. What general conclusion may we come to as to the principles and practices of the kindergarten?

III. Further Consideration of the Kindergarten

1. What anecdote of a child is quoted from Tolstoi's Childhood, Boyhood, and Youth? 2. Why are such tales as Miss Deland's The Story of a Child valuable? 3. What do we owe to Froebel? 4. What may we learn from the true Kindergartnerin? 5. Comment upon, 'Persons do not grow in a garden.' 6. Show that we must leave opportunity for the work of nature in education. 7. Give instances showing the intelligence of children. 8. Account for the pleasure children take in kindergarten games. 9. In what ways do teachers mediate too much? 10. Show the danger of personal magnetism in the teacher. 11. Show fully that the name 'kindergarten' implies a false analogy. 12. What might be said concerning the Froebel 'mothergames'? 13. Is the society of a large number of his equals in age the best for a young child? 14. Show the dangers of supplanting nature. 15. What would you say regarding the importance of personal initiative? 16. In what ways must parents and teachers sow opportunities? 17. Do 'only' children profit by the kindergarten? 18. In what ways should children be allowed some ordering of their lives? 19. Give a few of the lessons we may learn from the autobiography of Helen Keller. 20. What conclusions does Miss Sullivan, Helen Keller's teacher, arrive at with regard to systems of education? 21. Account for the success of the kindergarten in the United States. 22. What changes does Mr Thistleton Mark observe? 23. Give some of the comments of Dr Stanley Hall.

IV. Reading

1. Discuss the question of the age at which children should learn to read. 2. How did

Mrs Westey teach her children to read? 3. Give a few hints for teaching the alphabet. 4. How would you introduce a child to word-making? 5. Describe a lesson in word-making with long vowels, etc. 6. How should the child's first reading lessons help him to spell? 7. Give the steps of a reading lesson on 'Twinkle, twinkle, little star.' 8. Why is prose better in some ways than verse for early lessons? 9. Describe a second reading lesson on 'Twinkle, twinkle, little star.' 10. Show that slow and steady progress tends to careful enunciation. 11. Show how much a child might gain in a year's work on these lines. . 12. Contrast this steady progress with the casual way in which children generally learn to read.

V. First Reading Lesson
(Two Mothers Confer) [No questions]

VI. Reading by Sight and by Sound

1. Why is learning to read hard work? 2. What are the symbols children must learn ? 3. What do we definitely propose in teaching a child to read? 4. Can the symbols he learns be interesting? 5. Describe the stages of a lesson on 'I like little Pussy.' 6. How does Tommy learn to read sentences? 7. Describe Tommy's first spelling lesson. 8. How would you deal with the fact that like combinations have different sounds? 9. Show that his reading lesson should afford moral training to a child.

VII. Recitation 'The Children's Art'

1. What should we aim at in teaching children to recite? 2. How should we proceed? 3. What should we avoid? 4. Why may we expect success? 5. Distinguish between reciting and memorising. 6. Show that children have a, natural capacity for memorising. 7. How would you teach them to memorise a poem?

VIII. Reading for Older Children

1. To what two points must the teacher attend? 2. What is the most common and the monstrous defect in the education of the day? 3. How may we correct this defect? 4. What points require attention when the child is reading aloud? 5. What must the teacher be careful to avoid? 6. What is to be said for and against reading to children? 7. Should children be questioned about the meaning of what they read? 8. Why not? 9. Suggest a better test of their intelligence. 10. Why is the selection of a child's early lesson-books a matter of great importance? 11. What general rule should help in the choice of these? 12. How may the attention of children be secured during a reading lesson? 13. Give two or three hints with regard to careful pronunciation.

IX. The Art of Narration

1. Prove from your own observation that children narrate by nature. 2. How should this power be used in their education? 3. What points must be borne in mind with regard to a child's narrations? 4. Describe the method of a lesson.

X. Writing

1. How would you avoid the habit of careless work? 2. What printing should a. child do before he comes to write? 3. What stages should be followed in teaching writing? 4. What is to be said about copperplate headlines? 5. Why should children practise in text-hand? 6. What arguments are advanced in favour of a beautiful handwriting? 7. What is to be said for a beautiful basis for characteristic handwriting? 8. Suggest a way of using A New Handwriting.

XI. Transcription

1. Show the use of transcription before children write dictation. 2. What should children transcribe? 3. How should transcription help children to spell? 4. Why should text-hand and double-ruled lines be used? 5. Describe the proper position in writing. 6. How should children hold their pens? 7. What are the points of a good desk? 8. Describe a school-table for little children.

XII. Spelling and Dictation

1. Show how dictation may be made a cause of bad spelling. 2. What is the rationale of spelling? 3. What are the steps of a dictation lesson as it should be? 4. Show clearly what principle is involved. 5. What are the two causes of illiterate spelling?

XIII. Composition

1. Show that the exaction of original composition from school-boys and school-girls is a futility. 2. And a moral injury to the children. 3. Illustrate the sort of teaching that should be regarded as a public danger. 4. Upon what condition does composition 'come by nature'?

XIV. Bible Lessons

1. Illustrate the religious receptivity of children. 2. What Bible knowledge should children of nine have? 3. What would you say with regard to Bible narratives done into modern English? 4. Show fully why children should be made familiar with the text. 5. What conception should gradually unfold itself to them? 6. Distinguish between essen-

tial and accidental truth. 7. In what event may it be said that' the truths themselves will assuredly slip from our grasp'? 8. Why should care be taken lest Bible teaching stale upon the minds of children? 9. Describe the method of a Bible lesson. 10. What use would you make of illustrations? 11. What is to be said as to the learning by heart of Bible passages ?

XV. Arithmetic

1. Why is arithmetic important as a means of education? 2. How would you test a child's knowledge of principles? 3. Why are long sums mischievous? 4. What mental exercise should a problem offer? 5. What caution must be observed? 6. How may arithmetic become an elementary training in mathematics? 7. How should a child demonstrate 4 x 7 = 28? 8. How would you use buttons, beans, etc.? 9. Show how you would teach a child to work out an addition and subtraction table with each of the digits. 10. When would you introduce multiplication and division tables? 11. How would you teach division? 12. What is the step between working with things and with abstract numbers? 13. How would you introduce our system of notation? 14. Why? 15. Show fully how you would deal with 'tens.' 16. How long should a child work with 'tens' and units only? 17. What should follow? 18. What rule must be observed throughout? 19. How would you apply the same principle to weights and measures? 20. What part should parcels play at this stage, and why? 21. Show how the child should use a foot-rule. 22. How would you exercise his judgment as to measures and weights. 23. How does the idea of a fraction occur in this work with concrete quantities? 24. What should be the moral value of the study of arithmetic? 25. How does the inferior teacher instill a disregard of truth and common honesty in this study? 26. How would you deal with a 'wrong' sum? 27. What should the daily arithmetic lesson be to the children? 28. Discuss the ABC Arithmetic. 29. What is to be said against accustoming young children to the sight of geometrical forms and figures?

XVI. Natural Philosophy

1. Show that childhood is the time for gathering materials for classification. 2. What does Mr Herbert Spencer say as to the value of scientific pursuits? 3. Show that children are able to comprehend principles. 4. Mention some of the phenomena they might readily understand. 5. From the subjects taught successfully in a village school, write a list of questions which intelligent children should be able to answer. 6. 'The principles of natural philosophy are the principles of common sense.' Show how this statement should be a key to our educational practice.

XVII. Geography

1. Wherein lies the peculiar educational value of geography? 2. How is geography

commonly taught? 3. What sort of information about places do children and grown-up people enjoy? 4. Why is the geography learnt at school of little use in after life? 5. What should a child learn in geography? 6. How should he get his rudimentary notions? 7. How should children be introduced to maps? 8. Why should a child be made 'at home' in some one region? 9. Why is it well to follow the steps of a traveller? 10. Mention a few books useful in this connection. 11. How should maps be used in this kind of work? 12. How should a child get his first notion of a glacier, a canon, etc.? 13. What course of reading might parents aim at between a child's fifth and his tenth year? 14. How should young children get their lessons on Place? 15. How should they arrive at definitions? 16. What fundamental ideas should a child receive? 17. How should he be introduced to the meaning of a map?

XVIII. History

1. What is the intellectual and what the moral worth of history as an educational subject? 2. What is to be said of the usual ways of teaching English history? 3. What, if the little text-book be moral or religious in tone? 4. What is the fatal mistake as regards the early teaching of history? 5. What is the better way? 6. What should a child know of the period in which any person, about whom he is reading, lived? 7. What moral gain may he get from such intimate knowledge? 8. What manner of books must be eschewed? 9. What is the least that should be done to introduce children to the history of England? 10. Why is the early history of a nation better fitted for children than its later records? 11. Why are the old Chronicles profitable reading for them? 12. Name and comment upon a few of the Chronicles upon which children's knowledge of history should rest. 13. What effect on a child should the reading of such old Chronicles have? 14. Show that children should know something of the heroic age of their own nation. 15. What use may be made of Geoffrey of Monmouth's History of the British Kings? 16. From what authority should a child get the story of the French wars? 17. Why do Plutarch's Lives afford the best preparation for the study of Grecian and Roman history? 18. Give two counsels which should regulate the teaching of history. 19. Upon what principles should history books for children be selected? 20. Mention one or two books that lend themselves to narrating. 21. Comment upon Mr Arnold Forster's History of England. 22. How would you help children to clearness with regard to dates? 23. Mention two or three ways in which children's minds work if their history books are of the proper quality.

XIX. Grammar

1. Why is grammar uninteresting to a child? 2. Why is English grammar peculiarly hard? 3. Show that the Latin grammar is easier. 4. Show that the Latin, affords some help in the learning of English grammar. 5. Why should a child begin with a sentence and not with the parts of speech? 6. Write notes of one or two introductory lessons.

XX. French

1. How should French be acquired? 2. Show that the learning of French is an education of the senses. 3. What are our two difficulties in speaking French? 4. Show that these hindrances should be removed in childhood. 5. How? 6. How might the difficulty of accent be dealt with? 7. What half-dozen principles has M. Gouin made plain to us? 8. Show that the Series method enables a child to think in the new language 9. Trace fully the steps by which the author worked out his theory. 10. How does he treat the difficulty of spelling? 11. Illustrate the facility with which a child learns a new language.

XXI. Pictorial Art, Etc.

1. Upon what two lines should the art training of children proceed? 2. How should picture-talks be regulated? 3. What gains may we hope for from this kind of teaching? 4. Discuss the use of blobs in early drawing lessons. 5. What should be our aim in these lessons? 6. Children have 'art' in them. How should this fact affect our teaching? 7. What should we bear in mind in teaching clay-modelling to children? 8. Name methods of teaching singing and the piano which are to be commended. 9. What physical exercises would you recommend? 10. Name some handicrafts suitable for young children.

Part VI The Will—The Conscience—The Divine Life in the Child

I. The Will

1. How is the government of Mansoul carried on? 2. Show that the executive power is vested in the will. 3. What is the will? 4. In what respects may persons go through life without a deliberate act of will ? 5. Show that character is the result of conduct regulated by will. 6. What are the three functions of the will? 7. What limitation of the will is disregarded by certain novelists? 8. Show that parents blunder into this metaphysical error. 9. Show that wilfulness indicates want of will-power. 10. What is wilfulness? 11. What are the superior and inferior functions of the will? 12. Show that the will does not always act for good. 13. Show that a disciplined wilt is necessary to heroic Christian character. 14. How would you distinguish between effective and non-effective persons? 15. How does the will operate? 16. Show how incentives, diversion, change of thought are severally aids to the will. 17. What should be taught to children as to the 'way of the will'? 18. Show that power of will implies power of attention. 19. Show that habit may frustrate the will. 20. Show the necessity for the reasonable use of so effective an instrument. 21. By what line of conduct should parents strengthen the wills of their children? 22. How may children be taught to manage themselves? 23. Show that the education of the will is more important than that of the intellect.

II. Conscience

1. What are the functions of conscience? 2. What is implied in 'I am, I ought, I can, I will'? 3. What mistake is made by the inert parent with regard to the divine grace? 4. Show that conscience is not an infallible guide. 5. How does Adam Smith illustrate the fact that conscience is a real power? 6. What do we know of conscience? 7. Distinguish between a nascent and a trained conscience. 8. Show that refinement of conscience cannot coexist with ignorance. 9. What are the processes implied in a 'conscientious' decision? 10. What may be said of the instructed conscience? 11. What may be expected of the good conscience of a child? 12. Show that children play with moral questions. 13. How would you impart any of the moral ideas contained in the Bible to a child? 14. Show the use of tales in the training of conscience. 15. Show the extreme ignorance of a child's conscience. 16. How would you instruct children in the duty of 'kindness,' for example? 17. What is to be said of the conscience made effective by discipline?

III. The Divine Life in the Child

1. What is the 'very pulse of the machine'? 2. Show that parents have some power to enthrone the King. 3. Define as far as you can the functions of the soul. 4. What is the life of the soul? 5. Show by the illustration of the bee and the apple-tree what is the parent's part in quickening the Divine life in his child. 6. Show where the similitude of the bee and the apple tree fails. 7. By what two deterrent ideas is God most often presented to children? 8. What precautions must a mother take to secure that her children get inspiring ideas of God? 9. What considerations should help us to select the quickening thoughts proper for children? 10. How would you select fitting and vital ideas? 11. Show the danger of confounding 'being good' with knowing God. 12. What cautions will the mother observe as to the times and the manner of religious instruction? 13. Make some suggestions for the reading of the Bible. 14. How might a mother give her child the idea of God as Father and Giver? 15. How may children be brought up in allegiance to Christ? 16. How would you bring the thought of their Saviour home to children? 17. Show that the indwelling of Christ is a thought fit for children.